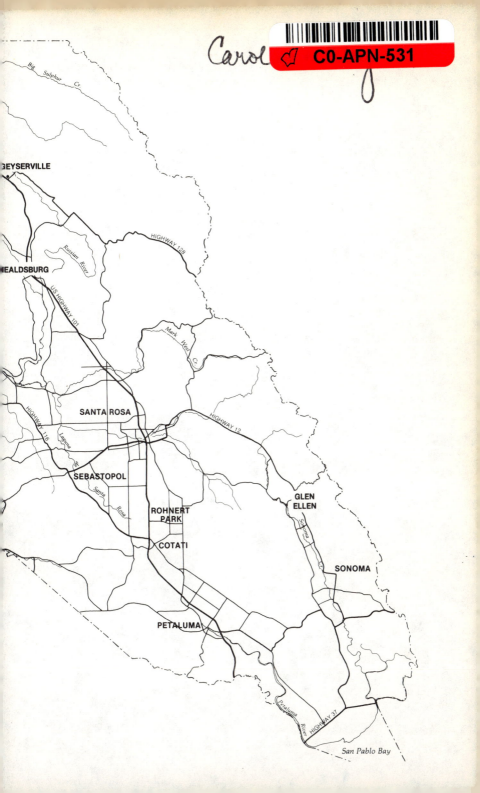

Carol

C0-APN-531

GEYSERVILLE

Big Sulphur Cr.

HIGHWAY 128

HEALDSBURG

Russian River

US HIGHWAY 101

Mark West Cr.

SANTA ROSA

HIGHWAY 12

HIGHWAY 116

Laguna de

SEBASTOPOL

Santa Rosa

GLEN ELLEN

ROHNERT PARK

Sonoma

COTATI

SONOMA

PETALUMA

Petaluma River

HIGHWAY 37

San Pablo Bay

Making the Most of
SONOMA

A California Guide
by Don Edwards

PRESIDIO PRESS

To my parents
Mac and Estelle Bethea Edwards

Copyright © 1982 by Don Edwards
All rights reserved

Published by Presidio Press
31 Pamaron Way, Novato, California 94947

Library of Congress Cataloging in Publication Data

Edwards, Don, 1948-
    Making the most of Sonoma.

    Includes index.
      1. Sonoma County (Calif.)—Description and travel—
Guide-books. 2. Sonoma County (Calif.)—History.
I. Title.
F868.S7E38   917.94'180453   82-3778
ISBN 0-89141-141-0   AACR2

Edited by Joan Griffin
Typeset by Helen Epperson

Printed in the United States of America

Contents

Introduction

This is the chosen spot of all the earth as far as nature is concerned," proclaimed Luther Burbank a century ago in praising Sonoma County. Sonoma always entrances visitors with its quiet, uncommon beauty: the rolling hills—green in winter, caramel-colored in summer—dotted with dairy cattle and white-washed farmhouses; the orchards and vineyards climbing up and down hills; the Russian River winding through redwood forests; the foggy coast, with jagged cliffs and hidden beaches.

Sonoma lies just an hour's drive north of San Francisco, and there are 1,450 miles of meandering country roads to explore. They lead to dozens of wineries; to family-run farms selling just-ripened produce; to acres of parkland; to the Russian River beaches; and to a long, unspoiled coast. Along the way are quiet country inns and roadside restaurants featuring local foods and wines.

Sonoma's vineyards, orchards, ranches, and farms fuel a $200 million annual agricultural powerhouse; the county is among the nation's top one hundred counties in agricultural sales. Few places can match Sonoma's cornucopia of fruit, nuts, vegetables, dairy products, eggs, nursery plants, beef, and pork. And Sonoma County's 27,000 acres of vineyards produce some of America's—and the world's— most coveted wines.

Over eighty bonded wineries dot the Russian River and Sonoma valleys, and most welcome visitors to taste, buy a bottle or case, tour their buildings, and picnic on the grounds. There are mammoth wineries such as Italian Swiss Colony, Sebastiani, Souverain, and Sonoma Vineyards, and small, family-owned wineries—some generations old, some just beginning production. The wine-country picnic is a popular Sonoma pastime: it begins with cheese (stop at one of the local cheese factories), sourdough bread (fresh from a Sonoma bakery), wines chosen right at the winery, plus just-picked fruits and vegetables, and perhaps locally raised and cured meats.

Traveling the Farm Trail is another favorite Sonoma activity. There are over 160 designated Farm Trails stops: look for the green-and-white Sonoma County Farm Trails signs along the country roads. You can buy apples, pears, prunes, peaches, corn, tomatoes, cherries, berries, mushrooms, eggs, poultry, turkey, even your Halloween pumpkin or Christmas tree, all directly at the farm. Some farmers will let you pick your own produce; many offer discounts for volume buying.

The bounty of Sonoma County isn't limited to the land. Bodega Bay is the Pacific Coast's second busiest salmon port, while the sea also yields Dungeness crab, red snapper, clams, and mussels. Deep-sea and shoreline fishermen flock to the Sonoma Coast, while the Russian and Gualala rivers are the haunts of steelhead trout fishermen. Divers brave the cold Pacific waters to go after that west coast delicacy, abalone.

The history and legends of this area also fascinate visitors. Sonoma is a Patwin Indian word meaning "land of chief nose," after an Indian leader with a prominent proboscis; romantics have translated Sonoma to mean "valley of the moon." Sonoma County is a microcosm of California's history, from the days of the Spanish padres and *Californio* settlers, through the Bear Flag Revolt, the Mexican War, the raising of the American Stars and Stripes, and the birth of California's wine-making industry. Historic spots include the Sonoma mission, Fort Ross (a nineteenth-century Russian outpost), General Vallejo's home, Luther Burbank's home and gardens, and Jack London's ranch.

This book is designed to help you make the most of your stay in Sonoma, whether it's for a day, a weekend, or longer. You can tour the local wineries, canoe down the Russian River, hike or ride horseback through redwood forests, go beachcombing and whale watching, or soar above the vineyards in a hot air balloon. Spend the night in a cozy country inn, in a lodge by the ocean, at a lively river resort, or camp out in one of Sonoma's eleven state parks, fifteen county parks, or numerous private beaches and campgrounds. And don't miss the exciting annual events around the county, from wine harvest celebrations and rodeos, to jazz or country-western music concerts.

Detailed information on lodging, camping, tours and excursions, transportation, rentals (from airplanes to horses), and annual events are provided in the Visitors Services chapter. Restaurants are suggested in each chapter, with most meals in the $5 to $10 price range. Prices and hours are given throughout the book, but these are subject to change. Telephone numbers are included so you can phone ahead for current information; the area code for all of Sonoma County is 707. There are also maps to help you find your way as you explore.

Enjoy your stay in the "chosen spot."

Don Edwards

Southern Sonoma

1

Petaluma's Dairylands

The dairy farms and poultry ranches scattered among the oak- and eucalyptus-dotted hills of southern Sonoma County today share the flat expanses of the Petaluma Valley with the busy town of Petaluma, burgeoning housing tracts, and a college campus. The completion of U.S. Highway 101 in the 1950s catapulted this poultry and produce seed farm region into the realm of commuter-dominated cities. An entirely new community evolved in Petaluma east of the freeway; and Waldo Rohnert's Seed Farm sprouted a new town, Rohnert Park.

The Petaluma Valley, flanked to the east by the Sonoma Mountains, pinched off in the west by the Merced Hills, forms a natural funnel for the mists and sea breezes that bluster through the Estero Gap (named for the estuaries near Bodega Bay). Drivers coming north on Highway 101 feel the temperature drop as they pass 1,558-foot-high Burdell Mountain in northern Marin County and enter Petaluma, two miles north of the Sonoma County line. Fingers of fog slither across the redwood tree-lined route of Highway 101 over Meacham Hill north of Petaluma, then scatter in the warmth of the Santa Rosa plain where the towns of Penngrove, Cotati, and Rohnert Park stand.

For decades the hills around Petaluma held thousands of chicken ranches, making the community the "Egg

Basket of the World." Herds of Holstein dairy cows and
beef cattle now have replaced the hens. Moderate temperatures, fog- and rain-fed grazing lands, and a large,
nearby urban market have made Petaluma a dairy center
for Sonoma and Marin counties. In these hills graze over
100,000 head of dairy stock, 40,000 beef cattle and calves,
and 20,000 horses; the silage grown here makes the region
the state's second largest hay producer.

The farmlands in southern Sonoma contain many
Farm Trails outlets, selling everything from chicken eggs,
pheasants, mushrooms, and Christmas trees to sausages,
cheeses, and the unique Crane melons. And for the first
time since Prohibition, Petaluma has its own winery, La
Crema Vinera.

Petaluma sits at the top of San Pablo Bay, connected to
it by Petaluma Creek, a saltwater estuary popular with
boaters and fishermen. The coastal Miwok Indians were
the first people to fish these waters, and in 1776 Spanish
explorer Fernando Quiros sailed through the marshland
looking for a waterway to Bodega Bay.

In 1834 a twenty-seven-year-old Mexican Army officer,
Mariano G. Vallejo, came to the edge of the Petaluma
Valley. Here he constructed his Petaluma Adobe, destined
to be northern California's grandest hacienda. Vallejo's
44,000-acre Rancho Petaluma was one of several Mexican
land grants covering the area. To the north, Rancho
Cotate was granted to Juan Castaneda, a soldier of Val-
lejo's, while another soldier, Juan Padilla, settled on
Rancho Roblar de la Miseria (Ranch of the Oaks of
Misery). A third rancho was owned by Antonio Ortega,
administrator of the Sonoma Mission, who lived on
Rancho Arroyo de San Antonio.

The city of Petaluma grew out of the marshland camps
that hunters built while looking for game to feed hungry
San Franciscans in the early 1850s. Oak forests and herds
of deer gave way to wheat and potato farms. Soon warehouses and piers were built beside the Petaluma River to
serve the flat-bottomed, square-rigged, two-masted hay
scows and the steam-driven paddleboats that hauled loads

of hay, eggs, dairy products, farm animals and produce, wine, lumber, coal, and quarried paving blocks to San Francisco.

Sharp-eyed Yankee businessmen and traders made Petaluma a shipping and manufacturing center; within five years of Petaluma's founding in 1852, the town boasted a major carriage and wagon factory, a cooperage, flour mills, a tannery, and a foundry, among other businesses. Petalumans built California's third railroad (the North Bay's first), opened the county's first bank, and made the Petaluma River the state's third busiest inland waterway, after the Sacramento and San Joaquin rivers.

Around the thriving commercial center, the town's prosperous merchants and bankers built elegant Victorian homes crowned with numerous iron front buildings. The homes and iron fronts escaped the 1906 earthquake and the mixed blessings of urban renewal—today Petaluma contains the best collection of iron front buildings on the West Coast, and many fine Victorian homes.

In the 1880s, Petaluma turned from a diverse manufacturing and shipping economy, and literally put all its eggs in one basket to become the "Egg Basket of the World." A Canadian poultryman, Lyman C. Byce, invented the first practical chicken incubator in Petaluma and marketed it on a mass scale. Danes opened Petaluma's first hatcheries and were followed by German, Italian, Portuguese, Japanese, and Jewish immigrant families. Petaluma was surrounded by thousands of chicken farms, while hundreds of hatcheries, scores of chicken feed mills, and related businesses employed hundreds of townspeople. The town boasted the world's only chicken pharmacy, and many scientific poultry innovations came out of Petaluma. As many as 600 million eggs per year were shipped to points as distant as Paris and Hong Kong.

The poultry industry began declining in the 1930s, and high labor and feed costs forced the concentration of ranches into the hands of a few large producers. The white Leghorn hens were replaced by cows and homes by the 1950s. At the same time the farming communities north of

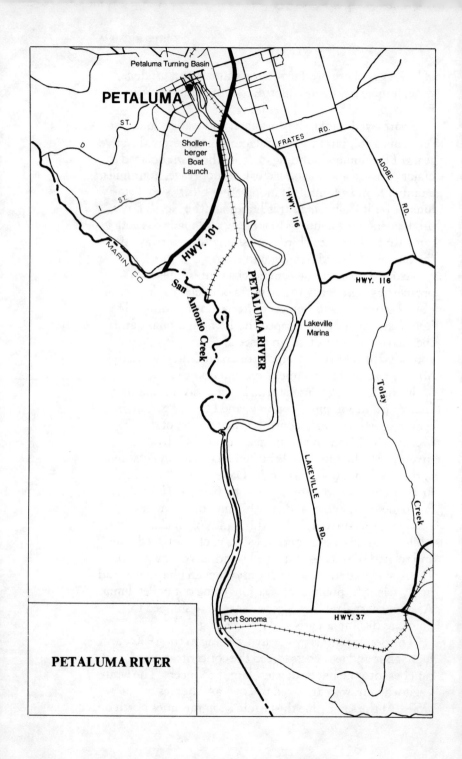

Petaluma Turning Basin

PETALUMA

ST.

D

Shollen-
berger
Boat
Launch

I ST.

MARIN CO.

HWY. 101

San Antonio Creek

PETALUMA RIVER

FRATES RD.

ADOBE RD.

HWY. 116

HWY. 116

Lakeville
Marina

Tolay

LAKEVILLE RD.

Creek

Port Sonoma

HWY. 37

PETALUMA RIVER

Petaluma, Cotati, and Penngrove found themselves
sharing land with the county's newest town, Rohnert
Park; and a state college, Sonoma State University, was
established in 1960.

Today, southern Sonoma County holds many attractions for visitors: Petaluma's historic neighborhoods,
fishing and boating on the Petaluma River, tracking down
the freshest produce at Farm Trail outlets, and attending
the many annual events in Petaluma—the Old Adobe
Fiesta at the Petaluma Adobe State Historic Park, the Ugly
Dog Contest, the World Championship Wristwrestling
Contests, and the Sonoma-Marin Fair.

Petaluma River

If you can beg, borrow, or buy a boat, a Petaluma River
cruise is a grand way to enter town. A leisurely cruise
brings you to downtown docking facilities, where you
can walk to many of Petaluma's restaurants, shops, and
historic attractions. You can still see much of the river by
car if you take the Highway 37 exit off Highway 101 and
turn north on Lakeville Road, then follow Highway 116
into Petaluma.

The Petaluma River is a sixteen-mile waterway surrounded by a large saltwater marsh rich in marine and
waterfowl life; along with the tidal wetlands of the San
Pablo Bay, it is the second largest contiguous wetland in
the San Francisco Bay Area, after Suisun Marsh. The
river's wide bends and long stretches make it a popular
water skiing spot, a yacht club mecca, and a fisherman's
nirvana. River scenery includes views of the Sonoma
Mountains, Burdell Mountain, dairy farms, and the
remains of piers from the waterway's commercial heyday.

For almost a century, steamboats and hay scows sailed
the waters between Petaluma and San Francisco, taking
farm products to the city and returning upriver with
manufactured goods. The steamboats were a dangerous
way to travel, as many riverboat captains—intent on

beating other boats to San Francisco—overworked their engines. The steamboats blew up, sank, and ran aground with great regularity. Petaluma's waterfront was hardly less safe, with waterfront toughs, saloons, sporting houses such as Fannie Brown's establishment, and bootleggers during Prohibition.

Today, the river is quiet, a relaxing way to spend the day. Start in the San Pablo Bay and plan to arrive outside the Petaluma River channel marker just after the tide begins to flood, as the channel is four feet deep and hasn't been thoroughly dredged. A depth-indicator is a very useful instrument for cruising in this area. In the river, the tidal current is a slow 1.5 knots and the tidal action is about one hour forty-five minutes later than the tides at the Golden Gate. Prevailing winds are from the northwest. (Complete navigational information on the river is yours by writing the Petaluma Chamber of Commerce, 314 Western Avenue, Petaluma, CA 94952.)

The channel leads to the first of three bridges that open on the river. This railroad bridge is normally open, but a bridge tender is on twenty-four-hour duty if it's closed. Just past the bridge is Port Sonoma Marina on the east bank, while on the west bank is the Black Point Boat Launch, with two concrete lanes, open during daylight hours.

Port Sonoma, immediately south of the Highway 37 bridge, is a privately operated marina built by dredging contractor William Boland, president of Shellmaker, Inc. It has about five hundred berths for boats up to sixty feet in length. The gas dock is open 7:30 to 4 on weekdays, 6:30 to 6 on weekends, with Union 76 products available, including regular gas and diesel II. They accept Master-Card, Bank of America and Union 76 credit cards. Over-night berthing costs $7; call 778-8055 for information. Port Sonoma offers rest room facilities with showers, tennis courts, picnic tables, dry boat storage, ships chandlery, yacht brokers, and a bait and tackle shop (sturgeon and bass fishing are good near here). Future plans include a restaurant.

If you're sailing all the way to the Petaluma turning

basin, call from Port Sonoma and arrange to have the
D Street drawbridge (a seven-foot clearance) raised. Tiny
and Gail Hultman are the bridge tenders; call them
approximately four hours before your arrival, 762-7030, or
call Petaluma City Hall, 763-2613, weekdays.

From Port Sonoma, it's twelve nautical miles to Petaluma. Channel depth is eight to eleven feet at low tide.
About three nautical miles up river is San Antonio Creek,
where a half-mile side trip will bring you to Mira Monte
Marina, with a fuel dock (Chevron products) and a snack
bar. Phone (415) 897-9785.

Visible both from the river and nearby Lakeville Road
is the ranch home of James G. Fair, one of California's
"Big Four" silver kings and U.S. senator from Nevada.
Fair had served as Petaluma's town constable until, jilted
by a local woman, he took off for the Nevada mines. His
Petaluma ranch was noted for race horses and wine;
Fair's daughter also built a mansion atop San Francisco's
Nob Hill, today the site of the Fairmont Hotel.

A short distance away, on the river's east bank, is the
Lakeville Marina and Gilardi's Restaurant, 5688 Lakeville
Highway (762-4900). The marina—with a boat launch,
twenty berths for boats, and rowboat rentals—is open 7 to
7 daily. Berthing fee is $3 per night. They have Standard
regular gas and oil, but no diesel fuel. Seafood and hamburgers are served at Gilardi's, along with beer, wine, and
occasional live entertainment. There's good bass fishing
nearby. You can also call from the Lakeville Marina if you
want the D Street drawbridge raised.

The wide curve above Lakeville is known as Cloudy
Bend; here, in 1883, the steamer *Pilot* exploded, killing
nine people. Favor the west bank from No. 4 and No. 5
flashing beacon as you pass this area. The river narrows
here for the last five miles of your trip; keep an eye out for
barges.

As you approach Petaluma, you'll pass Haystack Landing, where the Petaluma and Haystack Landing Railroad
route started in 1864. Petalumans used to gather here for
cockfights, bear and bull fights, and boxing matches. Here

is the river's second bridge, a railroad bridge usually left open and manned twenty-four hours daily.

Just before the railroad bridge is Shollenberger Boat Launch, operated by the Sonoma County Department of Parks and Recreation. This free boat launch has ample parking, picnic tables with grills, and rest rooms; it's always open. To get there by land, take Lakeville Street (Highway 116) and turn off onto Petroleum Avenue. Shollenberger Boat Launch is the proposed site for a 250-berth marina. Just beyond the boat launch, you'll pass beneath the Highway 101 overpass, seventy feet above you.

This section of the river is industrial. At the Basin Cut-Off, also called the McNear Canal, you'll see the remains of the steamboat *Petaluma*, victim of a 1914 fire. From here it's a short distance to the D Street drawbridge and the Petaluma turning basin.

Tiny Petaluma Harbor is a cramped place; the only docking areas for visitors are beside the Farrell House Restaurant and the Steamer Gold Landing Restaurant. About sixty sailboats can dock in the harbor; fees are $3 per day, including water and electricity. Overnight berthing is allowed for up to three days. If you are planning to bring a fleet of boats upriver, call Terry Michelson, Petaluma Chamber of Commerce, 762-2785.

Years ago steamers and scow schooners docked at this landing to load eggs, produce, and wine for hungry San Franciscans; the last of these scows, the *Alma*, can be seen today at the Hyde Street Pier in San Francisco. The steamer *Gold* is remembered in the name of the Steamer Gold Landing Restaurant in the Great Petaluma Mill. The restaurant highlights seafood, prime rib, chicken, and steak; it has a full bar, nightly entertainment, and dancing on weekends. The outdoor tables are especially popular for Sunday brunch (763-6876). Across the harbor is the Farrell House Restaurant, the Victorian home of a former Petaluma mayor. The building was moved to this spot to avoid demolition. It's open for lunch, dinner, and Sunday brunch, and has live entertainment (778-6600).

Farrell House, across the Petaluma River turning basin. (Redwood Empire Association)

The Town of Petaluma

The center of Petaluma, with its myriad of nineteenth-century business buildings and its tree-lined residential streets, reminds many of a midwestern town. Others see it as a mirror of San Francisco, with its fog, Victorian homes, and street-side flower stands. Downtown Petaluma was laid out to follow the curves of the river, which flows through the western part of town. In recent years Petaluma has expanded to the east, where new suburbs sprawl.

To get downtown, take the Central Petaluma/East Washington Street exit off Highway 101 and go west along East Washington Street, the main east/west route through town. A good place to begin your tour of Petaluma is the

Great Petaluma Mill. Turn left at Petaluma Boulevard
North and drive two blocks to the mill at 6-22 Petaluma
Boulevard North. There's free parking around the corner
at B and Second streets.

The Great Petaluma Mill began as a storehouse in 1854
(note the original stone wall), then expanded when two
Maine-born brothers, John and George W. McNear, used
it for shipping grain. The McNear family built railroads,
banks, and warehouses, leaving a number of buildings that
are the pride of Petaluma today.

The mill closed in 1964 and reopened in 1976 as a
shopping and dining complex, all because of actor/
entrepreneur Skip Sommer, who helped to launch restoration fever in downtown Petaluma. In the old feed mill and
in the adjacent brick building designed by Petaluma's own
architect Brainerd Jones are thirty-three shops offering
gifts, antiques, books, clothes, jewelry, plus dining at the
Steamer Gold Landing Restaurant and the Salad Mill.

A popular mill spot is Water Street Hot Tubs and
Saunas, with ten private rooms. They also have massage
tables and cool tubs for hot summer days. Water Street's
summer hours are 3 to 12, Monday through Thursday;
3 to 2 A.M., Friday through Sunday. In the winter they
open earlier, at 11 A.M. Rates are $5 per person per hour
weekdays, $6 weekends. Call 762-5277 for reservations.

The origin of the name Petaluma is unknown; some say
it means little hills, while others claim it's a Coast Miwok
phrase for flat back. If you'd like to learn more about
Petaluma's history, hike a block down B Street to the
corner of Fourth Street and stop in the Petaluma Historical Library-Museum. The stone and brick neoclassic
building was designed by architect Brainerd Jones after
Andrew Carnegie gave the city $12,500 for a library and
local citizens raised funds to complete the structure.
Today it holds Petaluma mementos, including an antique
fire engine purchased by the city in 1857, Indian artifacts,
a Petaluma River exhibit, plus displays of the town's agricultural and commercial past. Pick up a free copy of the
"Old Petaluma Walking Tour." The library-museum is

open Monday through Saturday, 11-4; Sunday, 1-4; phone 763-3208. Free admission.

You can also pick up a copy of the "Old Petaluma Walking Tour" at the chamber of commerce office, 314 Western Avenue, 762-2785. The chamber also has area maps, Petaluma River navigational information, Sonoma County Farm Trails maps, Sonoma County wineries location maps, the "Guide to Petaluma Antique Shops," and more. Hours are 8:30 to 5 daily, except Sunday.

Petaluma's prime claim to fame is wristwrestling, boosted by "Snoopy" of Charles Schulz's "Peanuts" comic strip. The televised world championship wristwrestling matches for men and women is one of the most requested shows on ABC's "Wide World of Sports." The event had humble beginnings two decades ago in a local tavern, but now—held annually on the second Saturday in October— draws capacity crowds to the Petaluma Veterans Memorial Building, 1094 Petaluma Boulevard South.

For cash prizes totaling $7,500, contestants in several weight categories square off, with elimination matches beginning at 1 P.M., finals at 8 P.M. Petaluma wristwrestling champions include the Dolcini brothers, Jim and Mike, while the 1980 winner was Georgia's "Man Mountain" Cleve Dean, whose six-foot, seven-inch frame tipped the weigh-in scales at 466 pounds.

For further details, write or call the Petaluma Chamber of Commerce, or call Bob Lipman at KTOB radio, 763-1505.

Petaluma Architectural Tour

Most of Petaluma's architecturally and historically inter-esting buildings and homes can be seen on foot, and there are many places to stop for shopping and eating. The city's outstanding architectural feature is the iron front buildings. The iron fronts, one of America's first attempts to construct prefabricated, fireproof buildings, are the forerunners of our high-rise structures. The fronts were factory-made in San Francisco, of cast iron or sheet iron

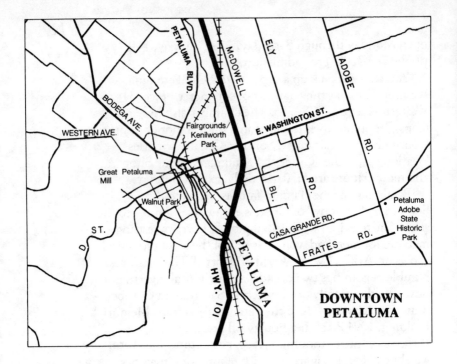

DOWNTOWN PETALUMA

(look for the foundry maker's insignia on the bottom of the buildings), and shipped upriver to Petaluma. The fronts were then hoisted into place and pinned onto underlying brick or wooden walls.

Trimmed with elaborate cornices, moldings, and crestings, the eye appeal of the iron fronts is now heightened by multicolored coats of paint. Look for the names of early day Petaluma entrepreneurs (McNear, Wickersham) or dates of construction on the iron fronts.

A good spot to start your walking tour is Center Park, directly in front of the Great Petaluma Mill on Petaluma Boulevard North. The Mission Trail Bell beneath the redwood trees commemorates *El Camino Real*, the King's Highway, the route created by Spanish and Mexican padres to link California's missions. Father Jose Altimira passed through the "land of the Petalumas" in 1823, on his way to found San Francisco de Solano Mission in the Sonoma Valley.

Across from Center Park are two McNear buildings, one of brick, built in 1911; the other a High Victorian Italianate iron front, erected in 1886. John McNear erected both structures. Today the brick building houses the Plaza Theatre, Sonoma County's premier movie house for seldom-seen flicks, from American classics to new releases and foreign films. The Plaza is open daily; call 763-7171 for shows and times. The prices are right too: adults $2.50, seniors $1.50, kids $1.

Petaluma's most graceful iron front is McNear's 1886 masterpiece, complete with mustachioed faces over the third-story arched windows. Downstairs, at 23 Petaluma Boulevard North, is Henry's Bar and Grill, with Italian cuisine and live entertainment nightly. (If Petaluma's streets give you a *deja vu* feeling, you've seen them before in *American Graffiti*, filmed in downtown Petaluma.)

In this same block is the Lan Mart Building, reputedly a former bordello, now a warren of shops and restaurants. Downstairs is 39 North, Petaluma's newest nightspot for dancing. Upstairs is Old Chicago Pizza, with deep dish delights, plus wine and beer.

Inside the Lan Mart Building is Marisa's Fantasia, a bazaar of crystal, china, and giftware, including a wide selection of Arni-Ferrandiz wood carvings. Each holiday season, Marisa's Fantasia has a Christmas display upstairs, across the hall from Old Chicago Pizza. Marisa's hours are 10-5:30, Monday through Saturday; closed Sunday. Other shops include the Fuji Store, with Oriental foods and gifts; and the Great Petaluma Desert, home of cacti and succulents. Most Lan Mart shops are open daily, except Sunday.

At the end of this block, between Petaluma Boulevard North and Kentucky Street, stands the Western Avenue Iron Front Block, composed of four iron front buildings. The first of these, with its Seth Thomas clock encased in a landmark clock tower, is the Masonic Hall, erected in 1882. Around the corner, at 15 Western Avenue, is a small, two-story Italianate cast iron front structure, originally the Arcade Saloon. The adjacent iron front, built in 1885, once was the New Model Saloon and is now

Andresen's bar. The flamboyant, brightly painted, three-story High Victorian Italianate iron front at 25 Western Avenue was built in 1885 for the Mutual Relief Association, one of a number of benevolent societies that flourished in nineteenth-century Petaluma. Much of its ornate facade resembles wood, but if you take a quarter and strike it against a column, you'll hear a distinctive metallic ring. Take a walk around the rear of this building to see a Coca-Cola sign honoring Petaluma's poultry past.

Nearby are two gourmet shops well worth a stop for picnic supplies. Pedroni's Delicatessen, 16 Western Avenue, has been operated by the Pedroni family for three generations. They have sandwiches to go, gourmet foods, meats, over a hundred cheese varieties, famous homemade potato salad, and a wide selection of wines from small California wineries. Pedroni's is open 9-6, Monday through Friday; 8-5, Saturday; closed Sunday. At 15 Fourth Street, John Pecora's North Bay Gourmet features many local products—from the Marin French Cheese Company, from the Sonoma Sausage Company, and from Sonoma and Napa wineries. Hours are 10-5:30, Monday through Saturday.

In continuing your walk up Petaluma Boulevard North, you'll spot another landmark, the neoclassic revival Wells Fargo Bank building. Built in 1926, its detailed terra cotta facing was made to resemble stone. A similar terra cotta-faced bank building anchors the opposite end of Petaluma Boulevard North at Washington Street.

Adjacent to the Wells Fargo Bank is a three-story iron front structure with a mansard roof, built in 1871 for the International Order of Odd Fellows. Next door, The Market Place, 119 Petaluma Boulevard North, has a fancy selection of gifts for brides and homemakers. Call 763-2671. Store hours are 9:30-5:30; open until 9 P.M. Thursdays.

An espresso coffee stop, with sandwiches, salads, quiches, omelets, and desserts, is the Unicorn Cafe, 134 Petaluma Boulevard North, across the street. Perry's Delicatessen, at number 139, features sandwiches and salads to go; they're open daily.

A perfect picnic spot with a view of downtown Petaluma is palm tree-lined Hill Plaza Park, reached by crossing Washington Street and continuing along Petaluma Boulevard North. The park is part of the Brewster and Oak Hill residential areas, where many early Petaluma merchants and bankers built their homes. All homes mentioned in this walking tour are privately owned and not open to the public, but you can view their interiors during the biannual fall tours given by Heritage Homes of Petaluma. This private preservationist society also hosts an annual Mothers Day Iron Front Tour. Call Jim Webb (762-3444) or Bill Lawrence (795-4089) for tour information and prices.

Kentucky Street, which forms the park's west boundary, and nearby Prospect and Liberty streets feature a kaleidoscopic landscape of architectural styles—Greek revival, Queen Anne, Eastlake, Italianate, bungalow-craftsman, and Bay Area shingle. At 219 Kentucky Street is an elaborate, two-story stick-style home built about 1870 by Louis Tomasini, a Swiss-Italian who came to California around the Horn in the 1850s and served as the first director of the Petaluma Dairymen's Council. His daughter Julia married Rudi Thompson, son of the founder of the Marin French Cheese Company. Next door is an Italianate home built by Giovanni Canepa of Genoa, a prominent Petaluma businessman. The house was later Petaluma's first hospital; now it's divided into apartments.

Behind Hill Plaza Park stands a colonial revival home constructed for Petaluma banker J. H. Gwinn by architect Julia Morgan, who designed many Bay Area buildings, as well as Hearst Castle. Gwinn donated the land for Hill Plaza Park. One block away, at 200 Prospect Street, stands one of the town's noteworthy Queen Anne homes, erected about 1892 for the widow of William Brown by her second husband, Leonard Haubrich, owner of the Arcade Saloon. The home's stained-glass windows were recently added, coming from Petaluma's Parent Funeral Home. Another Queen Anne, at 226 Liberty Street, was built at the turn of the century for Petaluma's poultry king, Lyman C. Byce.

Petaluma Victorian. (Don Edwards)

Return to Washington Street and proceed down Kentucky Street, which has several antique shops along the route. The brick building with columns of cast iron, at Washington and Kentucky streets, dates from about 1900, built by Giovanni Canepa's wife. At 149 Kentucky Street is the Maclay Building, erected in 1870 as Petaluma's Opera House for a cost of $25,000. This iron front was a theater until 1900, hosting many visiting dignitaries, including Mark Twain, Tom Thumb, Lotta Crabtree, President Rutherford B. Hayes, Gen. William T. Sherman, and William Jennings Bryan. Today the Maclay Building houses several shops, including Opera House Antiques, home of elegant home and office furniture.

Take time to visit Schreiner's Deli and Restaurant at 148 Kentucky Street. It's a German specialty shop with German, Dutch, and Danish foods, beer and wine, sausages and sandwiches, plus imports and gifts. They're open 8-5, Monday through Saturday, with lunch served 11:30 to 4. Gift-givers delight in the Apple Box, 124 Kentucky Street, a haven for gourmet kitchenware and country antiques. You can get a cup of coffee while browsing, and take home coffee beans or imported teas. The Apple Box is open daily, 9:30-5:30; until 9 on Thursday. From here, it's a two-block walk back to the Great Petaluma Mill via Western Avenue and Petaluma Boulevard North.

Walnut Park Walking Tour

Two blocks south of the Great Petaluma Mill is Walnut Park, with its distinctive bandstand, home to many annual events, including a "Spring in the Park" art show each May. Among several Victorian homes around the park is an Italianate home at 218 Fourth Street, built about 1875. Two blocks away, at Fifth and C streets, is St. John's, a British country-style church designed by English architect Ernest Coxhead for Petaluma's Episcopalians. The Congregationalists built a Gothic-style church at 16 B Street, today occupied by the Evangelical Free Church. A short walk away is St. Vincent's Catholic Church, 35 Liberty Street, built in a Spanish revival style. The red, shingled Five Corners Community Center, at Western Avenue and English Street, is a former church converted into a multi-purpose building; plays are occasionally performed here.

Elegant D Street

D Street forms the northern boundary of Walnut Park and runs west through the city's choicest residential section before entering dairy country. It's the route to the Marin

French Cheese Company and the Marin County communities of Nicasio and Point Reyes Station. From downtown Petaluma, it's a little far to walk to D Street, but you can park in the neighborhood and walk around.

In your tour of D Street, be sure to take a two-block detour to see two dwellings on Sixth Street. The Victorian farmhouse at 320 Sixth was built in 1862 by A. P. Whitney, pioneer grocer and Republican state senator from Sonoma County. The colorfully painted stick-style residence at 312 Sixth Street, virtually unaltered since its construction in 1882, was a wedding gift from Senator Whitney to his son Arthur. Arthur's son, Leslie Denman Whitney, was a founder of the Leslie Salt Company in the Bay Area. Today it's the private residence of internationally known photographer Ulric Meisel.

Back on D Street, at number 600, is a Julia Morgan-designed Spanish revival home with extensive formal gardens. A 2½-story Queen Anne residence at 758 D Street was built about 1890 by H. T. Fairbanks, who made his fortune in the mines. At 853 stands a federal-style two-story home with distinctive brickwork known as Flemish bond, while at 901 D Street is an antebellum-looking building constructed in 1902 for the Brown family, successful ranchers who hired local architect Brainerd Jones to design the home. The Bihn family, owners of one of the state's largest hatcheries, lived in the prominent Queen Anne home at 920 D Street, built in 1870.

All these homes are privately owned, but many are opened during the Heritage Homes of Petaluma tours. The next tour date is scheduled for the fall of 1982.

Petaluma Fairgrounds and Kenilworth Park

Just west of Highway 101, via the Central Petaluma/East Washington Avenue exit, is the Petaluma Fairgrounds and adjacent Kenilworth Park, focal point for many of Petaluma's recreational and cultural activities.

The annual Sonoma-Marin Fair takes place at the fairgrounds each June, sponsored by the Fourth District Agri-

cultural Association of the state of California. It's a five-
day event, with livestock and poultry exhibits, craft
displays, live entertainment, a rodeo, a carnival, and a car
demolition derby. Fair admission prices are $2.50 for folks
fifteen years and up, $1.50 for kids seven to fourteen; a
five-day admission ticket is $6.50. There are extra admis-
sion prices for live entertainment events (music by famous
names such as Hoyt Axton or local artists), the rodeo,
carnival and demolition derby. Call 763-0931 or 795-2963
for information.

The fairgrounds hosts many other events, including a
Fourth of July celebration, the Swiss Picnic each July, the
Sons of Italy picnic in August, and a weekly Flea Market
every Sunday from 7:30 to 4:30, with free admission and
free parking, no pets allowed. The fairgrounds speedway
holds super and street stock, spring and midget car races
Friday and Saturday nights from April to September. Call
763-7282 for details.

In conjunction with the Old Adobe Fiesta each August,
Petalumans trot out the region's homeliest canines for the
Ugly Dog Contest. The 1980 purebred winner was a Chinese Shar-pei, a medium-sized dog housed in the skin of an
animal twice its size. The Shar-pei's baggy, non-permanent
press skin overlaps all over its body, making it difficult to
see, breathe, or walk. The Ugly Dog Contest is held the
Saturday preceeding the weekend-long Old Adobe Fiesta.

Kenilworth Park, adjoining the fairgrounds, has lawns
and picnic tables, a recreation center, Petaluma's new,
copper-roofed library, and the Municipal Swim Center.
The park, at Payran and Washington streets, honors the
famous race horse Kenilworth, who was stabled north of
town and ran at the old racetrack here. The world's first
air mail flight started at Kenilworth Park on February 17,
1911, when Fred J. Wiseman flew his homemade airplane,
a "kite with an engine," from Petaluma to Santa Rosa—a
distance of fourteen miles—with a forced overnight stop
between.

The fifty-meter pool at the Petaluma Municipal Swim
Center is open between April and September. Hours are

1-5, weekdays; 12-6, Saturdays; 12-5, Sunday. Prices for children and adults range from 25 cents to $1. Call 763-4041.

East Petaluma

Highway 101 divides Petaluma into two distinct communities, with East Washington Street the main route linking the two. East Petaluma is a suburban "bedroom" community that sprang up in the 1950s and grew at an annual rate of 18 percent. Local municipal services became so strained that voters passed the "Petaluma Plan," a growth limit on housing, by an 82 percent affirmative vote. A 500-home limit annually went into effect, cutting growth to 6 percent a year. The Sonoma County construction industry took Petaluma to court and, in a landmark U.S. Supreme Court decision in 1976, the High Court ruled that Petaluma did have the right to curb development.

In addition to housing developments, east Petaluma contains the town's only winery, a park, several interesting shops, and General Mariano Vallejo's Petaluma Adobe, now preserved by the state.

La Crema Vinera is a new winery in a region that once had its own vinicultural reputation. After the 1906 earthquake, one of the Bay Area's largest wineries relocated in Petaluma. The firm, Lachman and Jacobi, had buildings covering ten acres, with a wine-storage capacity of 5 million gallons and a brandy-holding capacity of 500,000 gallons.

La Crema Vinera, located in an industrial park at 1314 Ross, produces Chardonnay, Pinot Noir, and under the Petaluma Cellars label, Cabernet Sauvignon. They're open by appointment and plan to move to a more rural setting, so call first, 762-0393.

Lucchesi Park, located two blocks north of East Washington Street on North McDowell Boulevard, offers boating, fishing, picnicking, tennis, and baseball on 31 acres of land. Named for Petaluma baseball star Mario "Moch" Lucchesi, the park is still being developed and will contain a senior center, a community center, and a performing arts center.

If horseback riding is what you want, continue down East Washington Street to Adobe Road, turn right and head for El Adobe Ranch, 3268 Old Adobe Road. You can ride for up to four hours in the Sonoma hills. The Pronzini family also runs El Adobe Ranch as a children's summer camp, so call first, 763-1011. Rates are $7 per hour. If you're not too saddle sore, stop at Jim Palm's Saddle Shop, 1326 Ely Road, off East Washington Street, and take a look at his custom saddlery, riding equipment, and tack room. The shop is open Monday through Saturday, 8-5.

To fortify yourself for more exploring, stop at nearby Cader Country Store, 1315 Ely Road, which features local poultry and oysters, among other goodies. They're open Tuesday through Saturday, 9-7; Sunday and Monday, 10-6. Lobster lovers can enjoy a "Maine event" with a stop at the Petaluma Wholesale Fish and Lobster Company, 1390 North McDowell Boulevard. Live Maine lobsters are kept inside ingenious storage tanks designed by Richard Daggett, a former employee at the University of California Marine Biology Laboratory at Bodega Bay and now the store's assistant manager. Open 10-6, Tuesday through Saturday.

Petaluma Adobe State Historic Park

Northern California's outstanding example of Mexican hacienda life still flourishes at Gen. Mariano G. Vallejo's Petaluma Adobe, at 3325 Adobe Road. Vallejo began construction of his ranch home in 1834 on the 44,000-acre Rancho Petaluma. His land grants eventually covered 175,000 acres, extending from Petaluma to his Rancho Soscol in Solano County; this plus his 50,000 cattle, 24,000 sheep, and 8,000 horses made him one of Alta California's wealthiest men.

Armies of Indian laborers tended his fields of wheat, barley, and corn, while multitudes of *vacqueros* followed

Bust of General Vallejo, Petaluma Adobe State Historic Park. (Redwood Empire Association)

the vast herds. Indian women spun, wove, and sewed all the hacienda workers' clothes and blankets, while black-smiths turned out tools. A tannery provided leather saddles, bridles, and other goods made from the cattle hides called "California dollars" because they were used in trade.

The Petaluma Adobe's rectangular design, with an inner courtyard, allowed for defense against both the Indians and the Russians, who were entrenched on the northern Sonoma coast. The mud walls were three feet thick and braced with redwood beams lashed together with rawhide thongs. The original thatched roof was replaced with redwood shingles by trapper George Yount, who later settled in the Napa Valley at Yountville.

The Vallejo family didn't live at the Petaluma Adobe full time, coming instead from La Casa Grande in Sonoma. From July to October of each year, the general supervised the *matanza*—the slaughter of steers for their hides, meat, tallow, and *manteca* (lard). In the spring, after the branding and earmarking of calves, the Vallejos held *meriendas* (outdoor picnics and parties), inviting owners of neighboring ranchos to gather and feast on slabs of beef roasted over beds of live-oak coals, accompanied by oven-baked breads and simple wines from Vallejo's vineyards. Indian musicians provided melodies for dancing the *jarabe* or *jota* (a waltz), and *vacqueros* performed riding and roping feats similar to those in today's rodeos. One Californio could well have had Vallejo in mind when he wrote of Mexican California, "We live here like princes."

On June 14, 1846, Vallejo was arrested by Americans staging the Bear Flag Rebellion in Sonoma. While he languished in jail, the Bear Flaggers and members of Gen. John C. Fremont's California Battalion stripped the Petaluma Rancho. Plagued with financial setbacks, Vallejo sold the Petaluma Adobe in 1857.

At age 72, Vallejo returned to view his old hacienda after a thirty-year absence. He wrote his son: "I ordered a picture taken of what was my old house . . . although almost in ruins, it nevertheless doesn't fail to show what it was in those days. . . . I compare that old relic with myself and the comparison is an exact one; ruins and dilapidation. What a difference between then and now. Then Youth, strength, and riches; now Age, weakness, and poverty."

In 1910, the adobe was purchased by the Petaluma Chapter of the Native Sons of the Golden West, which managed to preserve the remaining half of the hacienda until the state took title in 1951. Today, the Petaluma Adobe is furnished much as it was when Vallejo lived here. Local school districts bring students to stay over-night at the Adobe as part of the environmental living program. Reservations for the visits should be made six months or more in advance; call 762-4871.

Each August, Petaluma celebrates the Old Adobe Fiesta at the park, with a Sunday full of activities including demonstrations of pioneer crafts (adobe brickmaking, breadmaking, weaving, blacksmithing, tallow candle-making), Kashaya Pomo Indian dances, live music and entertainment, and a barbecue. Except for the barbecue, all events are free. Call the park office (762-4871) or the Petaluma Chamber of Commerce (762-2785) for more details.

The Petaluma Adobe State Historic Park is open 10-5 daily, except major holidays. Admission prices: kids 6-17, 25 cents; adults 18-61, 50 cents; over 61, 25 cents. Your admission ticket is also good at the Sonoma Mission, Sonoma Barracks, Vallejo's Sonoma home, and Benicia, if used the same day.

The route from the Petaluma Adobe State Historic Park to the town of Sonoma follows the same gap in the Sonoma Mountains that Padre Altimira and Mariano Vallejo used to enter the Sonoma Valley. Also known as Highway 116, Stage Gulch Road winds through dairy country.

Halfway between Petaluma and Sonoma are some folks who talk turkey to the tune of 52,000 birds a year. At 1555 Stage Gulch Road is the site of Willie Bird Turkeys No. 2, the Petaluma ranch of the Benedetti family's turkey empire, which includes ranches in Santa Rosa and Valley Ford, a store in Santa Rosa, and a Santa Rosa turkey restaurant. The Petaluma ranch is open to visitors only at Thanksgiving and Christmas time, when you can buy fresh or smoked turkeys. Tour groups are welcomed at Thanksgiving, but call ahead several days in advance, 763-2684.

The Petaluma Countryside

In the foggy hill country around Petaluma it takes as little as six acres to support one cow and her calf; the same pair of animals need up to twenty acres of range to live in the Sierra or the Central Valley. Coastal range-lands can be grazed longer, and the proof is in the staying power of Sonoma's dairy people, some of whom have been on the land for four generations.

The dairy farms here are small by California standards, between 300 and 500 cows on a Grade A dairy. But the

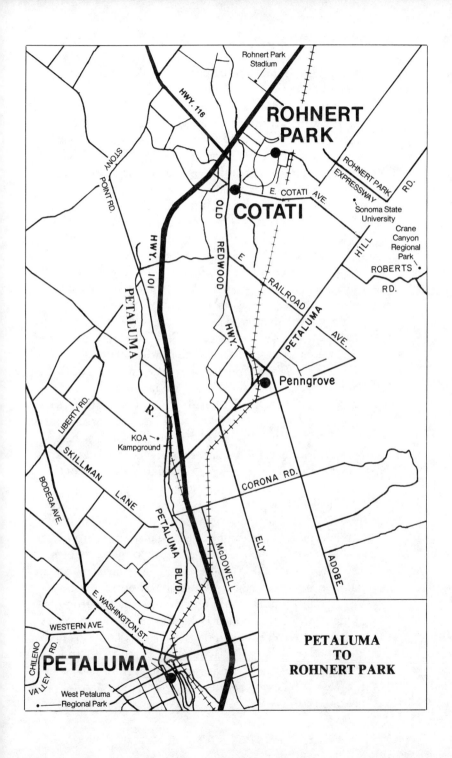

HWY. 116

Rohnert Park
Stadium

ROHNERT
PARK

ROHNERT PARK
EXPRESSWAY

RD.

STONY

POINT RD.

E. COTATI AVE.

COTATI

Sonoma State
University

Crane
Canyon
Regional
Park

HWY. 101

OLD REDWOOD HWY.

E. RAILROAD

HILL

ROBERTS
RD.

PETALUMA AVE.

PETALUMA

R.

Penngrove

LIBERTY RD.

KOA
Kampground

CORONA RD.

SKILLMAN LANE

BODEGA AVE.

PETALUMA BLVD.

McDOWELL

ELY

ADOBE

E. WASHINGTON ST.

WESTERN AVE.

CHILENO VALLEY RD.

PETALUMA

West Petaluma
Regional Park

PETALUMA
TO
ROHNERT PARK

descendants of midwestern farmers and of immigrants from Ireland, the Portuguese Azores, and the Italian speaking cantons of Switzerland have consistently produced award-winning dairy products. Other small farms scattered throughout the countryside grow a variety of produce—you can follow the Farm Trail and find everything from fresh eggs and vegetables to Christmas trees.

The Dairylands

Folks interested in touring a local dairy farm can call the Farm Advisory Office's dairy farm advisor at 527-2621, weekdays between 8 and 5. Allow two to three weeks for a tour to be arranged. Or you can drive through the countryside, with a stop to see how cheese is made.

Begin your dairyland drive by taking D Street out of Petaluma. The name changes to Red Hill Road, and nine miles out of town, just across the Marin County line, you're at the Marin French Cheese Company. Under their Rouge et Noir label, the Thompson family makes and sells Camembert, Breakfast, Brie, and Schloss cheeses. Cheesemaking tours are given daily from 10 to 4; the salesroom is open 9 to 5. You can bring picnic supplies or buy them here, including wine, beer, and sandwich makings, then picnic at one of the tables beside a lake with views of the cows that make this all possible.

The firm's founder, Illinois cheesemaker Jefferson A. Thompson, came to Sonoma County in the early 1850s and became a circuit-riding cheesemaker, going from ranch to ranch, making and curing a Colby-like cheese. In 1865, he bought the 700-acre Marin dairy farm, where the family has made cheese for four generations. Jefferson Thompson's sons learned French cheesemaking from French-Swiss cheesemaker Louis Cantel; the rest is history.

To return to Petaluma, drive back a half mile on Red Hill Road to Wilson Hill Road, drive three miles, and follow Chileno Valley Road for six miles until you come to the West Petaluma Regional Park. This free, county-operated park, with 171 acres, has open meadows and panoramic vistas of Petaluma and southern Sonoma and northern Marin counties. It's a good place for hiking, horseback riding, and nature study, but bring a jacket; it can get windy here. From the park, it's a two-mile drive back to Petaluma via Chileno Valley Road and Western Avenue.

The Farm Trail

Bodega Avenue wanders through the west Petaluma hill country with dozens of stops for farm fresh eggs, mushrooms, pheasants, meats, and Christmas trees. You'll also find antique shops and can even prearrange a stop at the U.S. Coast Guard Training Center. The long, low-roofed, slate gray chickenhouses standing empty along Bodega Avenue recall the days forty years ago and more when Sonoma County had more poultrymen than exist today in the entire state.

Petaluma's poultry business was largely a family affair; in 1915, a farm family could, for as little as $3,000, buy a five-acre chicken ranch complete with farmhouse, chickenhouses, horse, wagon, tools, and young chicks. Between 1,500 and 2,000 white Leghorn hens could be raised on the acreage and fed at a cost of about $1.40 per hen per year. Chickens, fed grain mixed with oyster shells to add calcium to their diet, produced thick-shelled, shippable eggs. Hens began producing at six months and laid 120 eggs each per year for an average of two and one-half years. The queen of egg-layers was "Lady Show You," a white Plymouth Rock hen who won the world's egg-laying title by dropping 281 eggs in one year. She starred in Walter Hogan's *The Call of the Hen*, a book modeled on Jack London's *The Call of the Wild*.

Although high costs have forced the concentration of the local poultry business into a few firms, you can buy fresh eggs at two locations, Miller Egg Ranch and Liberty Farms. But first a few stops along the way.

Bodega Avenue is fast becoming antique store row, and a good first stop is Junktiques, 307 Bodega Avenue, where

Petaluma's queen of collectibles, Sonia Bermingham, reigns. Junktiques is open 12-6, Wednesday through Sunday.

Locally caught fish and fresh Tomales Bay oysters, shellfish, plus cooked seafood and seafood cocktails (all take-out) are yours at Buchan's Fish and Oysters, 1105 Bodega Avenue, 763-4161. Don't miss Buchan's home-made chowder, especially right for those winter days you spend choosing just the right Christmas tree at one of the nearby tree farms. Buchan's is open 10-6, Tuesday through Thursday; 10-7, Friday and Saturday; 11-5, Sunday.

Turn north onto Lohrman Lane to reach the Christmas tree farms, many of which tag their trees (mostly Monterey pines) in November for tree hunters who start arriving right after Thanksgiving. Bob and Marilyn Larsen of Larsen Christmas Tree Farms make Christmas trees a full-time business, with three farms (391 Marshall Avenue, and 2043 and 2216 Magnolia Avenue). They're open from November 27 to December 24; weekdays, 10 to dusk; weekends, 9 to dusk. Call 762-6317.

Continuing west on Bodega Avenue, you'll pass another antique shop, Bobill Antiques, 3690 Bodega Avenue near Thompson Lane. Bobill's deals primarily in glass, china, and silver and carries a collection of 25,000 postcards. Open Tuesday through Sunday, 10-5.

One of the most popular Farm Trail stops is on Thompson Lane off Bodega Avenue—the Petaluma Mushroom Farm, at 782 Thompson Lane. Here you can buy the grocery store variety of mushroom, *Agarius Bisporus*, from button to stuffing size, priced per pound at $1.85 for jumbo, $1.60 for large, $1.50 for medium, $1.40 for button size, and $1.20 for mature mushrooms. Over 1,400,000 pounds of mushrooms a year are raised here, and there's great demand also for their mushroom compost. Thanksgiving is the busiest time for the Petaluma Mushroom Farm, which opens weekdays, 7-4:30; weekends, 10-4; phone 762-1280 or 795-1260. Their mushrooms can be dried or frozen too. Sorry, you can't put mushrooms on your credit card.

If you're after eggs, follow Thompson Lane north to

Skillman Lane and stop at 700 Cavanaugh Lane, home of the Miller Egg Ranch. The Millers raise a quarter of a million white Leghorn chickens here, and all egg processing is done at the ranch. Their fresh eggs are less than supermarket prices and the store is open weekdays, 9-5. Call ahead, 763-0921, especially at Easter, the busiest time of year for egg ranches.

Nearby, at 395 Liberty Road, is Liberty Farms with 700,000 laying hens. They do all their own operations, from feed milling to breeding and trucking, and market the eggs at the farm by the dozen or the flat. Liberty Farms is open all year, Monday through Friday, 8-4:30; call 762-7623.

While in poultry country, don't pass up a visit to the Krout Pheasant Farm, 3234 Skillman Lane, within cackling distance of the Miller Ranch and Liberty Farms. Jack and Verna Krout hatch about 20,000 birds a year, from the ringnecked Mongolian pheasant to the beautiful Lady Amherst. The Krouts also raise Chukar partridges, guinea hens, ducks, turkeys, and other birds. Visitors come to the farm to purchase birds for eating or for hunting clubs, and tours can be arranged by calling several days or a week in advance, 762-8613. They're open September 15 to January 1, Tuesday through Saturday, 1-5; folks wanting birds for the holiday season should call one week ahead.

Another fall and winter stop is the Pine Tree Farm, where kids will enjoy the petting corral with baby animals. Pine Tree Farm also has pumpkins, gourds, Indian corn, and Christmas trees. Open October 15 to December 20, 9-5 daily; call 763-4574. Pine Tree Farm, 50 Queens Lane, is reached by turning off Bodega Avenue onto Kings Road, then onto Queens Lane.

U.S. Coast Guard Training Center

The U.S. Coast Guard Training Center at Two Rock has tours of their eight different military schools, topped off with a lunch served on the base. This 800-acre site at 599 Tomales Road, off Bodega Avenue, is one of the largest operated by the Coast Guard. Your prearranged tour can include their emergency medical technician school, subsistence specialist school (for cooks!), store-keeper school, yeoman school, leadership and manage-ment school, radioman school, among others. The free, one and one-half hour tour begins at 10 A.M., after which a $2 lunch is served. For tour information, call two weeks to one month ahead, 778-2380, or write Commanding Officer, U.S. Coast Guard Center, Petaluma, CA 94952, Attention: Public Affairs.

The hamlet of Two Rock derives its name from two prominent boulders that have served as trailmarkers since Indian days when this was the route from San Rafael to Bodega and Fort Ross. A landmark is the Two Rock Pres-byterian Church, with its ancient cemetery and modern church.

Two miles west of Two Rock, at 9999 Valley Ford Road, is the Valley View Ranch, selling European-style, milk-fed veal. It's a gourmet treat at reasonable prices, but call first for an appointment, 762-8011.

North on Stony Point Road

You can take a city/country drive from Petaluma to Santa Rosa via Petaluma Boulevard North and Stony Point Road, the old stage route that connected the towns in pioneer days. Near Santa Rosa, Stony Point Road con-nects with Highway 12, which runs east to Santa Rosa and Sonoma, or west to Sebastopol. Along the way are sam-plings of sourdough bread, homemade sausages, country dining, lodging or camping, with a bit of history thrown in.

Begin in downtown Petaluma at the Great Petaluma Mill and drive north on Petaluma Boulevard North to number 389. Here's Lombardi's Petaluma French Bakery, with sweet and sourdough French bread, rolls, cookies, and some pastries, all baked fresh daily, and day-old bread too. The bakery dates back to 1921. It's open from 4:30 A.M. to 5:30 P.M., Monday through Saturday, except Wednesdays when it's open 6 A.M. to 5:30 P.M.

Several interesting restaurants beckon travelers along this route. In a Petaluma Victorian at 610 Petaluma Boulevard North, chef Michel Lalanne holds forth. He hails from a French family rich in culinary tradition, and his cuisine features dishes like roast duck with figs and sauteed chicken breast with raspberry sauce. The 610 Restaurant menu changes seasonally to take advantage of fresh produce; they're open for lunch, dinner, and Sunday brunch. Reservations suggested; 762-6625.

Lovers of hot, spicy foods can stop at Steve's Bar-B-Q, 841 Petaluma Boulevard North (park in the rear), or the Old Mexico Restaurant, 1484 Petaluma Boulevard North. Steve's offers barbecued beef and lamb ribs, pork shoulder, chicken, and hot links, plus sandwiches. Old Mexico's chef Luis Lopez uses family recipes to cook up gourmet Mexican delicacies to match his pitchers of margaritas.

Lovers of modern and traditional drama, innovative dance, and opera gather at the Cinnabar Theatre, 3333 Petaluma Boulevard North, where owner Marvin Klebe has converted the mission revival-style building, formerly a lodge and school, into a theater which seats fifty to seventy-five people. Write for program information or call 763-8920.

Stop to stock up on homemade sausages at the Batemon Meat Center, 3695 Petaluma Boulevard North. Batemon's makes many types of sausages, from the Danes' delight (bratwurst) to Italian and Polish sausages and linguisa, along with smoked meats, fresh fish, cheese and eggs. Hours are 9-6, Monday through Friday; 9-5, Saturday; phone 762-7253.

Stony Point Road begins a block before Petaluma Boulevard North reaches Highway 101 and parallels the freeway as it traverses the Denman Flats dairy country. The San Francisco/Petaluma KOA Campground is off Stony Point Road on Rainsville Road. With 282 RV or tent sites, pool, spa, store, dumpstation, laundry and playground, the KOA campground is a perfect base for exploring the region and a good jumping-off site for a trip to San Francisco. A San Francisco tour leaves from here; the eight-hour round-trip jaunt costs $22.50 for adults, $18 for kids ages 3-11. Call 763-1492 for campground or tour information.

Garden Valley Ranch near Petaluma. (Santa Rosa *News-Herald*)

Farther north, Pepper Road runs west off Stony Point Road and leads to two historic homes. The Garden Valley Ranch at 498 Pepper Road is Petaluma's first bed and breakfast inn. There are eight bedrooms in the Victorian home, twelve bedrooms in the carriage house, also a restaurant and swimming pool. The rose fields on the ranch are a Sonoma County Farm Trails stop, open to the public on weekends from May to Christmas, 10-5. The Queen Anne-style home was built in 1890 by Petaluma pioneer Harrison Meacham as a wedding gift for his daughter. Meacham owned 1,400 acres, including Meacham Hill between Petaluma and Cotati, now bisected by Highway 101.

A privately owned yellow farmhouse at Pepper Road and Pepper Lane was the site of Luther Burbank's first Sonoma County job when, in 1876, the young New Englander went to work for W. H. Pepper as a nurseryman. Burbank nearly died from a terrible cold he caught here. The Pepper house later was home to the famed race horse Kenilworth, winner of ninety-four major races.

In 1976 this section of Sonoma County became a work

of art as Christo's Running Fence. The Bulgarian-born artist put up an eighteen-foot-high white cloth fence from Penngrove to the Marin County coastline, twenty-four miles in all, and thousands came to view its serpentine route across the Merced Hills to the sea.

At the intersection of Roblar Road and Stony Point Road stands the Washoe House, the state's oldest extant roadhouse, now a restaurant and bar. Opened as a stage-stop inn in 1859, it was named for the Washoe mining district in Nevada. Tradition says President U. S. Grant spoke from the second floor balcony. Don't miss the dollar bills tacked to the barroom ceiling, left by locals who thought they might need additional cash next time they stopped in.

Penngrove and Cotati

From Petaluma, it's a ten- to twenty-minute drive to reach Cotati and Rohnert Park via Highway 101, but a country road alternative is to take Old Redwood Highway. The Penngrove/Redwood Highway exit off Highway 101 takes you to Cattlemen's Restaurant, a carnivore's heaven, or to Sonoma Joe's Restaurant. Like many of the Bay Area restaurants christened "Joe's," it serves the "Joe's Special"—a blend of ground beef, eggs, and spinach, with a local touch, fresh mushrooms. Sonoma Joe's features Italian cuisine and is open for lunch, dinner, and Sunday brunch.

The small town of Penngrove is one and one-half miles from the freeway and hasn't changed much since it was a prosperous poultry-raising community at the turn of the century. At 8 Ely Road, on Old Redwood Highway, is the Palace of Fruit, a good produce stand stop and open daily.

Between Penngrove and Cotati, at 10201 Old Redwood Highway, stands the Green Mill Inn with its Dutch-style windmill. Open since 1930, the Green Mill is famous for its smorgasbord and family-style dinners, plus country and western music in the lounge on weekends.

34

Cotati, like Penngrove and Rohnert Park, lies on the old Rancho Cotate land grant, a diamond-shaped piece of property given to Juan Castenada, a Mexican Army officer under General Vallejo. The name Cotate or Cotati honors an Indian chief of the same name. Rancho Cotate was patented to Thomas Page, a native of Chile and an early Sonoma County sheriff. It remained the largest undeveloped piece of real estate in Sonoma County until the coming of the Northwestern Pacific Railway.

Cotati's hexagonal town plan, one of two in the United States (Detroit is the other), was laid out in the 1890s by Newton Smyth as an experiment in city planning. The resultant Cotati Plaza, today a picnic spot, is bordered by streets named for Thomas Page's sons.

The town developed as a poultry center, with a comet flash of fame in its Cotati speedway, a wooden track built of 2 million board feet of lumber and four railcar loads of nails. Completed, it rose twenty-six feet into the air on the straightaways and nearly sixty feet on the curves. Race drivers who competed on the track included Barney Oldfield and Ralph DePalma. The Cotati speedway track lasted just two seasons, folding in 1922. Nothing of it remains today.

Like other nearby towns, Cotati changed with the coming of Highway 101 and the growth of Sonoma State University. A number of student-oriented businesses appeared in town, and Cotati even had several students on the city council in the early 1970s.

Today, Cotati is known as an entertainment center: its several clubs and restaurants highlight jazz, blues, rock and roll, and country and western bands. The Inn of the Beginning, at 8201 Old Redwood Highway, has been bringing many of the Bay Area's and the nation's finest entertainers to Cotati for years. It's a place for night people, open Wednesday through Sunday from 3 P.M. (noon on Friday) until 2 A.M. Call 795-9955 for schedule and cost of tickets.

A short walk away, across Cotati's tree-lined plaza, is 85 La Plaza, a cafe and wine stop housed in the old Cotati Women's Club. The restaurant offers hamburgers and omelets. Call 795-7622 for show times of live music and dancing.

Cotati cuisine, defined as California creations with continental touches, can be had at several places along the Old Redwood Highway in downtown Cotati. Among these is Susie's Cotati Cuisine, with a varied menu including vegetarian dishes, crepes, and salads; and Cafe Cotati, with Mediterranean rabbit, paella, and more.

Cotati's Plaza is the setting for the annual Cotati Jazz Festival, held in a club-to-club fashion with six local restaurants and clubs simultaneously hosting jazz ensembles. Call 795-5478 for information on this festival, held early each summer.

East Cotati Avenue is the best route to Sonoma State University. On the way, at 680 East Cotati Avenue, is the Lotus Sutra, a retreat house with a number of facilities: meditation room, nap room, sheltered patio, sauna, yoga room, and tables for massages done by licensed and unlicensed "drop-in" masseuses. The Lotus Sutra Retreat House has seven rules, including no sex, no dope, no liquor, and no chatter. Cost is $4 per visit, and it is open from noon to midnight, daily but Tuesday (when women only use the facilities from 10 A.M. to 10 P.M.). Call 795-1634 for massage reservations.

Sonoma State University

Sonoma State University, located east of Rohnert Park on 270 acres of former farmland, was established by the state legislature in 1960 to fill an educational void in the North Bay counties. Today it offers undergraduate liberal arts and science curricula, twelve master's degree programs, and selected professional programs to 5,500 students.

The campus information center is located on South Sequoia Way, north of East Cotati Avenue, and is open daily from 8 to 8 during the school year; 8 to 4:30, summers; 664-2880. Visitor parking is available near the center during the week; the parking fee is 50 cents (two quarters),

36

7 A.M. to 10 P.M., Monday through Friday; no fee on weekends.

As one of nineteen campuses of the California State University and College system—the largest system of track and field, soccer, cross-country, baseball, tennis, and wrestling. In all, the university has sixteen intercollegiate teams: seven for men, seven for women, two co-ed. Most events charge nominal fees; call 664-2357 for game schedules. The campus's newest athletic addition is the outdoor swimming pool, open to the community and students alike, with handicapped access.

Performing arts get top billing at the campus with plays from the pens of local playwrights and international favorites performed year around, along with dance recitals and musical concerts. Admission is generally $1-2 for students and seniors, $2-4 for the public. Call the box office at the Center for the Performing Arts in Ives Hall for reservations, 664-2353.

Foremost among the free lecture series is the President's public higher education in the world—Sonoma State has yet to develop the special identity that marks its sister schools. Sonoma State's successes include the "Sonoma Plan," now a model nursing program throughout America, and the university has one of the highest acceptance rates for graduates into medical, dental, optometry, and other professional schools.

In their infancies, Rohnert Park and Sonoma State squared off against each other in a classic "hip" versus "straight" conflict, but present relationships are greatly improved, and under current president Peter Diaman-dopoulos, the university is welding a positive link with many segments of the Sonoma County community.

The campus is a rich resource of cultural and recrea-tional activities for the public, from athletic events and plays to concerts and galaxy-gazing in the campus observa-tory. The school's Special Events office has information on most of these happenings; call 664-2712.

Sonoma State's sporting events spotlight the SSU Cos-sacks in intercollegiate matches in football, basketball,

Lecture Series, which brings national figures to campus. Past guests have included journalists Joseph Kraft and David Halberstam, scientist Linus Pauling, and playwright Sam Shepard. Various departments offer free, scheduled lectures with visiting professors throughout the academic year. Call 664-2712 for details.

A crowd pleaser among ongoing campus events are public viewing nights at the college observatory. Astronomy lectures are given, and through fourteen-inch, ten-inch, and eight-inch telescopes, you can view heavenly bodies. Call 664-2267 for times. Film buffs flock to the Sonoma Film Institute for American classic and foreign films. Tickets are $1.50 for Film Institute members, $2.75 for the general public. Call 664-2606 for times and dates.

Other free campus facilities open to the public include the 340,000-volume Ruben Salazar Library (fee for "special borrowers" card for non-students), the college museum in Darwin Hall, and the campus arboretum and garden of native and exotic plants east and north of campus. East of the school, in the foothills of the Sonoma Mountains, is the 450-acre Fairfield Osborne Preserve, managed by the Nature Conservancy, a private, naturalist organization, and used by the school's biology students. Interested non-student groups can visit the preserve by calling the biology department (664-2189) or the preserve's managers (795-5069).

A potpourri of annual events begins each May, including campus open house featuring lectures, exhibits, and demonstrations; musical events; children's plays; and tethered hot air balloon rides. The campus duck pond is the site for free summer concerts by local and Bay Area rock, blues, folk, and jazz artists, while each October frisbee flingers gather on campus for the State Frisbee Championships. Always popular is the annual Redwood Empire Jazz Festival held in Ives Hall each November on the Saturday before Thanksgiving, where young musicians from northern California and Nevada gather to compete for jazz awards. Call 664-2712 for details on all these events.

Rohnert Park

Rohnert Park, a teenaged town among the grand dames of Sonoma County, owes its existence to the freeway, where easy on/off access has made this primarily a commuter town. To some, Rohnert Park's relatively low-cost, expanding housing market, with planned neighborhoods and parks, and cul-de-sac streets, represents the best in city planning. Others feel the look-alike subdivisions clustered around fast food restaurants and franchise-dominated shopping centers call up their worst fears about future growth in Sonoma County and elsewhere.

In only two decades, Waldo Rohnert's Seed Farm, reportedly the world's largest, has erupted into Sonoma County's third largest city. Between 1970 and 1980, Rohnert Park experienced a 266 percent increase in population. By 1986 the buildable land will be gone and the town's population will be 36,000 people.

Baseball fans will want to take in Rohnert Park's top attraction; Class A California League baseball is played in the 2,000-seat Rohnert Park Stadium. From Highway 101, take the Rohnert Park Expressway west and turn at Labath Avenue. From April to August, the Redwood Pioneers battle teams from San Jose, Reno, Fresno, Stockton, and other California League cities, while fans eagerly watch young baseball hopefuls, knowing that they may see another Fernando Valenzuela or Chili Davis rise from the ranks.

The Redwood Pioneers have a player development contract with the California Angels, as the California League is a prime breeding ground for budding baseball prospects. The Pioneers play weeknight games starting at 7 P.M., while weekend action begins at 2 P.M., except on Sunday's double games, when the first ball is pitched an hour earlier. Box seats run $2.75, grandstand is $2.25, kids twelve and under and seniors pay $1.75, and women pay only $1.50 on Tuesday night. There are also student cards and season ticket rates. Call 584-7707 to ask about group nights, and you can charge season tickets by phone at all Emporium-Capwell and Macy's department stores. For season tickets, game schedules, and more information, write the Pioneers, P.O. Box 1667, Rohnert Park, CA 94928.

The Rohnert Park Expressway ends at Petaluma Hill Road, which runs south to Penngrove and north to Santa Rosa. This section of Sonoma County was among many settled by Missourians, in this case the Crane brothers, who left their name to many local landmarks and to a tasty melon that can still be bought at a Farm Trails stop.

A drive south on Petaluma Hill Road and east on Roberts and Pressley roads brings you to Crane Creek Park, 128 acres of hilly, oak-covered country. This county-run park three miles east of Rohnert Park-Cotati is an ideal hiking and picnicking spot.

A northward drive up Petaluma Hill Road, to number 5837, brings you to Herbs 'n Things, where Margaret and Franklin Martin raise and sell multitudes of herbs and flowering plants. They're open from April to September, 10-5 on Friday, Saturday, and Sunday. Phone 584-5134.

Crane Canyon Road runs east off Petaluma Hill. The home of pioneers Richard and Nancy Crane, built in 1868 from locally quarried stone, is set in a grove of trees near the intersections of these roads. After Petaluma Hill Road makes a bend, you'll find Crane Brothers Melons, 4947 Petaluma Hill Road, home of the original Crane melons, developed by crossing a Japanese melon with a cantaloupe. Open daily 10-6 from August 15 to November 15, 584-5141.

Another Petaluma Hill Road landmark is The Gables, at 4257, built in 1877 and still maintained as a private home by local authoress Zilpha Keatley Snyder and her husband. From here Petaluma Hill Road continues on into Santa Rosa.

Don Edwards

Santa Rosa

2

City of Roses

Santa Rosa, named after the Indian maiden baptized by Padre Juan Amoros on the feast day of St. Rose of Lima in 1829, is today northern California's largest city north of San Francisco and west of Sacramento. With an urban population rapidly approaching 90,000 people, Santa Rosa's homes, shopping centers, and industrial parks extend across the vast Santa Rosa plain or valley and around the hillsides of the Rincon, Bennett, and upper Sonoma valleys. This City of Roses—now Sonoma County's commercial, financial, industrial, real estate, medical, and governmental capital—is the county seat.

In its Indian era, this land contained forests of valley oaks, and the wild oats grew so tall here that a man on horseback could pass through them unseen. Giant California grizzly bears and herds of blacktailed deer tracked through the valleys. More than one European visitor compared the Santa Rosa valley to an English park.

Aside from her native Pomo peoples, Santa Rosa's first family was that of the widow Maria Ignacia Lopez de Carrillo, half-sister to Governor Pio Pico and mother-in-law of Gen. Mariano G. Vallejo. Accompanied by nine children ages two to eighteen, she journeyed 700 miles from her San Diego adobe to the Mexican frontier. Maria was granted 8,000 acres as the Rancho Cabeza de Santa Rosa (Ranch of the Head of the Santa Rosa Creek) in 1837, and the nearness of the *rancho* to Russia's Fort Ross undoubt-

42

edly prompted more than one local wag to comment that
Vallejo had sent his mother-in-law to the Russian front.

Quick in the saddle, handy with a gun, Maria was also
a gracious hostess, despite the dreaded Santa Rosa fleas
that haunted her adobe. Her eldest son, Ramon, was
widely known as a bear fighter, baiting the 1,000-pound
California grizzlies with a small sword and shield before
killing them with one quick thrust to the heart.

During the Bear Flag rebellion, two Americans,
Thomas Cowie and George Fowler, raided Dona Maria's
Santa Rosa adobe, looking for arms. Accounts differ, the
Carrillos saying that Ramon's wife was raped and killed,
the Bear Flaggers stating that Cowie and Fowler were
seized by Mexican bandits. Cowie and Fowler were murdered and buried near today's Community Hospital.
Tensions between the *Californios* and the Americans grew
until Maria fled to Tomales; most Spanish-speaking
families left Sonoma County, and the American settlers
barricaded themselves at Sonoma. The arrival of Gen.
John C. Fremont gave the Americans the upper hand.

Maria eventually died from a cold she contracted while
in hiding at Tomales; Ramon left the county, living the life
of a fugitive and vigilante until gunned down in Cuca-
monga. Today, the Carrillo Adobe, on an orchard
adjacent to St. Eugene's Cathedral in Santa Rosa, is
rapidly returning to earth, although protected by a roof
and fence.

The rival hamlets of Franklin and Santa Rosa sprang
up, then merged in 1854 as the town of Santa Rosa,
scarcely more than a trading post but brash enough to
want the county courthouse. Barney Hoen, one of three
ship-jumping German sailors who helped to found the
town, promoted Missourian William Bennett (Bennett
Peak and Bennett Valley bear his name) to run for state
assemblyman against Sonoma favorite, U.S. Army officer
Joe Hooker (later a Civil War general). Bennett beat
Hooker, then went to Sacramento to introduce a bill to
make a centralized town in each county the county seat.
The bill passed.

Local residents still had to approve Santa Rosa replacing Sonoma as county seat, and to help persuade the voters, a huge Fourth of July barbecue was held in Santa Rosa. An historian recalled the event: "The people came and saw and were conquered by the beauty of the place and the hospitality of the people who, on that occasion, killed the fatted calf and invited to the feast rich and poor, the lame, the halt, the blind—in fact everybody who had or who could influence or control a vote."

Sonomans refused to relinquish the records, so just before daybreak on September 22, 1854, several Santa Rosans, including "Peg Leg" Menefee, stole the county records and raced back to Santa Rosa. Maria Carrillo's son Julio donated the land for the courthouse; in later years he was reduced to selling tamales on the streets of the town his family founded.

Santa Rosa evolved as an educational center, with private academies, numerous public schools, and several colleges. The first of these was the Pacific Methodist College, originally founded in Vacaville by Southern Methodists. Santa Rosa's largely Southern-born population invited school officials to the town after Vacaville citizens burned the campus following the assassination of President Lincoln. The school is now gone; College Avenue memorializes it. The Christian College opened in 1872. When it folded eight years later, the Sisters of St. Ursula came from Ohio and bought the building to open the Ursuline Select School for Girls, today's Ursuline High School. In 1918, one of the state's first community colleges opened as Santa Rosa Junior College, which today has one of the strongest academic reputations in California.

In 1870, the San Francisco and Northern Pacific Railroad reached Santa Rosa; within five years the town exploded from 1,000 to 6,000 inhabitants. Mark McDonald, a Kentucky-born "colonel," arranged for a railroad to link up with the Central Pacific line and promoted the fruit-growing industries of the county. Soon carloads of apples, French prunes, canning cherries, walnuts, and other crops bearing the "Santa Rosa Brand Fruit" label were reaching eastern markets. McDonald also developed the town's water system (Lake Ralphine in Howarth

Memorial Park is named for his wife), started the town's library, and left Santa Rosa her finest mansion, "Mableton."

In 1875, a shy, slight New Englander, Luther Burbank, came to Santa Rosa, established a successful nursery, and by 1893 was able to devote his full time to plant experimentation. He advanced horticulture by decades, perfecting flowers at his Santa Rosa home and cultivating fruits at his Gold Ridge farm near Sebastopol. Burbank's almost psychic gardening techniques earned him the title "Plant Wizard".

Wizardry of another sort went on at Fountain Grove, a colony of the Brotherhood of New Life, under the guidance of spiritualist/poet Thomas Lake Harris, who arrived in Santa Rosa in 1875. New converts were separated from their spouses and money, awaiting their celestial mates in another world which was revealed to Harris in trances. Amid charges of adultery Harris left town, but the vineyards at Fountain Grove flourished, providing some of the state's finest wines.

Santa Rosa suffered severe damage in the 1906 earthquake, but the devastation in this farm town of 6,700 souls was upstaged by the earthquake and fire damage in San Francisco. Nearly 100 people died, the courthouse collapsed, and commercial Santa Rosa was destroyed. (A second major earthquake in 1969 did far less damage and no lives were lost.)

The opening of the Golden Gate Bridge in 1937 stimulated Santa Rosa's and Sonoma County's growth; the entire area more than doubled in population between 1940 and 1960. The completion of Highway 101 in the 1950s divided Santa Rosa in two and fostered the development of homes and shopping centers, including Coddingtown Shopping Center, named for developer and former Santa Rosa city councilman and mayor Hugh Codding. Agriculture is now a minor industry in Santa Rosa; the area is chiefly dominated by manufacturing and service businesses, including Hewlett Packard, Optical Coating, and National Controls.

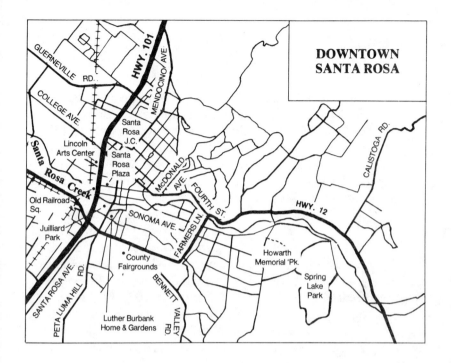

Downtown Santa Rosa

Between earthquakes, urban renewal, and moderni-
zation, it is surprising downtown Santa Rosa has
any pre-twentieth-century structures left, but there
are many, interspaced with modern office buildings and
shopping complexes. To reach the downtown district, take
the Downtown Santa Rosa exit off Highway 101 and drive
east on Third Street to Old Courthouse Square. Don't
look for a courthouse here; it was torn down years ago; but
the square, with its fountain and trees, is a gateway to
shopping and dining along the Fourth Street Mall, Santa
Rosa Plaza Shopping Center and, with a little walking,
Old Railroad Square, the eating/entertainment center of
town.

   Many of downtown Santa Rosa's streets have parking
meters, but there are parking garages at Third and D

46

streets, and Fifth and Beaver streets; parking lots at Second and E streets, and along B Street in front of the Santa Rosa Plaza Shopping Center. Santa Rosa Plaza shoppers can find parking next to Macy's or Sears, and if you're headed for Old Railroad Square, there's free parking underneath the freeway. Downtown's lettered streets, A through F, run north/south; numbered streets run east/west.

Old Courthouse Square is a major transit center for Santa Rosa Municipal Transit, Sonoma County Transit, and Golden Gate Transit. The square is bounded by Fourth Street on the north, Third Street to the south, and bisected by Santa Rosa Avenue, which changes name but not direction, continuing north as Mendocino Avenue.

The Santa Rosa Chamber of Commerce Information Center, 637 First Street, has maps and information about Santa Rosa, Sonoma County, and the Redwood Empire. Guides available here include Sonoma County Wineries Location Map, Sonoma County Stay-A-Day booklet, Sonoma County Farm Trails Map, and Redwood Empire Visitors' Guide. The chamber is open weekdays, 8:30-5:30; Saturdays, 10-3; 545-1414. Near the chamber of commerce is the modernistic Santa Rosa City Hall, at Santa Rosa Avenue and First Street. Built in 1970, it is set in a parklike locale.

Fourth Street Mall

Santa Rosa's Fourth Street Mall, with its wandering, tree-lined pedestrian walkways and two lanes of traffic, is succeeding in keeping a lively downtown livelier, connecting long-time Santa Rosa stores with the newer retail giants—Macy's, Sears, Mervyn's—that anchor Santa Rosa Plaza's $70 million regional shopping complex. Santa Rosa has rescued a declining downtown and integrated a regional shopping center into its heart, a situation almost unique in California.

A focal point of the Fourth Street Mall is Rosenberg's Department Store, a streamlined modern-style structure

(1937), housing a mercantile establishment known to generations of Santa Rosans. Across the mall stands Corrick's, 637 Fourth Street, with fine giftware, stationery, books, household items, and cards. Corrick's is open daily, but not Sunday, from 9 to 5:20. Close by is Sweeney's Open Book, Fourth and D streets, a well-known bookstore.

When you get hungry, you have a lot of choices. At 717 Fourth Street is Katiusha's Restaurant with lunches of Russian and American food. In the same block, Arrigoni's Market, a landmark in downtown Santa Rosa since the early 1900s, has deli delights, hot food, and sandwiches to go or eat there. Mac's Kosher Style Delicatessen, 630 Fourth Street, is a lunch-time favorite.

Fronting Old Courthouse Square is the Great Bombay Trading Company, formed when the 1½-foot-thick brick walls of three adjacent hotels were cut open to create a collection of shops and restaurants. Joe Frogger's Restaurant and Bar has dining and entertainment nightly, except Sunday. Upstairs is Tachibana, a Japanese hibachi steak house featuring *teppan*-style cooking done by chefs at your table. Tachibana and the Ukiyoe bar are open daily; call 523-0941. Other stores at the Great Bombay Trading Company include contemporary women's fashions at Boog and Fox, and one-of-a-kind jewelry creations at A Study in Gold. Next door to the Great Bombay Trading Company is the Courthouse Cafe, 535 Fourth Street, serving lunch and dinner while highlighting Sonoma County's first wine bar.

South of the Fourth Street Mall stand two palate-pleasing places, Traverso's Gourmet Foods, Wines and Liquors, and the Marshall House. Traverso's, at Third and B streets, carries a hearty selection of gourmet foods, including Italian cold cuts, more than a hundred domestic and imported cheeses (Laura Chenel's locally made California chevre goat cheese is one), sandwiches and salads to go, plus one of the county's grandest wine, champagne, and liquor displays. Among their hard-to-find wines are vintages from the Pat Paulsen Vineyards, made at the

48

former presidential candidate's Cloverdale winery. They're open daily from 8:30 to 5:30, except Sunday.

The Marshall House, a restaurant open for breakfast, lunch, dinner, and brunch, resides in one of Santa Rosa's oldest homes, the 1876 Victorian built by James Marshall, a brother of the Marshalls who settled the little town of Marshall in Marin County. The home contains many of the original furnishings and fixtures, while the food comes from some of the town's oldest recipes. The Marshall House is at 835 Second Street; call 542-5305 for reservations.

Santa Rosa Plaza

An archway connects the Fourth Street Mall to the Santa Rosa Plaza Shopping Center, a regional complex that will have 130 retailers and 3,000 parking spaces when completed in 1982. Long after the last store opens, Santa Rosa Plaza's legal battles will continue between its developer, Ernest Hahn of El Segundo, and rival developer Hugh Codding, builder of Santa Rosa's Coddingtown Center, Montgomery Village, and other commercial projects in Sonoma County and elsewhere.

Both Hahn and Codding had eyed downtown Santa Rosa for development in the city's pre-urban renewal days, but after city officials opted for urban renewal funds and selected Hahn as developer, Codding sued both Hahn and the Santa Rosa Redevelopment Agency on grounds that federal antitrust laws had been violated. The controversy raged—with counter-suits, court fights, financial crises, and political roadblocks—while blocks of Santa Rosa's city center stood vacant.

In 1980, the first section of the plaza was completed with the opening of Sears, followed by the openings of Macy's and Mervyn's department stores. Macy's $18.5 million building features a unique design, square on the first floor, octagonal on the upper two floors. The plaza's five parking structures are interconnected, allowing drivers to traverse the entire complex.

Old Railroad Square

A drive or walk beneath Highway 101 from the Santa
Rosa Plaza brings you to Old Railroad Square, centered
around lower Fourth Street, the Northwestern Pacific
Railroad Depot, and Railroad Park. Renovated from a
skid-row past, the collection of turn-of-the-century stone
and brick buildings now houses shops, restaurants,
cabarets, a hot tub palace, a theater, and Santa Rosa's
only bed and breakfast retreats. But first a little history.

Santa Rosa's "Battle of the Tracks" took place near
here in March 1905 when railroad workers of the Petaluma
and Santa Rosa Electric Railway attempted to lay a cross-
over track on the California Northwestern Railway's main
line, thereby completing the Sebastopol to Santa Rosa
electric line. California Northwestern's steam-spouting
locomotives were brought to the battleline, challenging
the electric line's work crew. The combatants were egged
on by a crowd of 3,000 townspeople. Curses and rocks
filled the air, and in desperation a director of the electric
line flung himself across the tracks. A locomotive stopped
just inches from the official, who became the center of a
tug-of-war. The Santa Rosa police arrived to break up the
fracas, and the electric line eventually did reach town.

Many of Old Railroad Square's buildings, like the railroad depot and the Western Hotel (along with other structures in Sonoma County such as St. Rose Catholic
Church in Santa Rosa, Jack London's Wolf House, and
Hop Kiln Winery in Healdsburg), were built by Italian
stonemasons. From northern Italy's Massa-Carrara district, they included Peter Maroni, Massimo Galeazzi,
Angelo Sodini, and Natale Forni. Basalt quarries in Rincon and Sonoma valleys yielded building blocks for the
local edifices and also cobblestones for San Francisco's
city streets.

A good starting point for taking in Old Railroad
Square is Railroad Park. Luther Burbank most likely
planted the trees here. Across the street, the two-story
stone Western Hotel, built in 1903, is now a bed and

breakfast stop. The renovated twenty-room hotel has a lounge and a restaurant.

Behind the Western Hotel is the Marquee Theatre, 15 Third Street, with melodrama and vaudeville performances year 'round. Show times are 8 P.M., Wednesday through Saturday. Prices for Wednesday shows are $4.50 for all ages; $6 for adults, $3.50 for kids on Thursday; $7 for adults, $4 for kids on Friday and Saturday. Tickets can be bought at the door, or call 545-1906, Wednesday through Saturday, noon to 6 P.M. Don't miss their annual Thanksgiving to Christmas presentation of Charles Dickens's *Christmas Carol*.

Across the parking lot from the Marquee Theatre is Sourdough Rebo's Old Santa Rosa Fish House and Longbar, spotlighting homemade sourdough bread, hearty seafood dishes, and live entertainment, Thursday through Saturday. Sourdough Rebo's is open for lunch, dinner, and brunch. Theatergoers attending the Marquee can get a dinner-theater package if they ask. Sourdough's number is 526-6400.

Across the street from Sourdough Rebo's, at 208 Wilson Street, is a red brick building containing La Gare Restaurant, with French cuisine served nightly except Monday. La Gare also has a theater-dinner package for Marquee Theatre audiences. Call 528-4355. A few doors down is a good lunch spot—the Third Street Station, offering hamburgers, sandwiches, beer, and wine.

Magnolia's of Railroad Square, at 107 Fourth Street, is another example of innovative renovation. It's a storefront jazz showplace, drawing people nightly for cocktails, live music, and dancing to jazz, rock, and country sounds. Call 526-9787.

Across the street is the Omelette Express Restaurant, open daily for breakfast and lunch, and Sunday for brunch. Skylights and ferns, along with artwork by local artists, set the mood for this meal-or-coffee stop.

Antiques and collectibles are offered at several Fourth Street shops: Collector's Showplace, at number 11, spotlights Oriental rugs; the Blue Goose, number 125, has fine oak furniture; and Whistle Stop Antiques, number 130, is a bazaar of three dozen antique dealers featuring furniture, rugs, books, and collectibles. In the same block is Dan Blackwelder's Sweet Potato, an eclectic dime store with two floors of modern-day madness, from chemical warfare coats and art deco housewares to campy greeting cards and message-laden T-shirts. Sweet Potato is open daily, 10-6 weekdays, 10-5 weekends.

Around the corner at Fifth and Davis streets is a hot tub haven, Just for the Health of It. Their redwood tubs rent for $5.50 per person per hour before 7 P.M., $6.50 per person per hour after 7 P.M., with a minimum of two people. They also have a Kohler Environment Suite, designed to duplicate the effects of tropical sun, steam, rain, even Chinook winds. There are also exercise facilities and cool tubs for hot weather. Just for the Health of It is open 11 A.M. to midnight, Sunday through Thursday; 11 A.M. to 2 A.M., Friday and Saturday.

Italian restaurants have been a part of the Old Railroad Square district since the early 1900s, and two, Lena's and Michele's, carry on this tradition. Lena's, at West Sixth and Adams streets, is not only popular for their Italian specialties but also for banquets and dancing. Call 542-5532. Michele's, at Seventh and Adams streets, long noted for Italian and American cuisine, also features dancing and banquet facilities. Call 542-2577. Both are open daily.

New Orleans jazz sounds fill Old Railroad Square every August when the annual Dixieland Jazz Benefit Festival pulls into town. Nine jazz and blues bands fill local restaurants and entertainment spots. Tickets run $7 and can be bought at Sweet Potato or at Santa Rosa music stores.

Three blocks south of Old Railroad Square is the Pygmalion House, 331 Orange Street (Olive Park neighborhood), a bed and breakfast inn within a century-old Queen Anne home. They have two large bedrooms and one small bedroom (the bath is shared), and serve a full breakfast. Call 526-3407.

Lincoln Arts Center

A few blocks north of Old Railroad Square is the Lincoln
Arts Center, Davis and Eighth streets, located in an old
elementary school. Home of the Sonoma County Arts
Council, the center houses a ballet school, a radio station,
and a fine art printer. It is also the stage home of the Santa
Rosa Players, performers of musicals, tragedies, and
comedies. Call 544-STAR for show times (October to May)
and prices, or write Santa Rosa Players Community
Theatre, 709 Davis Street, Santa Rosa, CA 95401.

The Sonoma County Arts Council publishes several
free guides, including the Sonoma County Craft Map,
spotlighting local artisans and craftspeople, and the Guide
to Sonoma County Art Galleries. For these guides, send a
self-addressed, stamped envelope to Sonoma County Art
Galleries, 709 Davis Street, Santa Rosa, CA 95401; or call
528-8220.

Luther Burbank Home and Gardens

The next time you crunch into a potato chip, pinch
a plum, crack a walnut, or pick a daisy, you can
thank Luther Burbank, the Santa Rosa "Plant
Wizard" who produced hundreds of new plants to eat and
enjoy. Burbank's austere home, his glass-roofed greenhouse, carriage house, and gardens are a short walk or
drive from downtown Santa Rosa, at the corner of Santa
Rosa Avenue and Sonoma Avenue, near City Hall.

When twenty-six-year-old Luther Burbank arrived in
Santa Rosa in 1875, the town was in the grip of a depres-
sion following the collapse of the Bank of California.
Overproduction of wheat had exhausted the soil of the
Santa Rosa valley, and phylloxera (a grapevine louse)
threatened to destroy Sonoma County's vineyards. Yet
Burbank knew he could make horticultural history here.

Luther Burbank in his Santa Rosa garden. (Luther Burbank Property Advisory Committee)

In his fifty-three-year sojourn in Santa Rosa, Burbank developed over eight hundred new plants—an average of one new plant every twenty-three days. By his death in 1926, Santa Rosa had become a booming farm town centered in the nation's eighth richest agricultural county.

Today it is virtually impossible to enter a grocery store, produce stand, or nursery without laying your hands upon some plant improved by the "Plant Wizard." His experiments, which resulted in more than 25 marketable vegetables and over 250 salable fruits, paralleled the rise of American large-scale fruit production, preservation, and handling. Above all, Burbank had a sharp Yankee sense of what people wanted in food and flowers. Among his creations are the Burbank potato, thornless berries, the Shasta daisy, Santa Rosa plums, spineless cacti, plus new varieties of apples, cherries, peaches, quinces, nectarines, potatoes, corn, squash, peas, lilies, roses, dahlias, gladioli, and poppies.

Burbank ranked alongside Henry Ford, Thomas Edison, and Harvey Firestone as the epitome of an early twentieth-century self-educated, self-made American genius. Ford, Edison, and Firestone were among the many famous people who traveled to Santa Rosa to see Burbank. Others included Ignace Paderewski (who played the piano that is now in Burbank's home), Helen Keller, Jack London, President William Taft, William Jennings Bryan, John Muir, and the Belgian king and queen.

Yet Burbank often found time to trade seeds and plants with local residents who leaned over his white picket fence. The horticulturist's unscientific methods (he would raise thousands of plants of a single species, pick out a handful to propagate, and destroy the rest), his haphazard record keeping, and his mystical way with plants made scientists of the time label him a charlatan. But Burbank's legacy was the development of plant breeding as a science.

Burbank's modified Greek revival-style home, now open to the public, was occupied by him from 1885 until 1906, when he moved into a larger home nearby (now gone). The same year he moved, an earthquake destroyed downtown Santa Rosa, yet left his glass-paned greenhouse almost untouched. A decade later, Burbank married his secretary, Elizabeth Waters. He was 67; she, 27.

Burbank died in 1926 and was buried beneath the cedar of Lebanon tree which stands today in front of his home. In 1958, Burbank's widow deeded the property to the city of Santa Rosa. The Stark Brothers Nurseries and Orchards Company of Missouri have exclusive rights to Burbank's plant creations, while the Smithsonian Institute preserves many of his papers.

Burbank's home and gardens, a National Historic Landmark, are maintained by the city, with Don Flowers as gardener, and by the Burbank Advisory Committee, which provides docents for tours. The Burbank gardens, with spineless cacti and roses, are open all year during daylight hours, free of charge. The home can be toured from spring through fall, Tuesday through Sunday from noon to 3:30 P.M. Admission is $1 for adults, children under sixteen free with adult. Special tours can also be arranged; call 576-5115. There's also a small gift shop inside the carriage house.

Santa Rosans pay tribute to Burbank each May with the Luther Burbank Rose Festival, sponsored by the Santa Rosa Junior Chamber of Commerce. Floats created with thousands of roses are the highlight of a parade which begins in front of Burbank's home and winds its way through Santa Rosa's streets to the Veterans Memorial Building. Carnival rides and folk dancing at the Sonoma County Fairgrounds complete the weekend of activity. For information, call the Santa Rosa Chamber of Commerce, 545-1414.

Juilliard Park

Across Santa Rosa Avenue from the Luther Burbank Home and Memorial Gardens is Juilliard Park, a popular picnic spot and site of the Church of One Tree, home of the Robert L. Ripley Memorial Museum. Juilliard Park consists of nine grassy acres, with lily-padded ponds, arched bridges, and picnic tables; playground equipment is available at the Luther Burbank School to the west. The park was originally the home of Charles Juilliard, pioneer fruit grower (one of his relatives founded the famous Juilliard School of Music in New York City). Charles's son Frederick donated the Juilliard home-site to the city in 1931 for use as a park.

The Church of One Tree, on the north side of the park, was mentioned in a 1939 "Believe It or Not" cartoon drawn by Santa Rosa native Robert Ripley. The Victorian Gothic revival church, built in 1875 by Santa Rosa's oldest religious congregation, the Baptists, came from one 275-foot-high redwood tree, 18 feet in diameter and over 3,000 years old, cut on the Drake Ranch near Guerneville. The building held 300 worshipers. Since 1971 the church has contained Ripley memorabilia.

Robert L. Ripley, cartoonist, broadcaster, and one of America's most traveled men, was a high school dropout who was fired from an early job at the San Francisco *Bulletin* and *Chronicle*. His first cartoon, born almost by

56

accident in the pages of the New York *Globe*, launched
Ripley's "Believe It or Not" series, which he penned for
thirty years. Although Ripley died in 1949, "Believe It or
Not" cartoons still appear in hundreds of newspapers,
drawn by his successors; his search for the bizarre and
unusual has spawned television programs such as *Real
People* and *That's Incredible*.

Ripley owned a priceless Oriental art collection, many
devices of torture, and countless curios, but his most
beloved possession was the door from his childhood home.
Ripley is buried in Santa Rosa Memorial Park; after his
death, Santa Rosa citizens gathered many of his personal
effects for display and the Robert L. Ripley Memorial
Museum was opened.

The museum, at 492 Sonoma Avenue, is open to the
public at varying times, depending on the season of the
year. Open daily from 11 to 4, May 16 to August 31;
Thursday through Monday, September 1 to December 14
and February 16 to May 15. Closed December 15 to
February 15. Telephone 528-5233.

Santa Rosa Avenue

The route south from the Luther Burbank Home and
Juilliard Park is Santa Rosa Avenue. Along this stretch are
many of Santa Rosa's motels and hotels, plus trailer parks
that welcome overnighters, but very few of the town's
restaurants.

Santa Rosa's largest hotel, the 300-room El Rancho
Tropicana at 2200 Santa Rosa Avenue, is a major con-
vention center and summer training camp for the Oakland
Raiders. To reach the hotel from Highway 101, exit at
Hearn Avenue and drive north on Santa Rosa Avenue.
El Rancho features swimming pools, tennis courts, lounge
with live dance bands, restaurant, and coffee shop. Recre-
ational vehicles may use the parking lot for overnight
stays; check with the office, 542-3655. The Santa Rosa
Airporter van provides service between the hotel and the
San Francisco International Airport.

The Oakland Raiders, 1980 Super Bowl champions, use El Rancho's two football fields and other facilities from the first of July until the middle of August. The first week in August the Raiders line up for autographs and photos at their annual Family Day at Santa Rosa Junior College's Bailey Field.

Architectural Tour

S everal Santa Rosa neighborhoods, with their well-groomed Victorian homes, manicured yards, and wide, tree-lined streets, recall the days when the town was a prosperous farming community. This small-town atmosphere has been captured in several films made in Santa Rosa, including Alfred Hitchcock's *Shadow of a Doubt* and Walt Disney's *Pollyanna*.

A good spot to begin your architectural tour is in the center of town at the Santa Rosa Plaza shopping complex, where you'll find two surviving examples of early-day Santa Rosa. The first is the Hoag House, a steep-roofed, gingerbread home on First Street, opposite Sears. Built in 1860, it is the city's oldest continuing residence. The other is Santa Rosa's old post office, a 1,700-ton hunk of reinforced masonry moved, inches at a time, 800 feet north to make way for the shopping plaza. The Roman-Renaissance revival building, designed by James Knox Taylor and erected in 1906, will eventually become a county historical museum. The old post office is located on Seventh Street near Santa Rosa Plaza.

Nearby B Street contains a number of century-old Italianate Victorians and the St. Rose Catholic Church (1900), lovingly constructed of local basalt by Italian stonemasons.

Mendocino Avenue, which runs north from Old Courthouse Square, features several architectural gems. At 550 Mendocino Avenue is the Episcopal Church of the Incarnation, built in 1873. A turn right onto the next street, Cherry Street, will reward you with a number of Queen Anne-style homes, including the Sweet Home, at number 607, which was built circa 1880 for J. S. Sweet, former mayor and founder of Sweet's Business College (today's Empire Business College). A block north, at 521-525 College Avenue, are two bungalows converted into La Province Restaurant, specializing in French cuisine.

At 727 Mendocino Avenue, near College, stands the Belvedere House, a Queen Anne-style home built by Petaluma architect Brainerd Jones. It now houses shops, a hot air balloon company, and The Restaurant at the Belvedere. The Restaurant, serving continental cuisine, is open daily for lunch and dinner, brunch on the weekends, and spotlights a piano bar. Airborn of Sonoma County headlines champagne balloon flights; call 528-8133.

McDonald Avenue

McDonald Avenue, Santa Rosa's toniest Victorian neighborhood, became home to the city's business and professional people after the railroad opened the town to the outside world in 1870. From Mendocino Avenue, drive eight blocks east on College Avenue to Monroe Street, north one block to Twelfth Street, and one block east to McDonald Avenue.

Among the first homes here was "Mableton," 1015 McDonald Avenue, built in 1877-78 by Santa Rosa developer Mark McDonald, for whom the avenue is named. Mableton was modeled after a Mississippi plantation; the home, carriage house, and grounds cover half a city block. McDonald planted the blue-green eucalyptus trees in front. The 1½-story home was used in the filming of Walt Disney's *Pollyanna*.

The best way to view the lovely old homes on McDonald Avenue is to park your car and walk. Please note: all of these homes are privately owned and not open to the public. Start in the 800 block, with number 824, once home of Congressman Thomas J. Geary. The Boston-born Sonoma County politician sponsored the congressional bill that excluded Chinese immigrants from America.

Geary's Chinese Exclusion Act was the culmination of a shameful period in Sonoma County history when Chinese laborers and merchants were forced from their homes and out of the county because of economic competition with Caucasian workers.

Across the street, at number 815, is the Eastlake and Queen Anne-style home built in 1878 for Dr. and Mrs. Augustus Wright. The home at 825 McDonald Avenue dates from 1880 and was the residence of Frank P. Grace, former county sheriff and co-owner of the Grace Brothers Brewery in Santa Rosa. A block up, at 925, is the former Thomas Hopper home, which was owned by the president of the Santa Rosa Bank, reputedly the county's wealthiest man and a financial wizard, who nonetheless was unable to read or write.

Opposite Mableton is an antebellum-style home at 1020 McDonald Avenue, where Ernest L. Finley, publisher of the Santa Rosa *Press Democrat*, lived. Today it is home to Finley's successor, Evert Person, and his wife. Another newspaper publisher, Thomas L. Thompson, lived in a similar antebellum-style home at 1104 McDonald Avenue. Thompson served as U.S. ambassador to Brazil under President Grover Cleveland.

Santa Rosa Junior College

S anta Rosa's early educational efforts spawned its two-year community college, Santa Rosa Junior College. Opened in 1918 as one of the first California community colleges, it has an outstanding academic reputation, plus being an educational bargain. Annual fees are about $50, compared to nearly $190 at Sonoma State University, or over $7,000 per year in tuition at Stanford University. Total yearly costs for a Santa Rosa Junior College student living at home run about $1,700.

Located on 93 acres at 1501 Mendocino Avenue, Santa Rosa Junior College has an enrollment topping 24,000 students—in both day and evening programs. Academic emphasis centers on general education, transfer education to four-year institutions, occupational education (over fifty programs), and developmental education for inadequately prepared students.

Among the multiple college activities open to students and visitors alike are athletic events, plays, concerts, lectures, plus annual events such as A Day under the Oaks and, sponsored by the Santa Rosa Arts Council, the Artrium. Santa Rosa Junior College's athletic teams are part of the Camino Norte Conference, and intercollegiate competition for men and women includes baseball, basketball, cross-country, football, golf, gymnastics, soccer, softball, swimming, tennis, track and field, volleyball, water polo, and wrestling. For more information, call the physical education department, 527-4237.

One of the college's and the town's hottest summer attractions is the Summer Repertory Theatre, a nationally recognized company and the largest semiprofessional theater ensemble in northern California. Each July and August, comedy, tragedy, musicals, and serious drama are spotlighted in the Luther Burbank Auditorium. For information or tickets, call 527-4342 or write Summer Repertory Theatre, Luther Burbank Auditorium, Santa Rosa Junior College, 1501 Mendocino Avenue, Santa Rosa, CA 95401. Ticket box office is open 10 A.M. to 10 P.M., Tuesday through Sunday, during the summer season. For other thespian presentations held during the academic year, call 527-4342.

The college's Community Services office schedules events such as a series of midday lectures, music and dance programs, mini-courses, a scholar-in-residence series, a classical music concert series, and Sunday movies. The Community Services office will issue a Senior Citizens Gold Card for any person sixty years and older for free admission to athletic events and reduced admission to many other campus events. For information, call 527-4371.

The first Californians and other native Americans are well represented at the school's Native American Museum in Bussman Hall. There are collections of Pomo basketry,

Navajo textiles, New Mexican blackware pottery, among other exhibits. The museum is open daily except Saturday, 10 to 4. Groups interested in tours can call 527-4479 or 527-4325.

Arts and crafts of northern California artisans are showcased at the college in the art gallery, open daily except Saturdays from noon to 4. Each June, a three-day free art festival, Artrium, is sponsored by the Sonoma County Arts Council and the Community Services office, and funded by Sonoma County and the city of Santa Rosa. The artistic creations are judged and awarded prizes. Artrium visitors are also entertained by jugglers, fire eaters, and hot air balloon rides. Call 527-4371 for information.

Each year during the same weekend that Santa Rosans hold the Luther Burbank Rose Festival, Santa Rosa Junior College hosts an open house—A Day under the Oaks. This is a chance to tour campus facilities and learn more about the college: that, for example, the college has its own 285-acre farm near Forestville, or that among the many outstanding instructors is Cathy Mitchell, co-winner of a Pulitzer prize for news reporting on the activities of Synanon, a controversial drug rehabilitation community. A Day under the Oaks also features athletic events, native American dances, and musical happenings. Call 527-4371 for information.

The college's newest additions include the eighty-seven-seat planetarium, with a dome forty feet in diameter and twenty-seven feet high. Many of the planetarium's shows are open to the public; call 527-4371 for dates. Admission is $1.50; students and Gold Card holders pay 75 cents. Scheduled to open in 1982 is a new field and gymnasium, with seating for 2,000 spectators.

Near the college is the Santa Rosa Swim Center, 533 Ridgeway Avenue, with three swimming pools—one for diving, one for competitive swimming, and a shallow one for instruction. It's open 1:15-4:45 P.M. daily from the second week in June until Labor Day, weekends in spring. Call 528-5115 for prices.

62

Sonoma County Fairgrounds

The nucleus of many annual Sonoma County events is the 185-acre Sonoma County Fairgrounds, with its racetrack and grandstand, rodeo arenas, theater, exhibition buildings, and pavilions. To reach the fairgrounds, exit Highway 101 at Highway 12 and travel east along Bennett Valley Road for less than a mile; from the downtown area, Santa Rosa Avenue leads to Highway 12.

The biggest annual event here is the Sonoma County Fair, which draws over 400,000 participants for two summer weeks in July or August. Other yearly celebrations include the Farm and Ranch Show, the Health and Harmony Festival, the Scottish Gathering and Games, and the Sonoma County Harvest Fair. A number of horse shows are also held here throughout the year, as well as many other events. There's even a golf course at the fairgrounds, a nine-hole, par-29 course, which is excellent for beginners. Open daily. Fees: $3.50 weekdays, $4.50 weekends. Call 546-2469.

The Sonoma County Fair is not only Sonoma County's biggest crowd catcher, it's also a major Bay Area event, with fairgoers drawn by thoroughbred horse racing and pari-mutuel betting. Races are run Monday through Saturday; post time is 1:20 P.M.

Flower lovers come to the fair to see the Hall of Flowers, where a floral feast unfolds each year, while rodeo fans flock to professional rodeo events at the Chris Beck Arena. Live entertainment, with emphasis on country and and western stars or blues singers, is held at the Redwood Theatre and at other spots around the fairgrounds. But top fair attractions continue to be the farm animals— goats, chickens, cattle, lambs, pigs. For many of the animals, it's their one moment of stardom before the livestock auctions.

The Winner's Circle at the Sonoma County Fair. (Santa Rosa News-Herald)

Best of all are the fair's admission prices: $3 for adults (13 years and up), children seven to twelve $1. Racetrack admission fee is $1.50, and an "express ticket" lets you in both the main gate and the racetrack gate for $3. For information on the Sonoma County Fair, call the Fair Association, 545-4200, or the Special Events office, 528-3247.

The Scots pull out all the stops, including the ones on their bagpipes, when they gather at the fairgrounds for the Scottish Gathering and Games. Staged by San Francisco's Caledonian Club each Labor Day weekend, these Scottish events are the second oldest and largest in America. Highlights are the athletic feats, such as the caber toss, putting the stone, and five-a-side soccer. The caber is a telephone pole-sized log thrown end over end into the air; best score is 12 o'clock in direct line with throw. There are highland dances, bagpipe bands, and Scottish foods too. Admission is $7 adults ($10 both days), $1 children under twelve.

64

Tickets through BASS outlets, (415) 835-4342 or (408) 297-7552.

Sipping and stomping are the main events at the Sonoma County Harvest Fair, with wine competition and judging open only to wines made in Sonoma County. Fairgoers get a chance to taste some of the prize-winning vintages and buy bottles to take home. Among the footloose events at the fair is the World Championship Grape Stomp, where competitors have five minutes to turn grapes into two gallons of juice. Other happenings include hayrides, free concerts (Jesse Colin Young performed in 1981), and exhibits of the agricultural richness of the county, everything from apples to pygmy goats. The two-day fair, held the first full weekend in October, costs $2 for adults, $1 for kids seven to thirteen, children under six free. Wine tasting fee is $3.00. Call 545-4203 for more information.

Other events held at the fairgrounds include the 4-H Chicken-que (barbecue and parade) in May, a flea market every Sunday from October 25 to April 1, plus antique shows, home shows, and car shows. For further information, call 545-4200.

Sonoma County Farmer's Market

Across Bennett Valley Road from the fairgrounds is the Veterans Memorial Auditorium, site of the Sonoma County Farmer's Market. Local farmers and backyard gardeners gather in the parking lot to sell fruits, vegetables, honey, eggs, houseplants, cut flowers, herbs, dried nuts in the shell, and some processed foods. The Farmer's Market is open from 9 A.M. each Wednesday and Saturday between May 16 and November 24. Free admission.

Bennett Valley

Bennett Valley Road parallels Highway 12, then branches off to the right just past the Sonoma County Fairgrounds. Bennett Valley—squeezed

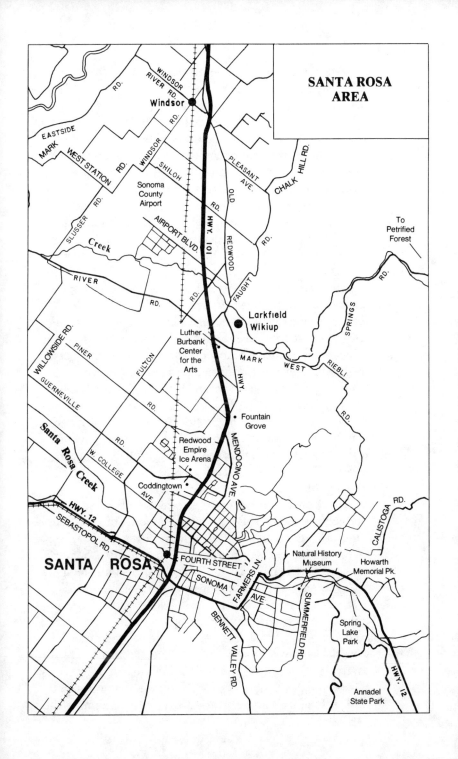

between Taylor Mountain and the Sonoma Mountains on the west, Bennett Peak (Yulupa to the Indians) and Bennett Ridge to the east—has been ranching and farming country since the days when Missourian William Bennett settled here. (As state representative, Bennett introduced the legislative bill that made Santa Rosa the county seat.) Issac De Turk, one of California's top vineyardists and a force in the state Viticultural Commission, had his vineyard Yulupa here. His round winery barn still stands in Santa Rosa on Donahue Street near Old Railroad Square.

Killed by Prohibition, grape growing is again a going concern in Bennett Valley. Although this area is part of the Russian River watershed, Bennett Valley's warm microclimate places it within the Sonoma Valley appellation. Matanzas Creek Winery, 6097 Bennett Valley Road, one of Sonoma County's newer wineries, was the 1981 Harvest Fair sweepstakes winner with its 1979 Chardonnay. Winemaker Merry Edwards is producing Cabernet Sauvignon, Chardonnay, Pinot Noir, Gewurztraminer, and Semillion wines. Matanzas Creek Winery is open by appointment only, 542-8242.

If you turn off Bennett Valley Road onto Grange Road, which becomes Crane Canyon Road as it heads toward Rohnert Park, you'll pass the Bennett Valley Grange on Grange Road. This is America's oldest grange hall (1873) and it's still in use.

There are a number of ways to relax in Bennett Valley. For you active types, Bennett Valley Golf Course, 3330 Yulupa Avenue, has eighteen holes, with a par-70 rating. Green fees are $4.50 weekdays, $7 on weekends; 528-3673. Exercise for the mind is offered at the Genjo-ji Zen Center on Sonoma Mountain. The peaceful atmosphere and lovely grounds provide a pleasant backdrop. Visitors are welcome every Saturday for meditation instructions, meditation, work practice, lecture, and lunch. Meditation workshops, weekend retreats, and guest residency are also available. Genjo-ji is at 6367 Sonoma Mountain Road, off Bennett Valley Road; 545-8105. You can follow Bennett Valley Road to Warm Springs Road in the Sonoma Valley.

Montgomery Village

ighway 12 continues through Santa Rosa via
Farmers Lane. This section of Santa Rosa, called
Montgomery Village, was built by Hugh Cod-
ding, the local developer once featured in *Life* magazine
for building a home and church in a matter of hours.

In the Montgomery Village Shopping Center is a
unique shop, John Ash and Company, at 2324 Montgomery Drive. This is a restaurant, a wine shop, and a
wine-tasting center all in one. John Ash offers fine French
and California cuisine, plus a selection of hard-to-find
wines from Europe and America. The weekly wine tastings
attract imbibers bent on increasing their wine knowledge,
and when John Ash hosts dinners, his wines are often
accompanied by their creators, such as Joseph Swan of
Swan Vineyards in Forestville. The restaurant is open for
lunch, dinner, and brunch; call 527-7687. You can get on
John Ash's mailing list by writing to P.O. Box 2617, Santa
Rosa, CA 95405.

If you want to continue on your way to the Sonoma
Valley, follow Farmers Lane to its junction with Fourth
Street and Highway 12. Here stands the newly refurbished
Flamingo Hotel, built in 1952 by Hugh Codding. The
Flamingo has 150 units, an Olympic-sized swimming pool,
six championship tennis courts, a lounge with live enter-
tainment, a dining room, and a coffee shop. The Empire
Room, which can accommodate up to 600 people, is avail-
able for meetings, banquets, and receptions. Call 545-
8530. The Airport Express operates an airport shuttle
between the Flamingo and both the San Francisco and the
Oakland airports. Call 526-1360, twenty-four hours a day.

Codding Museum of Natural History

A short drive east on Montgomery Drive will bring you to
Summerfield Road and the Codding Museum. Santa Rosa
developer and big game hunter Hugh Codding has created

museum dioramas of polar bear, cougar, leopard, gazelle, tiger, bighorn sheep, and other animals in their native habitats, from Africa to India, from the arctic to the desert. Carvings by local artist Elwin Millerick are also on display. The Codding Museum of Natural History, 557 Summerfield Road, is free and open from 1 to 5, closed Monday and Friday. Tours and orientation lectures can be arranged with thirty days' notice by calling Ben Cummings, 539-0556.

Santa Rosa Parklands

Santa Rosans are uniquely fortunate to have a chain of parkland—a city, a county, and a state park interconnected so that it is possible to hike from one to another. The city's Howarth Memorial Park begins at Summerfield Road and connects with the county's Spring Lake Park. A lake and a reservoir make these two parks popular for fishing and boating. Adjacent Annadel State Park, much larger in area, is known for its hiking and horse trails. Follow Highway 12 to Montgomery Drive, then go east to find your way to these parks.

Howarth Memorial Park

Howarth Memorial Park is one of the city's oldest and largest parks, a 152-acre urban oasis with lawns shaded by oak trees, picnic facilities, a lake with a boathouse, a children's amusement park, six tennis courts, a lighted softball field, and hiking trails, some of which lead to Spring Lake Park. Howarth Park is the most heavily used of the three parks. Each Sunday during the summer free concerts are held here, featuring concert bands and jazz ensembles.

The park is named in memory of Leonard Howarth, a British-born bank clerk who amassed a $6 million fortune from a Washington timber mill and upon his death donated $75,000 to a park fund. Santa Rosa developer Mark McDonald used this property to establish the city's water system; the resulting reservoir was christened Lake Ralphine after McDonald's wife.

A children's favorite is Big-K Land, an amusement park created by the Santa Rosa Kiwanis service club. There's a miniature train, a merry-go-round with century-old handcarved horses, and live ponies, 25 cents a ride. Kids also enjoy petting the animals at the animal farm built by the Optimist Club. Both Big-K Land and the animal farm are open daily 1-5 in summer, and weekends in fall; 528-5132.

Swimming is prohibited at Lake Ralphine, but you can fish and rent sailboats, canoes, rowboats, and paddleboats if you're a qualified boater. The summer boating season runs from June 13 to September 7, 10 to 5 daily. Boat rental fees vary from $2 to $3 per hour. There's also a boat launch, costing $1.50 per launch or $4 for a yearly permit. No motorboats are allowed on Lake Ralphine, and only boats under twenty feet in length may use the lake. The Santa Rosa City Parks and Recreation Department sponsors sailing and boating classes here; call 528-5115.

Spring Lake Park

This county park has 320 oak-studded acres; a 72-acre lake containing bass, bluegill, and trout for year-round fishing; and a warm spring-fed swimming lagoon with 3 acres of sandy beach. Spring Lake is a multiuse park, popular with fishermen, swimmers, boaters, joggers, hikers, bicyclists, equestrians, and campers.

Boats can be rented here in summer—canoes, kayaks, sailboats, rowboats, paddleboats, tubes. There's a launch ramp on the west side of the lake. No powerboats are allowed.

Camping facilities include twenty-nine family-type campsites for RVs and tenters, plus five walk-in campsites and one large group campsite (up to 100 people maximum) with centrally located showers and rest room facilities. There are 200 picnic units with barbecue pits.

Spring Lake Park may be reached via Newanga Avenue

off Summerfield Road or by taking Montgomery Drive to
Channel Drive and Violetti Road. Day use fee is $2.00;
camping fees are $5 for RVs and tents, $1 for walk-in
camping. For more information, call or write Sonoma
County Regional Parks, 2403 Professional Drive, Suite
100, Santa Rosa, CA 95401, 527-2041; or Spring Lake
Park, 539-8092.

From Spring Lake Park you may hike or horseback ride
into Annadel State Park; if you're driving, continue on
Montgomery Drive to Channel Drive for the entrance to
Annadel.

Annadel State Park

On almost any level, Annadel State Park is a microcosm of
Sonoma County, be it geology, geography, ecology, history, or people. Its volcanic past left it rumpled and rolling,
with an old volcano, Bennett Peak, on its south flank.
Annadel's canyons are dark with redwoods, Douglas firs,
and laurels; her grassy meadows stand crowded with California black oaks, live oaks, and Oregon oaks. Blacktailed
deer and wild pigs roam about, while over 130 bird species
flock to Ledson Marsh.

Pomo and Wappo Indians held uneasy truces here while
they came to dig for obsidian; a lucky hiker may still find a
perfectly formed arrowhead. As part of Scotsman William
Hood's Los Guilicos Rancho, the land was used for ranching; then vineyards, orchards, and hop fields were planted.
Italian stonemasons quarried basalt blocks from the hillsides, used for San Francisco streets.

The name Annadel dates from its dairy farm days;
then, under mining and real estate magnate Joe Coney,
Annadel became a rich man's preserve, a hunting and
riding club. Eleventh-hour negotiations kept the land
from becoming subdivided, and Santa Rosa businessman
Henry Trione engineered the financing to preserve the
5,000 acres which today compose this state park.

Annadel is a free, day-use park, a place for hikers,
equestrians, fishermen, and nature lovers. Twenty-five-

Annadel State Park. (Don Edwards)

acre Lake Ilsanjo (named for Joe and Ilsa Coney) is stocked
with black bass and bluegill; it's about a three-mile hike
from the parking lot on Channel Drive. Swimming and
boating are prohibited in the lake. Trails are steep in many
places, so wear good hiking shoes. Bring your own water.
Annadel State Park is open daily from one hour before
sunrise to one hour after sunset. For more information,
write Annadel State Park, c/o Sonoma Area, P.O. Box
167, Sonoma, CA 95476; 996-1744 or 539-3911.

72

Santa Rosa Farm Trails

S cattered amid Santa Rosa's blossoming housing tracts and industrial parks stand reminders of the city's agricultural past—weatherworn barns and water towers, disintegrating hop kilns, unpruned orchards. Yet a wide variety of farms are left, many open for visitors.

West of Highway 101 and near Highway 12 are two well-known farm outlets—Imwalle Gardens and the Dutton Ranch. Imwalle Gardens, 685 West Third Street, is a produce bazaar with tomatoes, corn, beans, pickling cucumbers, onions, pumpkins, nursery bedding plants, garlic, mushrooms, and eggs. Joseph Imwalle, a native of Hanover, Germany, began Imwalle Gardens in 1895 and delivered produce door to door in horse-drawn wagons. The wagons are gone, but little else has changed on this farm. Joseph Imwalle III, grandson of the founder, and his family are regular winners of the "one farm family" exhibit competition at the annual Sonoma County Harvest Fair. Imwalle Gardens are open all year Monday through Saturday, 8:30-5:30; and Sunday, 11-4, from March to June; 546-0279.

The Dutton Ranch, 2808 Sebastopol Road, sells apples, apple juice, pears, peaches, walnuts, honey, and dried fruit (pears, apricots, and apples) in a barn decorated with antique farm equipment. Their custom-made gift packs can be shipped anywhere in the U.S. Dutton Ranch is open daily 9-6, August through December; 545-8447.

Guerneville Road, which runs between Highway 101 and Highway 116, is a pleasant way to get to the Sebastopol apple country or the Russian River resort region. At 2481 Guerneville Road is the Organic Grocery, one of northern California's largest and most complete stores of its kind, highlighting a wide variety of fruits and vegetables, plus body care products, massage and exercise tools, books, and housewares. The Organic Grocery is open Monday through Thursday, 10-7; weekends, 10-6. Call 528-FOOD.

Sunnyside Eggs, 2971 Guerneville Road, sells fresh

eggs, dairy products, luncheon and breakfast meats. Hours are 9:30-5:30, Monday through Saturday. To order eggs, call 542-3332.

Nearby is Willowside Meats, 3421 Guerneville Road, with homemade sausages—Polish, Italian, and summer— plus custom processing of domestic meats or wild game. Open all year 8-6, Monday through Friday; 8-4, Saturday; 546-8404.

Northwest of Santa Rosa in the Piner Road area, Martin Lambert, Jr. offers Gravenstein and Rome apples, dried pears, prunes, and walnuts. Open daily from August to November at 3964 Coffey Lane; 544-1653.

Winemakers are most likely familiar with this area. They head for Sonoma Grapevines, Inc., 1919 Dennis Lane (off Coffey Lane), to select grape scion or grape root-stock varieties. Also sold here are tropical plants, African violets, fuchsias, palms, and ferns. Open all year Monday through Friday, 8-4:30; 542-5510. Once the grapes are ready to be crushed, the next stop is Great Fermentations, 860 Piner Road #25, where Nancy Vineyard or Byron Burch stock supplies for winemaking and brewing.

East of Santa Rosa, an unusual farmland tour is yours at The Earthworm Company, 3675 Calistoga Road, off Highway 12 near Spring Lake Park. Tours are offered on weekends and Wednesdays, and gardeners can learn exactly how earthworms enrich the soil. Tour fees are $15 per couple or $8 per person, but fees are credited toward the purchase of earthworms or earthworm castings. Call 539-6335.

Santa Rosa even has its own snail ranch (well, not everybody raises horses). This is the brain child of Francois Picart, a French transplant who raises snails for escargot lovers across the country. Picart can't keep up with the demand, so he advertises locally for gardeners to turn in their pests for profits. (Yes, those big brown snails in northern California are edible.) Picart is also turning his attention to truffles, a mushroom that grows underground on oak tree roots. For more information, write F. Picart Snails, P.O. Box 6801, Santa Rosa, CA 95406.

For those of you who would like to see larger farms, the

annual Back-to-the-Farm Day takes place in May, with bus tours to local dairies, egg ranches, or produce farms. Write the Environmental Forum, P.O. Box 4874, Santa Rosa, CA 95404.

Coddingtown

Sonoma County's most well-established shopping center can be reached via Steele Lane, or by taking the Guerneville Road/Steele Lane exit off Highway 101 and driving west. Coddingtown opened in 1962, built by prolific developer Hugh Codding of Codding Enterprises, Rohnert Park. Department stores in Coddingtown include Emporium-Capwell, Penney's, and Liberty House; the complex includes a number of restaurants, movie theaters, and specialty shops. The Exxon station at Coddingtown, on Guerneville Road, has extra-wide gas pump spaces for RVs.

Adjacent to Coddingtown is Los Robles Lodge, 925 Edwards Avenue, with ninety guest rooms, heated pools, hot tubs, dining room, and cocktail lounge with entertainment and dancing. Los Robles Lodge also has banquet and convention facilities, 545-6330.

Redwood Empire Ice Arena

The Redwood Empire Ice Arena, 1667 West Steele Lane off Guerneville Road, is a Swiss chalet-style structure near Coddingtown Shopping Center. This ice skaters' heaven is the brain child of "Peanuts" cartoonist Charles Schulz of Santa Rosa. The arena offers a full range of skating—figure skating, ice hockey, broomball, skating classes—and many world champion skaters have glided across the ice here, including Tai Babilonia and Randy Gardner. The Redwood Empire Ice Arena

hosts the Santa Rosa Junior Hockey Club, with programs
for boys of all ages, and it sponsors adult hockey games
and a competitive broomball league. Special concerts are
also held here, featuring top entertainers such as Bob
Newhart, Seiji Ozawa, Helen Reddy, and Liberace.

The arena is open daily, but hours vary, with mornings
reserved for programs and classes. Current hours:
12:15-1:45, Monday and Wednesday, 4-5:30, Tuesday,
Thursday, and Friday; 12:30-5, weekends. There are also
evening hours: 8:30-11, Monday and Wednesday for
adults only; 7:30-9:30, Tuesday and Thursday; 8-11,
Friday and Saturday. Admission prices: $3.25 for adults,
$2.75 for teens twelve to seventeen, $2.25 for children
eleven and under. Skate rental fee is 75 cents. The stained-
glass windows depicting Snoopy of "Peanuts" fame lead to
the coffee shop, which opens at 7 A.M. There's a gift shop
too. Phone 546-7147.

The Redwood Empire Ice Arena is perhaps the most
public gift Charles "Sparky" Schulz has given to Sonoma
County, but he's a behind-the-scene contributor to many
charitable organizations. A native of Minnesota and a
county resident since 1958, Schulz began his cartoon strip
in 1950, and today "Peanuts" is read in over eighteen
hundred newspapers in sixty-five countries worldwide.
The antics and adventures of "Peanuts" characters—
Charlie Brown, Snoopy, Lucy, Linus, Peppermint Patty,
Woodstock, and others—are also seen in television specials
that have become a part of holiday traditions for many.
Santa Rosans get a special chuckle when they see a cartoon
item with a local twist.

Fountain Grove

Travelers heading north out of Santa Rosa along
Highway 101 can't miss a landmark (on the right):
a red, round barn, a physical reminder of nineteenth-century mysticism and twentieth-century wine-
making at Fountain Grove Ranch. In the latter half of the

76

nineteenth century, Sonoma County led the state in
communes, with no less than four. The most famous and
long-lived was Fountain Grove, started in 1875 when the
spiritual leader of the Brotherhood of the New Life,
Thomas Lake Harris, came west from New York to open a
branch of his commune.

Harris believed that through Divine Respiration, or
"New Breath," man could commune directly with God,
whom he saw as a bisexual deity. He preached a mixture of
brotherhood and socialism flavored with highly esoteric
sexual beliefs. This spiritualist/poet, with his patriarchal
beard, commanding voice, and penetrating black eyes
"like revolving lights in two dark caverns," gathered a
select group of his followers at Fountain Grove. Among
these were the English Lady Oliphant and her son Laurence, who had given up his seat in Parliament, and Baron
Kanaye Nagasawa, a young Japanese nobleman. Harris
built an Adams-Georgian-style mansion, separate quarters
for men and women, and Russian-style barns, including
the round barn still visible from the freeway. The mansion
was the scene of parties and dances, with wines from the
colony's own vineyards. The Fountain Grove colonists
believed their vintages were infused with "divine and
celestial energy."

When new converts arrived at Fountain Grove, Harris
separated husbands from wives, parted them from their
money, and took over their spiritual, financial, and sexual
lives. According to Harris's theology, earthly marriage was
to be avoided in favor of celestial bliss. Critics charged
that Fountain Grove was a hotbed of adultery and free
love, and it was a woman who proved Harris's undoing.

Alzire Chevaillier, a reporter, infiltrated Fountain
Grove and invaded Harris's inner sanctum; there she
found the mystic with his feet in the lap of his secretary,
Dovie Lee Waring. Harris explained such a position stimulated the "Internal Respiration" or "New Breath," which
came from the Divine Spirit.

Following Chevaillier's devastating articles in Bay Area
newspapers, Harris and the hooka-smoking Miss Waring
fled Fountain Grove. Laurence Oliphant sued Harris for

misuse of his family's funds and was awarded a considerable sum. He later left to settle in Palestine and work for a new Zion.

Baron Nagasawa remained at Fountain Grove, developing some of the state's finest vineyards and best wines. Among the many who visited Nagasawa at Fountain Grove were poet Edwin Markham, Luther Burbank, and viticultural giant Frederick Bioletti.

After Nagasawa's death in 1934, the vineyards remained untended until two German refugees, Kurt Opper (later winemaster at Paul Masson Winery) and Hans Kornell (who today has his own winery in the Napa Valley) came to restore the Fountain Grove label to greatness. They left after Fountain Grove's owner, Errol Mac-Boyle, died and his widow sold the property.

Today a portion of Fountain Grove Ranch is occupied by Hewlett Packard, a microwave technology firm. The Santa Rosa plant, with 3,000 employees, is one of the largest of the Palo Alto-based company. Free 1½-hour tours of Hewlett Packard are offered to the public; it's an opportunity to see the research, development, and manufacture of high-frequency transistors and integrated circuits. For tours, call 525-1400 two weeks prior to the desired tour date, or write Hewlett Packard, 1400 Fountain Grove Parkway, Santa Rosa, CA 95404.

Luther Burbank Center for the Arts

Farther north of Santa Rosa and east of Highway 101, at 50 Mark West Springs Road, is the new Luther Burbank Center for the Arts, future home of the Santa Rosa Symphony. The center became a reality in September 1981 when the Christian Life Center, a religious organization, was forced to sell its holdings as part of bankruptcy proceedings. A group of influential Sonoma County residents, members of the Luther Burbank Foundation, bought the property and are now

renovating the main sanctuary. Foundation members—
including Santa Rosa financier Henry Trione; developers
Hugh and Nell Codding; and Evert and Ruth Person,
owners and publishers of the Santa Rosa *Press Democrat*—
plan to use the 1,900-seat facility for touring concerts and
plays, as well as local performances, and it will be the
home of the Santa Rosa Symphony. Actor Raymond Burr
also envisions a theater school at the center, under his
direction.

The Santa Rosa Symphony, fifty-four years of age in
1981, has gained a sterling reputation in the Bay Area. For
more than a quarter of a century the symphony conductor
has been Corrick Brown, a Santa Rosa native and head of
the family's stationery store on the Fourth Street Mall.
Season tickets range from $15 (for students and seniors) to
$50. Individual concert tickets are $7. For ticket information, call 54-MUSIC or write the Symphony Association, P.O. Box 1081, Santa Rosa, CA 95402.

Mark West Springs Road

From Highway 101, Mark Springs Road winds
through the countryside, then connects with roads
leading into the Napa Valley.

On Mark West Creek, the Hijar-Farias colony briefly
flourished in 1834. This group of Mexico City artisans
came to frontier California as the Mexican government's
only attempt to colonize her northernmost province. The
colony's teachers, printers, silversmiths, and tailors scattered across California, forming an enriching mosaic of
talent among the pueblos and *ranchos*.

Englishman Mark West moved onto his Rancho San
Miguel here in 1840, opening a store and starting one of
the county's first schools. The mineral springs resort that
grew up nearby attracted many visitors, including the
utopian Alturias commune in 1894. Under the leadership
of Edward Biron Payne, a Berkeley Unitarian minister, the
Alturians (so named for William Dean Howells's utopian
novel *A Traveler from Alturia*) formed a rural consumer

cooperative movement in Sonoma County. Although it failed, Payne remained in Sonoma County, settling near Glen Ellen, where his wife's foster daughter, Charmian Kittredge, first attracted the attention of her future husband, Jack London.

The famed Mark West Lodge, 2520 Mark West Springs Road, location of the state's oldest living grapevine, served travelers for 108 years before burning to the ground in 1979. Czech restaurateur Rene Pavel rebuilt the lodge and now serves fine meals in Victorian elegance. Diners select calf sweetbreads, poached salmon, pheasant, or filet mignon, complemented by Sonoma County, French, and German wines. The Mark West Lodge is open for dinner Tuesday through Sunday and for Sunday brunch. Call 546-2592 for reservations.

Petrified Forest

Ten miles from Santa Rosa via Mark West Springs Road, Porter Creek Road, and Petrified Forest Road are the stony remains of a redwood grove flattened by a lava flow 6 million years ago. The Petrified Forest was first excavated by "Petrified Charlie" Evans, a nineteenth-century prospector. Since 1860, visitors have traveled to view the 126-foot-long "Monarch" redwood and other fossil flora. Robert Louis Stevenson mentioned the forest in his book *Silverado Squatters*. Today you can take a self-guided tour, picnic on the grounds, and also visit the museum and gift shop. The forest is at 4100 Petrified Forest Road; open daily 9-6 summer, 9-5 winter. Adults $2, children under ten free, special group rates; 942-6667.

Sonoma County Airport

A riving farther north on Highway 101 and exiting at Airport Boulevard will take you to the Sonoma County Airport. Located northwest of Santa Rosa, this 950-acre airport, owned and operated by Sonoma County, is home base for nearly three hundred

80

private and business aircraft. The airport's two paved runways, fully equipped control tower, and paved and lighted taxiways serve a number of scheduled passenger and air freight service airlines.

Airport services include regular aviation and jet fuel, engine repair and parts, ground school and flight instruction, charters, air taxi, aircraft rental, air ambulance, Cessna and Piper dealerships, taxi and car rental. D's Airport Inn and a cocktail lounge are located within the airport terminal. Sonoma County Airport administration office number is 542-3139. This number is not to be used for calling airlines or tenants.

Hot Air Balloons and Airplanes

L ittle did the French know when they launched the first hot air balloon in 1783—with a sheep, a duck, and a rooster as passengers—that they'd launched a craze. The craze has spread to Sonoma County, and you can see what it's all about by taking a flight over vineyards and wooded hills.

Sonoma's clear skies and interesting cross breezes make the region an ideal spot for manned balloons. Your flight will begin with a "whoosh" as the wicker basket beneath the balloon leaves the ground. Then there's silence and awe-inspiring vistas. Although modern aeronauts use compact propane burners to inflate the balloons and "ripstop" nylon envelopes that don't tear when punctured, the wind still has the final say on the landing spot. A ground crew keeps track of your flight so that when the balloon lands, you will have transportation back to your car.

Manned hot air balloon flights in Sonoma County, many complete with champagne, run from $50 for a halfhour flight to $90 for a one-hour flight. Sonoma Thunder operates out of Sonoma; call 996-1112 or 938-5131. Rides from Flights of Fantasy are reserved exclusively in Sonoma County at the London Lodge in Glen Ellen, 938-8510, or

Santa Rosa News-Herald

in San Francisco at (415) 921-5280. In Santa Rosa, call Airborn of Sonoma, 528-8133; Skyline Balloons Champagne Flights, 539-3209; or Thunder Pacific, 546-7124.

If you want something faster, hop on over to the Sonoma County Airport for an airplane charter from National Flight Service, Redwood Aviation, or Sonoma Valley Flyers. A round trip to Gualala for two in a Cessna 172 runs about $65.

For scenic tours and exciting aerobatic rides in a 1940-vintage two-seater biplane, see pilot Chuck Hunter at Aerosport, located at the Schellville Airport, 23982 Arnold Drive (Highway 121). Hunter offers three types of biplane rides: a straight-flying scenic tour over San Pablo Bay near Sears Point; a modified scenic flight with a loop and a roll; and, shades of the Red Baron, an exhilarating, terrifying, full aerobatic flight over the airport. The quarter-hour flights cost $30 to $40; call 938-2444.

Wine Institute

Northern Sonoma County 3

Wine Country

The meandering Russian River and the volcanic ridges of the Mendocino highlands and the Mayacamas Mountains dominate much of sparsely populated northern Sonoma County. The river tacks back and forth across the valley between hillsides and benchlands before turning west toward the Pacific Ocean. To the east there is evidence of the violent volcanic activity that occurred in this area's recent geologic history: majestic Mount St. Helena, the Bay Area's tallest peak, dominates the horizon, and at The Geysers, steam hisses through openings in the ground.

The Pomo and Wappo Indians first populated these valleys along the Russian River, followed by Russian explorers from Fort Ross. Mexican soldiers and American trappers settled massive Mexican land grants in the 1840s, bringing the first grapevines to the red-soiled hillsides. Following the Mexican War, the great *ranchos* were overrun with squatters and a prolonged "squatters war" erupted.

The *ranchos* were divided, and enormous cattle herds and grainfields gave way to prune orchards and hop fields. German, French, and especially Italian settlers pioneered grape growing, while colonies of landless immigrants, socialists, and religious devotees created communities and communes like Icaria, Preston, and the Italian Swiss Colony at Asti.

The arrival of the San Francisco and North Pacific Railroad in 1871 made Healdsburg a major fruit canning and shipping center, with prunes, peaches, apples, cherries, pears, and wine sent throughout America. Visitors rode the rails to vacation along the Russian River or to bathe at mineral hot springs like Skaggs Hot Springs and Lytton Hot Springs. Thousands made the arduous stagecoach trip to The Geysers, nineteenth-century California's second tourist attraction after Yosemite.

Prohibition killed the local wineries, and after Repeal, those that reopened produced bulk wines for wineries outside of the area. The Russian River Valley wine renaissance began in 1970, when Los Angeles oilman Russ Green purchased Simi Winery and planted grapes amid the prune orchards of the Alexander Valley. Long-established wine-making families were joined by corporate heads, ex-actors, former journalists, doctors, and engineers, all eager to transform the Russian River Valley into the born-again wine world it is today.

There are now dozens of wineries throughout the Russian River Valley, producing vintages rivaling those of the Napa Valley and Europe. You can select wineries for a tasting tour by following the wine tour routes suggested in this chapter. Many small wineries are open by appointment only, so it is best to call ahead. Along the route, you can also pick up locally grown fruits and vegetables at many area farms or at the Healdsburg Farmer's Market.

Many visitors come to northern Sonoma to fish or canoe in the Russian River; Lake Sonoma, when it is completed in 1984, will also be a prime recreational spot. The Russian River Valley hosts many annual events, from fairs, musicals, and art shows to wine tastings, canoe races, and harvest festivals. And for the hiker and the Sunday driver, the quiet countryside of northern Sonoma is a visual feast. In spring, the wild mustard blooms amid the vineyards, and prune orchards are white with blossoms; in fall, the vineyards blaze with color—scarlet, orange, and gold.

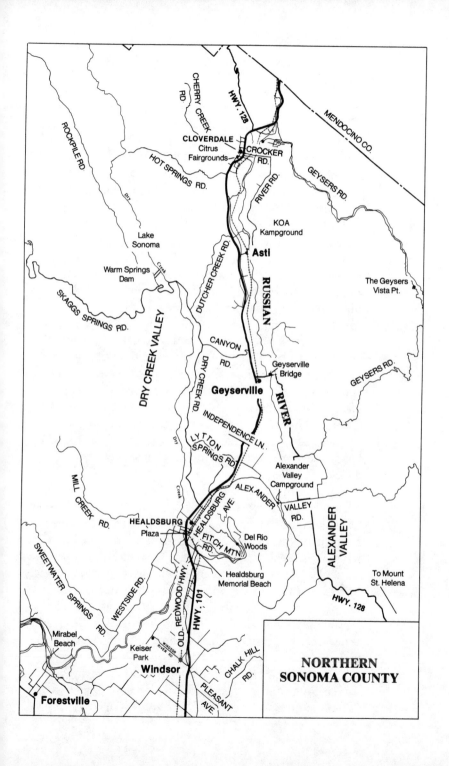

NORTHERN
SONOMA COUNTY

86

Windsor

The unincorporated community of Windsor lies north of Santa Rosa on either side of Highway 101 along the route of the Old Redwood Highway. The home of several wineries, two campgrounds, and produce farms, it is also known for aquatic fun on the waterslides of the Windsor Waterworks.

Pioneer mail carrier Hiram Lewis dubbed the town Windsor after the numerous oak groves here which reminded him of the parkland setting of England's Windsor Castle. The community that began here in the 1850s was the center of an agricultural area, producing grain, wine grapes, poultry, hops, and prunes. Today wine grapes are again a primary crop.

Windsor still has several pioneer structures, including an octagonal barn, 105 feet across and 105 feet high, built in 1868 and today the stable for Mount Weske Arabians at 1601 Mount Weske Drive off Brooks Road. Windsor's historic Methodist church building is now Chappell's Old Church Antique & Collective & Sandwich Shoppe, 251 Windsor River Road, near downtown Windsor, where you can eyeball antiques while having a piece of their delicious homemade pie.

Two Farm Trail stops worth an exit off Highway 101 at Shiloh Road are the Windsor Iris Gardens, 6842 Hembree Lane, and the DuVander Orchards, 221 Pleasant Avenue. Each spring the Windsor Iris Gardens hosts an open house where hundreds of blooming irises attract visitors for viewing and sales. They're open all year on weekends from 11 to 5, weekdays by appointment, 838-4640. Iris blooming season runs from March to May. DuVander Orchards highlights Gravenstein apples, Bartlett pears, Elberta and other freestone peaches during the month of August, open from Monday to Saturday, 10-6; 838-2174.

Windsor's hot in summer, but you can beat the heat with a trip to the Windsor Waterworks and Slides. Their "Doom Flume" is a series of four huge waterslides, each more than 400 feet long. Water riders sit or lie down on foam mats which carry them through the cascading series of tunnels, slopes, and valleys on a continuously flowing stream of water, and then plunge into the receiving pool before hiking up the stairs to start again. Children should be at least six years old to ride the Doom Flume. The oak tree-covered grounds also feature a huge family swimming pool, hot tubs, and picnic areas with barbecue pits.

The Windsor Waterworks and Slides is open 10-6, weekdays; 10-8, weekends, from Easter until early fall. Rates are $2.75 per one-half hour for the slides and hot tub; $2.50 for adults, $1.50 for children 12 and under in the day use area (pool and picnic area). All-day plan is $9 for adults, $8 for kids 12 and under, group rates available. Take the Windsor Exit off Highway 101 to the Old Redwood Highway and Conde Lane to reach the Windsor Waterworks and Slides at 8225 Conde Lane, 838-7760.

Adjacent to the Windsor Waterworks is the Camperlodge R.V. Park, 8225 Conde Lane, with 106 sites for all types of recreational vehicles, full and limited hookups. This oak-shaded park has tent and camping areas also, plus hot showers, laundry, grocery store, recreation room, swimming pool, and dump station. Groups and clubs are welcomed; call 838-4195. Nearby is Windsorland R.V. Trailer Park, 9290 Old Redwood Highway, with fifty-six full hookup sites, laundry, recreation hall, pool, and playground. Call 838-4882.

Windsor Winery Tour

Landmark Vineyards, 9150 Los Amigos Road, is aptly named, for visitors taking the Windsor exit off Highway 101 and onto Los Amigos Road soon spot the double row of great cypress trees bordering the lane that leads to the winery. Besides the winery building, on the property there's a 1930s Spanish-style home once owned by San Francisco millionaire civic leader William Matson Roth and the 1849 ranch house built by the pioneer Hembree family.

88

The Mabry family founded the winery in 1975 and currently produces 15,000 cases of wine annually: Chardonnay, Cabernet Sauvignon, Johannisberg Riesling, Pinot Noir, Gewurztraminer, Chenin Blanc—all 100 percent varietals and estate bottled. Landmark Vineyards is open for informal tours, sales, and tastings on weekends, 10-5, or by appointment, 838-9466. There are picnic tables too.

Sonoma Vineyards is the home of wine innovations, from their futuristic-style winery building to their Piper-Sonoma sparkling wines (a joint effort of the winery and French champagne maker Piper-Heidsieck). The winery is located at 11455 Old Redwood Highway, three miles north of the Windsor exit off Highway 101.

Established by Rodney Strong, formerly an actor, now winemaster, Sonoma Vineyards today is the North Coast's biggest single grape grower and one of the region's largest premium wineries. Sonoma Vineyards' 1,600 acres of grapes produce 650,000 cases of wine annually, expertly handled in the cruciform-shaped winery designed to minimize the handling of wine from crush to finished product. True to his theatrical background, Strong has incorporated an open air Greek Theatre into the winery design.

Sonoma Vineyards' vintage-dated wines include Cabernet Sauvignon, Chardonnay, Pinot Noir, Johannisberg Riesling, Petite Sirah, Gamay Beaujolais, Zinfandel, and French Colombard among others, and the winery has a large mail order business under the Windsor Vineyards label (you can also get personalized Windsor Vineyards labels). Other varietal wines are available under the Rodney D. Strong label.

Sonoma Vineyards currently produces Blanc de Blanc and Blanc de Noir champagnes, made literally one bottle at a time in the *methode ancien*. Piper-Sonoma sparkling wines will be marketed soon, and an $8 million sparkling wine complex, with a 100,000-case capacity winery, a visitors' center, and a theater for live performances, is under construction. Although Piper-Sonoma sparkling wines will be made in the French *methode champenoise* (where the champagne is fermented in the same bottle you buy), Strong prefers to call his results sparkling wines, reserving the title champagne for the products of the Champagne region of France. The sparkling wines will be produced from early ripening, cool climate Chardonnay and Pinot Noir grapes from Sonoma Vineyards' outstanding "Chalk Hill," "River East," and "River West" plantings.

Sonoma Vineyards is open 10-5 daily, with tours on the hour, tasting, retail sales, and a picnic area. Mailing address, P.O. Box 368, Windsor, CA 95492, phone 433-6511. From Sonoma Vineyards you can take Old Redwood Highway 1.2 miles into Healdsburg with a stop at the Healdsburg Plaza.

Healdsburg

Dominated by the conical, tree-covered slopes of 991-foot-tall Fitch Mountain, this farming community of 7,250 people began in 1852 when Harmon Heald, an Ohio-born, Missouri-bred forty-niner, opened a store and cabin under the oak trees where the Healdsburg Plaza is today. Heald died of consumption at age 34, but the tiny hamlet took his name and survived.

Centuries before Heald arrived, the Southern Pomo and Wappo Indian tribes camped along the banks of the Russian River, where Healdsburg's beaches are today. Healdsburg was part of the Rancho Sotoyome granted in 1841 to Henry Delano Fitch, a Massachusetts sea captain and brother-in-law to the wife of Gen. Mariano G. Vallejo. In 1829 Fitch had shocked Mexican California by eloping with Josefa Carrillo, after Governor Jose Maria Echeandia issued an edict banning their marriage. Josefa had reportedly spurned Echeandia, and sympathetic relatives spirited Josefa and Fitch away on a ship to Chile where they were wed. Although Fitch never lived at his Rancho Sotoyome, Fitch Mountain immortalizes his brief visit to the region,

where he installed a mountain man, Cyrus Alexander, as
overseer of his ranch.

After Healdsburg was established, the late 1850s saw a
series of squatters wars that rocked the area, and state
militiamen were finally called in to rid the *ranchos* of
squatters. These conflicts lasted more than seven years
and at one time involved over one thousand men.

Early American settlers, of English and Scotch-Irish
ancestry, were mainly Missouri farmers who grew grain
and raised cattle in the fertile valleys around Healdsburg.
The coming of the railroad in 1871 made Healdsburg the
center of orchard crop industries, with pears, apples,
cherries, and peaches, but most important were the French
and Imperial prune crops that made Healdsburg the
"buckle of the California prune belt." In the early 1900s,
Healdsburg boasted of a number of canneries, and Sunsweet Growers still has an active processing plant in town.

Vinicultural interests grew with the coming of German,
French, and Italian settlers who introduced European
grapes and old-world winemaking methods. Prohibition
killed the wineries, and after Repeal local vintners shipped
their wines to the East Coast in freight cars for bottling.
Only in the last decade have local wineries replaced prune
production as Healdsburg's major industry, and several
annual festivals now spotlight local wines.

Healdsburg and the surrounding area grow 18,000 acres
of grapes, but there are a number of other local agricultural crops, including almost 5,000 acres of prunes, 1,000
acres of apples, 600 acres of pears, and small acreages of
kiwifruit. There are also nurseries and Christmas tree
farms; dairy, sheep, and cattle ranches. Many local Farm
Trail stops offer these local products for sale.

Healdsburg's Russian River location has made it a
favorite spot since its founding. Public and private beaches
draw swimmers, canoeists, and fishermen, while several of
the town's historic Victorians are now bed and breakfast
stops. The town is a focal point for Sonoma County's
growing Chicano and Mexican-born population, reflected
in an annual Latin American fiesta.

Healdsburg Plaza

Harmon Heald laid out the town's plaza in 1856 and, unlike Sonoma's Plaza, the surrounding buildings have been changing ever since. The town's main thoroughfare, Healdsburg Avenue, forms the west boundary of the Plaza; Center Street is the east boundary; Plaza Street is the northern boundary; and Matheson Street, the Plaza's southern boundary, continues east as Fitch Mountain Road, which leads to the Russian River.

Healdsburg Plaza, with its redwood and palm trees, its fountain and park benches, is an ideal picnic spot. Many annual events are held here, including the Russian River Wine Festival, the Fiesta Latinamericana, and the Healdsburg Harvest Hoedown. Each May local wineries set up booths in the Plaza as part of the Russian River Wine Festival, which also features food, arts and crafts, and live music. Tasters purchase a souvenir glass and three tastings for a nominal fee, and additional tasting tickets are available.

The Fiesta Latinamericana, held around September 20 each year, commemorates Mexican Independence Day and the independence of several other Latin American countries from Spain. The Plaza becomes a bilingual bazaar of games, dances, songs, and theater; and kids can try to break a piñata. Mexican foods and drinks are also served. The activities are free and begin at noon.

The Healdsburg Harvest Hoedown, held in early October, spotlights homemade baked goods, jams and jellies, free balloons, live music, free hay rides, and then square dances to work off the pounds. This free event starts at noon.

The Healdsburg Chamber of Commerce, near the Plaza at 217 Healdsburg Avenue, is the place to pick up more information on these and other annual Healdsburg events. Also available are Healdsburg maps and literature, free Russian River Wine Road maps highlighting more than two score wineries in the Russian River Valley, and current Sonoma County Farm Trails maps. Watch for

signposts near the wineries which denote the Russian
River Wine Road routes. Chamber manager Helendale
Barrett and Meredith Driesback staff the office, 9-4,
Monday through Friday; 10-4 on weekends. Phone
433-6935.

Take a walk around the Plaza before moving on and
pick up locally baked bread, cheese, meats, and other
picnic items to go with wines from the local wineries. The
Salame Tree Deli, 304 Center Street, is an Italian deli-
restaurant offering over one hundred cheeses, two score
types of meat, locally dried fruit, regional wines, beer, plus
hot food and sandwiches to go. Open daily, except Sunday. Vivian Gromm's Pic-A-Deli, 109 Plaza Street, features
homemade soups, sandwiches, quiche, and ravioli. It's
open daily, except Sunday.

Pick up some sweet and sourdough French bread,
croissants, brioches, and French pastry at the Costeaux
French Bakery, 421 Healdsburg Avenue, near the Plaza.
Costeaux's is open Wednesday through Saturday, 7:30-5;
Sunday, 7:30-12:30. Plasberg Liquors, on the Plaza at 306
Center Street, also carries many local wines and picnic
items. Open daily. La Luna Market, 434 Center Street,
offers Mexican deli items.

If you're in the mood for elegant dining, try the Wine
Country Restaurant, 106 Matheson Street on the Plaza,
which features such dishes as New York steak, chicken
cordon bleu, and shrimp scampi. The Wine Country
Restaurant also has a full bar and live entertainment. Call
433-7203.

Gifts, quilts, kitchenwares, and home decorating items
are found at the Wild Rose, 113 Plaza Street. There will be
more shopping stops once the hotel/restaurant/shopping
complex on the west side of the Plaza is completed.

Take a peek at Healdsburg's history at the Edwin Langhart Museum, 133 Matheson Street, one block east of the
Plaza. This free museum has frequently changed exhibits
of Healdsburg's Indian, pioneer, and agricultural past. The
annual toy and doll show each Christmas is a favorite with
kids. The museum is open 12-5, weekdays; Saturday, 1-4.

The Healdsburg Farmer's Market, two blocks from the Plaza at the corner of East and Haydon streets, offers fresh, locally grown produce from vegetables, fruits, nuts, eggs, and honey to dried fruits and cut flowers. It's open Tuesdays, 5-7 P.M.; and Saturdays, 9-12, from mid-May until the early fall.

South of the Plaza lie several restaurants and two motels. There's Chinese cuisine at the House of Sonoma, 146 Healdsburg Avenue, 433-6267. The Works, at number 131, spotlights Swiss-Italian cooking, while Giorgio's Pizza and Italian Restaurant, 25 Grant Avenue, serves lunch and dinner in a converted farmhouse south of town, 433-1106. Jose Ramirez' Tamaulipeco Mexican Restaurant dishes up homemade delights, 433-5202. On Healdsburg Avenue are two motels: L & M (433-9934) features waterbeds and kitchenettes, while the Fairview (433-5548) has a heated pool.

Fitch Mountain

The shady slopes of Fitch Mountain and the nearby Russian River beaches have been tourist attractions since Healdsburg's founding. Today you can drive around Fitch Mountain, past Healdsburg's Victorian homes, and then circle back to the center of town.

Start with a drive from the Plaza east along Matheson Street, named for Scottish-born Roderick N. Matheson, a Healdsburg pioneer who helped establish the Russian River Institute (a prominent early day school). Matheson went to Washington to attend Lincoln's inauguration and stayed to become a colonel in the 1st California Regiment during the Civil War. He died of wounds received on a Virginia battlefield in 1862.

Matheson Street contains several residences built by pioneer families. Two homes of interest are the A. W. Garrett house at 403 Matheson, a small Queen Anne cottage, and an 1890s vintage Queen Anne mission revival home at 423 Matheson Street. Both are privately owned, not open to the public.

94

Once out of the city limits, Matheson Street becomes Fitch Mountain Road. At 9095 Fitch Mountain Road is the public, nine-hole, par-35 Tayman Park Municipal Golf Course. It's open daily, hosts men's and women's clubs, and has a modern pro shop and clubhouse. Weekday rates are $3; weekend rates, $5. Call 433-4275.

The Russian River beaches below Fitch Mountain are privately owned, including one at Del Rio Woods, 2795 Fitch Mountain Road. There is parking and public access to the river here, and the summer dam at Del Rio Woods Beach makes this a popular swimming, fishing, and canoeing spot.

Among the many resorts that have existed over the years around Fitch Mountain is Villa Chanticleer, established in 1910 as a resort for San Francisco's French community. One of the villa's owners was French-born Lucien Delagnes, who would meet visitors at the Healdsburg Depot and bring them to the "villa," where they feasted on ham, rabbit, homemade sausages, fresh cream and butter, and local wines. He took his guests on excursions to the Sonoma Coast via Skaggs Springs Road, or to see the hissing fumaroles at The Geysers.

Today the Villa Chanticleer, 1248 North Fitch Mountain Road, is a city-owned facility for meetings, banquets, dances, and picnics on the seventeen-acre site. Two annual events are headquartered here—the Spring Blossom Tour and the Wine Symposium. The Villa is a good starting or ending point for the self-guided Spring Blossom Tour, which includes visits to the orchards of the Russian River Valley, a barn sale in Geyserville, a pioneer exhibit at historic Alexander Valley Community Church, and lunch at the Alexander Valley Community Hall. The two-day event is free. The Wine Symposium is a spring event, where tastings of unreleased wines from the Russian River area precede a gourmet dinner and discussions on the wine industry. Advance reservations are required. For details on both events, call the chamber of commerce office, 433-6935.

Fitch Mountain Road becomes Powell Avenue once you're back in residential Healdsburg. The Wine Bibbers Inn, a bed and breakfast retreat in town, is reached by taking University Street off Powell to Monte Vista Avenue. At 603 Monte Vista, Jayne and Don Headley have turned two homes on the old Rafanelli family property into exquisitely decorated hideaways for up to fourteen people. The homes and their bedrooms are named for local wineries—the Landmark House has four bedrooms, while the Foppiano House has three. Make your reservations a month in advance during the summer, a week during the winter; 433-3019.

The Grape Leaf Inn, 539 Johnson Street (three blocks from Healdsburg Plaza), is one of Healdsburg's newest bed and breakfast inns, located on a street with a number of eye-pleasing Victorian homes. The seventy-year-old home was restored to turn-of-the-century decor and has four bedrooms, each named for a local grape variety. Advance reservations a must, 433-8140.

You can tour Fitch Mountain on foot during the annual Fitch Mountain Footrace and Health Fair, held each June. A nominal fee is charged for the ten-kilometer (6.2 miles) course or the shorter four-mile run. The chamber of commerce has details, 433-6935.

Healdsburg Memorial Beach

Just south of the Russian River Bridge on Old Redwood Highway is Healdsburg Memorial Beach, a popular swimming, canoeing, and picnicking spot. The bathhouse and concession, with lifeguards on the beach, is open from June to September. Parking fee is $2.

Canoe rentals are nearby, at Trowbridge Recreation Inc., 20 Healdsburg Avenue. Grumman canoes are rented for $25 per day, per trip, including life jacket, paddles, and canoe transport between beaches. Call 433-7247. River canoe trips are detailed in the Russian River chapter.

Sunsweet Growers

Across Healdsburg Avenue from Trowbridge Recreation Inc. is Sunsweet Growers, 25 Healdsburg Avenue, where you can buy (usually at a ten-pound minimum) dried apricots, pears, and peaches, pitted and unpitted prunes, raisins, walnuts, figs, and mixed fruit packages. The holiday season is the best time to pick up the fruit. The sales office, located in a mobile home just inside Sunsweet's gates, is open weekdays from 7:30 to 11:45 A.M. and 12:45 to 4:30 P.M. There are occasional one-half to one hour tours of the plant as well; call 433-3332 for arrangements.

Sunsweet's main production is in prunes, which arrive here in 1,400-pound bins after being picked the end of August and early September. The plump prunes are washed, then drained and spread on trays; they get their wrinkled look from a 15-hour, 184-degree stint in the dehydrator.

Most are French prunes, direct descendants of the cuttings brought to the Santa Clara Valley by Frenchman Pierre Pellier in 1856. Luther Burbank launched Sonoma County's commercial prune industry by delivering 20,000 young trees to rancher Warren Dutton in 1882, and soon Sonoma County was second only to Santa Clara County in statewide prune production. In 1970 Sunsweet Growers handled about 171,000 tons of prunes in Healdsburg; today the annual prune harvest is only one-fifth as large. The lowly prune just can't compete with vintage-dated wines; vineyards have replaced orchards.

Healdsburg Winery Tour

Healdsburg's half-dozen wineries include some long-established wine names—Simi, Foppiano, Cambiaso—that now share notability with newcomers like Clos Du Bois, Sotoyome, and Balverne.

Just as some wineries blend different grape varieties to make the right wine, so Simi Winery blends tradition and innovation to make it a favorite Healdsburg stopping

Simi wines aging in European oak barrels. (Simi Winery)

place. From Highway 101, take the Dry Creek exit, drive east 400 yards, and turn left at the traffic light. Simi is one mile north. If you're already in Healdsburg, follow Healdsburg Avenue northward.

The Simi brothers, Pietro and Guiseppe, natives of Montepulciano in the Tuscan hills of Italy, started the winery in 1876. After their sudden deaths, Guiseppe's teenage daughter Isabelle managed the winery until her marriage to local banker Fred Haigh. They operated the winery during Prohibition, making sacramental wines. In

1970, Russell Green, former president of Signal Oil Company, bought the winery from Isabelle Simi Haigh and carried on a tradition of women enologists by hiring Mary Ann Graf, who now has her own wine laboratory in Healdsburg. Zelma Long is currently the winemaker.

Today France's largest wine and spirits company, Moet-Hennessy, owns this historic, stone winery beside the railroad tracks and has just completed a $4.5 million modernization project. Simi's tasting room, with its stone fireplace, is a nice spot on chilly winter days, where you can taste several of Simi's dozen different wines, including Chardonnay, Chenin Blanc, Gewurtztraminer, Cabernet Sauvignon, Zinfandel, and Pinot Noir.

Simi Winery, 16275 Healdsburg Avenue, is open daily 10-5 for tasting and sales; tours are given at 11, 1, and 3. Picnic tables are located on the redwood-shaded grounds. Phone 433-6981.

Opposite Simi Winery sits Belle de Jour, a bed and breakfast inn with two bedrooms and shared bath in a small Victorian home at 16276 Healdsburg Avenue. Call 433-2724 or 433-7892.

As most of Healdsburg's wineries are located south of town, you can reach them by following Healdsburg Avenue southward until it becomes Old Redwood Highway. On your drive down Healdsburg Avenue, note the brick winery building on your right, once the pre-Prohibition home of the Oliveto Winery and Distillery.

An in-town winery near the Plaza is Clos Du Bois, 5 Fitch Street, open by appointment, 433-5576. The winery makes five wines, including Cabernet Sauvignon and Chardonnay.

Just out of town, take Grant Avenue off Healdsburg Avenue and follow it to the end, where the Cambiaso Winery is found. Cambiaso Winery began in 1934, when the Cambiaso family started in the 1852 country home that now stands next to the winery buildings. The winery is currently owned by the Likitprakong family of Thailand; Cambiaso's winemaker is Bob Fredson, fourth generation

member of a well-known Dry Creek Valley wine family,
who oversees the making of nine wine varieties at this
mid-sized Sonoma County winery. Cambiaso Winery is
open 10-4 daily for retail sales; tours and tastings by
appointment, 433-5508.

Farther south are two wineries—one old, one new.
Foppiano Vineyards, 12707 Old Redwood Highway,
433-7272, is one of California's oldest family-owned
wineries, in continuous operation since 1896. The winery
is friendly and informal; Louis Joseph Foppiano and his
sons, Louis M. and Rod, are proud of the Russian River
appellation on their wine bottles. Foppiano Winery currently produces Cabernet Sauvignon, Pinot Noir, Petite
Sirah, Zinfandel, Chardonnay, Sonoma Fume, Chenin
Blanc, and Sonoma White Burgundy. They're open daily
10-4:30 for retail sales; tasting and tours by appointment.
Picnic tables too.

A short distance away, on the other side of Highway
101, is Sotoyome Winery, located atop a red-soiled hill at
641 Limerick Lane. Opened in 1973, the winery preserves
the name of Capt. Henry Fitch's Sotoyome Rancho upon
which Healdsburg is built. The compact winery, a gem of
small-scale winemaking, is open by appointment,
433-2001. Four wines—Cabernet Sauvignon, Chardonnay, Petite Sirah, and Zinfandel—are offered here.

Balverne Cellars, two miles south of Sotoyome Winery,
at 10810 Hillview Road, has made a name for itself. Its
Healdsburger white wine was served by President Reagan
to German Chancellor Helmut Schmidt at a 1981 White
House dinner. Healdsburger is made from a blend of
Gewurztraminer, Johannisberg Riesling, and Scheurebe
grapes and is sold locally. The winery is open by appointment only, 433-6913.

North of Healdsburg at Lytton Springs is another
winery. Take Highway 101 north and exit at Lytton
Springs Road. The Lytton Springs Winery, 650 Lytton
Springs Road, produces Zinfandel. Open daily 9-5 for
sales, 433-7721.

Geyserville

Six miles north of Lytton Springs is the community of Geyserville, a time-tested village nestled in a major fruit and grape growing region. Founded in 1851 as a stage stop for travelers bound for The Geysers or Mendocino County, Geyserville was described in the 1877 *Atlas of Sonoma County:* "At present there is one store in the village, one post office and express-office, one saloon, one hotel and one blacksmith-shop. The hill-land about Geyserville is well adapted to fruit-culture, especially to the growth of wine-grapes. It would not surprise us if the wines of that section would become famous."

The early American and German vintners settling here soon attracted Italian winemakers to Geyserville, and many of the area's Italian winemakers descend from the immigrants who came between 1890 and 1919. Eight local wineries today are open to the public, and there are several country inns and fine restaurants. Geyserville is also a stop for Russian River canoe parties.

Geyserville, at the junction of Highway 128 and Highway 101, is a good starting point for trips to the Alexander Valley, The Geysers, Dry Creek Valley, or Lake Sonoma. Highway 101 bypasses the town, so take the Geyserville exit off the freeway and follow Geyserville Avenue into the village.

A favorite pit stop for bicyclists, picnickers, canoeists, and campers is the Geyserville Grocery, Geyserville Avenue at Highway 128. Here you can buy picnic supplies, sandwiches to go, and wine and beer. They're open daily 8 to 6, closed on Sundays in winter. Across the street are rentals and sales of canoes, kayaks, and rafts. California Rivers, 21001 Geyserville Avenue, is open 9-5 daily, except Sunday in winter. Call 857-3872.

A Geyserville attraction in the making is the Sonoma Wine Market, 21225 Geyserville Avenue, a complex of wine-oriented shops and restaurants, with a planned inn nearby. No opening date has been set for the complex, located in the old Geyserville High School.

A Geyserville landmark since 1936 is Catelli's The Rex Restaurant, on Geyserville Avenue, serving Italian cuisine for lunch and dinner, including specialties like rabbit, scampi, sweetbreads, steak, seafood, and pasta. The full bar has an excellent selection of local wines. Call 857-9904.

Geyserville has four country inns, three in town and one located on a country ranch. The most unique is the Isis Oasis, 20889 Geyserville Avenue, a series of structures surrounded by 8½ acres of wooded land, once the Baha'i World Faith School. Owner Lora Vigne has combined her artistic talents and her fascination with ancient Egyptian culture to decorate and renovate everything from the turn-of-the-century farmhouse where she lives to the two-story guesthouse with twelve rooms. About the grounds are a 100-seat theater, a dining hall, a swimming pool, a massive Douglas fir tree dubbed the meditation tree, and a yurt (a round, half tent, half cabin affair). Guests get a generous breakfast and complimentary bottle of wine, and there's no charge to see the caged ocelots, pygmy goats, and peacocks near Vigne's home. Call a week in advance for reservations, 857-3524.

Across from the old Geyserville High School are two new bed and breakfast inns, operated by Robert and Rosalie Hope, former Guerneville resort owners. The Hope-Bosworth House, 21238 Geyserville Avenue, 857-3356, was built in 1904 by the Bosworth family, Geyserville pioneers. It has three bedrooms, one bath, and an antique shop. Next door is the six-bedroom Hope-Merrill House, a large Eastlake stick-style Victorian home built between 1870 and 1885. Some rooms have private bath. Dinners by reservation; call 857-3945.

The Campbell Ranch, 1475 Canyon Road (Canyon Road exit off Highway 101), offers three guest rooms in a country setting. You can enjoy tennis, swimming, hiking on the 35-acre ranch, and the personal attention of Mary

Jane and Jerry Campbell who serve a full breakfast and homemade pie and coffee every evening.

Geyserville's two annual events are seasonal celebrations. The first is Geyserville's May Festival, held at Hoffman Grove, Highway 101 at the Canyon Road exit, complete with the traditional May Pole dance, racing in the Grape Box Derby, and food booths. The May Festival is held the first Sunday in May. The Geyserville Fall Colors Tour is held the last weekend in October, with self-guided tours through the brilliantly colored vineyards, picnicking and wine tasting at regional wineries, and an old-fashioned country buffet at the Geyserville Grange Hall. Write the Geyserville Chamber of Commerce, P.O. Box 276, Geyserville, CA 95441, for details.

Geyserville Winery Tour

Most of Geyserville's eight wineries are within easy access of Highway 101. Winery ownership runs from corporate (Geyser Peak, Nervo) to cooperative (Souverain) and family-owned (Trentadue, Pedroncelli, Pastori, Mazzoni, Vina Vista), so you have your pick of large and small.

South of Geyserville at the Independence Lane exit off Highway 101 are Trentadue, Nervo, and Souverain wineries. Trentadue, located east of the freeway at 19170 Old Redwood Highway, began in 1969, a decade after Leo and Evelyn Trentadue left family ranches in the Santa Clara Valley to plant grapes here. Among their varietals are Chardonnay, Johannisberg Riesling, French Colombard, Zinfandel, and Cabernet Sauvignon. Their label displays "32," which is "trentadue" in Italian. Trentadue Winery is open daily 10-5 for tasting, retail sales, and picnics, and they have an extensive gift shop; 433-3104.

Near Trentadue Winery, at 19170 Old Redwood Highway, is a two-story Victorian home built in 1870 on ten acres known as Heart's Desire Nursery. The nursery was developed by Andrew Bouton, a good friend of Luther Burbank.

Nervo Winery, 19550 Geyserville Avenue, with its distinctive stone building, began in 1896 when Frank Nervo, Sr. and his bride, Maria, arrived in Sonoma County from Venice. When farmers were still traveling nearby Old Redwood Highway by horse and buggy, Nervo encouraged them to use his winery as a rest stop, probably the original "tasting room" in Sonoma County. Nervo Winery today is part of the Joseph Schlitz Brewing Company's California holdings, and the winery is primarily a sales outlet and aging center. Nervo offers a variety of wines, including "Winterchill White." Open daily 10-5 for tasting and sales, picnic area too; 857-3417.

Across the freeway stands Souverain Winery, on Independence Lane. Architect John Marsh Davis designed the modernistic facility in the style of the hop kilns that once dotted the North Coast country. It is a fitting motif, for Souverain represents the combined efforts of more than three hundred North Coast (Sonoma, Napa, and Mendocino counties) grape growers to create sixteen 100 percent varietal wines.

Co-winemakers Patrick Heck (of Korbel's Heck family) and Bob Mueller oversee production of wines like Cabernet Sauvignon, Chardonnay, and Charbono (all made with 100 percent North Coast grapes, hence the North Coast appellation on the wine bottles). Tours are given on the hour 10-4 daily; tasting, 10-5 daily; retail sales and gift shop too; 433-6918.

Souverain is one of two Sonoma County wineries with its own restaurant, which turns out such palate-pleasing dishes as fresh Dover sole, rack of lamb, and sweetbreads, served with Souverain wines and vistas of the Alexander Valley. Restaurant is open for lunch and dinner; reservations recommended, 433-3141. Souverain Winery also hosts special events, including art shows, theater performances, and the Hollyberry Faire (arts and crafts) during Thanksgiving weekend.

North of Geyserville, at the Canyon Road exit off Highway 101, stand Geyser Peak, Pedroncelli, Pastori,

Souverain Winery, Geyserville. (Redwood Empire Association)

Mazzoni, and Vina Vista wineries. Geyser Peak's dual
attractions are its wines and its moonlight walks along two
trails near the winery, with vistas of 3,470-foot-high
Geyser Peak. Begun in 1880 by German vintner August
Quitzow, the winery made bulk wine and vinegar after
Prohibition; it was acquired by the Joseph Schlitz Brewing
Company in 1972.

Today Geyser Peak occupies fourth place in sales
volume among U.S. premium wineries. (Almaden Vineyards, Paul Masson Vineyards, and Sebastiani Vineyards
fill the first three slots. Gallo is not included; it's in a class
all by itself.) The wines are marketed under the Geyser
Peak, Summit, and Voltaire labels. Geyser Peak Vintage
wines include sixteen varieties from Burgundy to Brut
California Champagne, while Summit wines appear in
the portable wine-in-a-box and six-ounce cans (Burgundy
and Chablis, with pop-tops). Geyser Peak is open daily for
tasting, retail sales, tours by appointment, 433-6585. Picnic
facilities available.

There are two hiking trails at Geyser Peak; the Panoramic Trail winds up behind the winery among vineyards,
while the Margot Patterson Doss Trail (named for the Bay
Area's best known walker/writer) takes you down past
vineyards to the Russian River, one of the few spots where
you can reach it on foot. It's a good picnic stop. Nocturnal
hikers can sign up for moonlight walks (limited to twenty
people) by calling wine writer Mildred Howie, 433-5349.

Charmingly rustic J. Pedroncelli Winery, tucked two
miles up Canyon Road from Highway 101, was born in
1927 when John Pedroncelli bought the property. His
sons, John and Jim, make dry table wines from vineyards
along Canyon Road and in the Dry Creek Valley. Over
100,000 cases are produced annually, including French
Colombard, Chenin Blanc, Gewurztraminer, Johannisberg Riesling, Pinot Noir, Zinfandel, Gamay Beaujolais,
Chardonnay, and Cabernet Sauvignon. J. Pedroncelli
Winery is open 10-5 daily for tasting and retail sales; tours
by appointment, 857-3619. From here you can take Canyon Road to Dry Creek Valley and Lake Sonoma or
return to Highway 101.

Pastori Winery, 23189 Geyserville Avenue, dates to
1914, when Constante Pastori, a native of Italy, began
making wine here. In 1975, Constante's son Frank regen-
erated the winery, which now produces North Coast
appellation wines, all vintage dated and estate bottled.
Pastori's wines include Cabernet Sauvignon, Pinot Noir,
Pinot St. George, Zinfandel, Beclan Cabernet, Chenin
Blanc, French Colombard, Muscat Canelli, and Burgundy. In addition to tending sixty acres of vines, Frank
Pastori is winemaker, cellarmaster, business manager, and
tasting room host, so tasting room guests may have to wait
for him to shut off the tractor and drive to the winery
before they get a sip. Pastori Winery is open 9-5 daily for
tasting and retail sales; 857-3418.

Mazzoni Winery, 23645 Redwood Highway, is open
mainly for retail gallon sales. The founder, Guiseppi Mazzoni, left his home near Carrara, Italy, at the end of the
nineteenth century and, after working in the Bay Area,

founded his winery in 1912. Mazzoni was one of the
pioneer vineyardists who cultivated Zinfandel, and over
the decades the winery has changed little; 857-3691.

Nearby Vina Vista Winery, on Chianti Road, was once
part of Guiseppi Mazzoni's property and today is operated
by the Nelson family, who make a number of 100-percent
varietal wines. Open by appointment only, 969-3160.

Asti

North of Geyserville the grassy, oak-shaded hills
close in on the Russian River Valley. The red soil
here reminded Italian settlers of the Mount Ferat
district back home; it was christened Asti after the famed
Italian wine region. Here the Italian Swiss Colony was
founded, now one of the largest, most historic, and most
visited wineries in the world. Today, marketed under the
Colony label, the twenty-three wines of Italian Swiss
Colony stand for good wine at affordable prices.

In 1881, Andrea Sbarboro, a prominent (if slightly
eccentric) San Francisco Italian businessman, formed a
cooperative agricultural association for jobless Swiss and
Italian immigrants in California. Influenced by the collec-
tivist theories of John Ruskin and Robert Owen, and
backed by Italian-American business interests, Sbarboro
bought 1,500 acres four miles south of Cloverdale for his
colony. The workers were given room, board, and $35 per
month, $5 earmarked for a profit-sharing plan to build a
winery. The workers balked at this arrangement, and
Sbarboro reorganized the colony as a private venture,
bringing in Pietro Rossi in 1888 to run Italian Swiss Colony's winery. Enologist Rossi was soon winning gold
medals with his wines.

Despite its name, the Colony was a community of
many nationalities, with its own railroad station, post
office, school, and church. The neat rows of Italian grape
varieties (Barbera, Grignolino, Charbono), the stone
winery buildings, and Sbarboro's Pompeiian-style villa,

Casa de Vetti, became a favorite attraction; visiting royalty couldn't pass it up on their California tour.

Sbarboro, a practical joker, rigged the grounds of his villa with hidden sprinklers so he could spray guests if they flopped down to rest in the wrong hammock. He also enjoyed watering his visitors as they sat at a banquet table. The villa and grounds still stand behind the winery, *sans* sprinklers.

After Prohibition, Italian Swiss Colony became one of the top three wineries in America. A winery symbol was its Tipo Chianti, red and white table wines dressed in straw-covered Italian *fiaschi*. Today the winery is part of the Heublein-United Vintners Association.

Italian Swiss Colony, with its redwood tanks (including the largest one known), stainless steel fermenters, and modern crushing station, is an excellent place to see how wine is made on a large scale. Tours lasting twenty minutes to one hour are given daily 10-4. The tasting room is open daily 9-5; retail sales and delicatessen also, plus picnic tables. The Colony's old champagne vault can be rented for parties of up to 100; call 894-2541. Each August, the Asti Art Festival is held on the winery grounds.

Near the Italian Swiss Colony entrance is the unique El Carmelo Catholic Chapel, named after Our Lady of Mount Carmel. Originally a plant conservatory for young grapevines, the wine barrel-shaped structure became a chapel in 1907 and seated 125. It's now closed.

The Asti Store, Cafe and Deli on Asti Store Road is a favorite stop for picnickers, canoe trippers, and wine bibbers. Asti is also a popular Russian River canoe trip launching spot; see the Russian River chapter.

Cloverdale

Cloverdale, Sonoma County's northernmost community, located thirty-two miles north of Santa Rosa, has long been a gateway to Mendocino and points north. Today this town of 3,800 people is a popular spot for fishing, swimming, and canoeing in the Russian River, wine tasting at several local wineries, camping in nearby campgrounds, boating and camping in soon-to-be-completed Lake Sonoma, or visiting the steaming geysers in the Mayacamas Mountains to the east.

In 1846, Mexican Governor Pio Pico granted 8,766 acres called Rancho Rincon de Muscalon to Francisco Berryessa (a relative of the Berryessas whose Napa land grant today is Lake Berryessa). Berryessa and others sold the *rancho* for $1,000 in 1851, and a section of it became the town of Cloverdale the same year. The railroad arrived in 1872, and Cloverdale became the center of a fruit, wine grape, and ranching region.

A Cloverdale woman, returning from a Panama trip with oranges, planted the seeds and began "citrus fever" in the area. Residents planted grapefruits, lemons, tangerines, and varieties of oranges for home and commercial use, making Cloverdale California's northernmost citrus growing region. There are no commercial citrus groves today, but many Cloverdale homes are landscaped with citrus trees, and each February the town holds a four-day Cloverdale Citrus Fair. Exhibits are created from thousands of citrus fruits, and there are a parade, live entertainment, and carnival rides. Admission costs $2.50 for adults, $1.50 per day for kids six through seventeen. Call the Cloverdale Chamber of Commerce for details, 894-2862.

In the last half of the nineteenth century, Cloverdale had several colonies, of which the Italian Swiss Colony was the most successful. In 1881, a group of French-speaking socialists migrated to Cloverdale from Iowa to form a utopian commune.

Calling their colony Icaria Speranza after ideals espoused in the French novel *Voyage en Icarie*, the Icarians farmed their 850 acres in common, growing peaches and prunes, and making Zinfandel wine. Icaria Speranza dissolved in 1887, partly because new recruits had to be fluent in French. Many of the Icarians remained in Sonoma County and opened their own wineries.

Just north of Cloverdale, at Preston, the mysterious and charismatic Madame Emily Preston established her Church of Heaven in 1876. Many came to join her around the old meeting house (still standing and visible from Geysers Road north of town), while others sought her help through madame's mail order medicines (a favorite was a concoction of turpentine, saltpeter, vinegar, and egg, to be taken externally or internally). Despite her claims of immortality, Madame Preston dropped dead one day while washing dishes, and the colony disbanded.

Cloverdale's more conventional church-goers built the Good Shepherd Episcopal Church in 1886, today an eye-pleasing sight on Main Street, while Congregationalists erected a stone church, now covered with ivy, on the town's main thoroughfare, Cloverdale Boulevard.

Just south of Cloverdale, Highway 101 becomes two lanes and continues through town as Cloverdale Boulevard. Traffic can back up here during summer holiday weekends, and there are plans to build a Cloverdale bypass to ease congestion.

Before exploring this area, a good stop is the Cloverdale Chamber of Commerce and Tourist Center, Owl Plaza on Cloverdale Boulevard. Pick up free copies of the Russian River Wine Road brochure and the Sonoma County Farm Trails Map, or choose from their wide selection of literature on attractions in Sonoma and Mendocino counties. Office hours: 9-7 daily from Memorial Day to Labor Day; 9:30-4, Tuesday through Saturday, Labor Day to Memorial Day. Phone 894-2862.

The Cloverdale Citrus Fairgrounds, site of the Citrus Fair, is located at Cloverdale Boulevard and Railroad Avenue. Among the events held here is the Old Time Fiddle Contest. Each January juvenile and adult fiddlers compete for prize money, playing two tunes: a hoedown and a waltz. Admission to the day-long event is $4 for adults, $2 for kids. For details, write to the Cloverdale Historical Society, P.O. Box 433, Cloverdale, CA 95425.

Every September the Cloverdale Harvest Fair is held at the Citrus Fairgrounds. This is a weekend to enjoy wine tasting, grape stomping, mechanical bull riding, a salmon barbecue, harvest exhibits, plus live entertainment from bluegrass bands to the Los Lupenos de San Jose Mexican folkloric dancers. There's free admission to the fair, but fees for wine tasting, barbecue, and Los Lupenos. Call the Citrus Fair office (894-5790) or write P.O. Box 445, Cloverdale, CA 95425.

Cloverdale's City Park, situated four blocks west of Cloverdale Boulevard on Second Street, is a mid-town picnic spot. The park hosts the annual Fourth of July Celebration and Turtle Races, which include a barbecue.

The Russian River forms the east boundary of town, and Crocker Road is the launching spot for many Russian River canoe trips.

Cloverdale's restaurant choices include Mama Nina's, one mile north of town on Highway 101, justly famous for homemade pasta and minestrone soup, steaks and seafood. You can dine outdoors on their deck, and the full bar features many local wines. South of town is Papa John's Restaurant, 225 Theresa Drive, serving Italian specialties, including family-style dinners on Monday nights. Open for lunch and dinner.

Next to Papa John's Restaurant is Boucher's Liberty Lake R.V. Resort, at the Dutcher Creek exit off Highway 101. Open all year, this large campground has a six-acre lake and a golf course, plus camping sites for tents and RVs; call 894-5512. Cloverdale's second year-round campground is the KOA Campground, 26460 River Road, near Asti. Set amid sixty acres of oak- and pine-covered rolling hills near Palomino Lakes, this campground offers tent sites and campsites for RVs, plus a swimming pool, stocked fish ponds, and hiking trails; call 894-3337.

Besides three motels in town, Cloverdale sports a bed and breakfast stop one block off Cloverdale Boulevard at 302 North Main Street. Tom and Judy Hayworth refurbished this Queen Anne Victorian mansion of twenty rooms into the Vintage Towers Bed and Breakfast Inn. The architecturally unusual home, built by Simon

Pinschower, wealthy merchant and mining executive, has three tower suites—one round, one square, and one octagonal. Five guest rooms are available. The Hayworths can provide bicycles, inner tubes, and canoes for guests, also a twenty-five-foot sailing sloop harbored at a nearby lake. Call 894-4535.

Cloverdale Winery Tour

Prior to Prohibition, Cloverdale had dozens of wineries, but after Repeal, the handful left sold only bulk wines. Things have changed; there are now three wineries around Cloverdale, and in the near future comedian Pat Paulsen, Cloverdale resident, will probably open his winery to the public.

Le Bay Winery, 26900 Dutcher Creek Road (take Dutcher Creek Road exit off Highway 101), is the old Rege Winery, once famous for furnishing house wines to San Francisco's North Beach restaurants. The winery underwent a metamorphosis when purchased by Doug Shaffer of Houston and Helen Dauphiney, Bay Area psychologist/farmer/sailor. Shaffer and Dauphiney are making premium wines of mostly local grapes, including Chenin Blanc and Chardonnay. Le Bay Winery is open for tasting and retail sales 10-4, Wednesday through Sunday; 894-3191. Picnic area too.

Arroyo Sonoma, with its new tasting room in town at 723 South Cloverdale Boulevard, is another old-time Cloverdale winery with a new face. Formerly Bandiera Winery, Arroyo Sonoma produces Arroyo Sonoma, Bandiera, and Potter Valley premium wines, such as Cabernet Sauvignon, Zinfandel, Sauvignon Blanc, Johannisberg Riesling, Grey Riesling, and Colombard Blanc. Their tasting room is open daily 8-4:30, 894-4295.

Across the Russian River is Cordtz Brothers Cellars, 28237 River Road, reached by taking First Street off Cloverdale Boulevard in town. In its first year of operation, Cordtz won a gold medal at the Los Angeles County

Fair for their Zinfandel. Other Cordtz varietals include
Sauvignon Blanc and Gewurztraminer. Open for tours
and tasting 10-4:30 daily, picnic tables on the grounds
under ancient oak trees; 894-5245.

Alexander Valley

The lush Russian River bottom land of the Alexander Valley extends north from Healdsburg to
the outskirts of Geyserville. From Healdsburg, you
can take Alexander Valley Road off Healdsburg Avenue
(Dry Creek exit off Highway 101), or you can follow Highway 128 south from Geyserville as it cuts through the
9,000 acres of the Alexander Valley. Most of the wineries
are located along Highway 128.

The warm Alexander Valley has been compared to the
Bordeaux region of France, and its rich variety of grapes—
Cabernet Sauvignon, Chardonnay, Zinfandel, Johannisberg Riesling, Gewurztraminer, and White Riesling
(especially late harvest)—have produced award-winning
wines. The Alexander Valley is an appellation of origin
used by both Sonoma and Napa winemakers.

First, a little history before beginning your wine tour.
The Alexander Valley was part of Capt. Henry Fitch's
Rancho Sotoyome, and the land-rich Fitch hired Cyrus
Alexander to oversee the 35,487-acre *rancho*. Alexander, a
Rocky Mountain fur trapper, came here in 1840 and
within four years had his own land, an adobe home, and
vineyards. Alexander's neighbor, Franklin Bedwell,
another trapper-turned-farmer, brought seeds from the
Russian orchards near Fort Ross, and the valley's orchards
were born.

Moses Carson, brother to frontiersman Kit Carson,
took over management of Rancho Sotoyome, while Alexander organized a church and school for settlers. Cyrus
Alexander's second home, his family graveyard, and the
pioneer schoolhouse are all located on the Alexander
Valley Vineyards winery grounds.

A succession of crops—hay, hops, prunes, pears, apples —were grown before grapes were again planted. In 1959, when Los Angeles oilman Russell Green planted his first fifty acres of vines in the Alexander Valley, there was only one winery. Green bought Simi Winery in 1970, then encouraged his associate, Harry Wetzel, to start his own winery, Alexander Valley Vineyards. Denver oilman Thomas Jordan also struck wine gold in the Alexander Valley. Today the Alexander Valley is a vast carpet of vines beneath the rocky ridges of the Mayacamas Mountains, and presently there are seven wineries—River Oaks, Sausal, Soda Rock, Johnson's Alexander Valley, Alexander Valley, Field Stone, and Jordan.

Alexander Valley Winery Tour

If you are following Alexander Valley Road out of Healdsburg, River Oaks Vineyards, at Lytton Station Road and Alexander Valley Road, could be your first stop, but tours are by appointment only, (415) 456-7310. (Note that many of the small wineries can give tours only with some notice.)

At 2411 Alexander Valley Road is the Alexander Valley Campground, a popular starting/stopping place for Russian River canoe trips. Besides RV campsites (no hookups), there are campfire pits and rest rooms. Call 433-1320 for reservations.

After crossing the river, follow Highway 128 south. At Jimtown, a settlement named for general store owner Jim Patrick, you can stop for picnic supplies at the Alexander Valley Store and Lounge, 6487 Highway 128. Nearby is the Alexander Valley Church, begun in the 1850s by Cyrus Alexander. The present church building dates from 1896.

Sausal Winery, 7370 Highway 128, gives tours by appointment only, 433-2285. It's owned by the Demostene family, long-time valley residents, now making Zinfandel from family vines.

Soda Rock Winery, 8015 Highway 128, 433-1830, is an historic winery given new life when it reopened to the public in 1981. The tasting room is open daily 10-5, and there's a garden picnic area too. Pears and grapes in season are yours at Rancho Sotoyome, 8329 Highway 128, from September 1 to October 15; call 433-2319 for hours.

Just beyond is Johnson's Alexander Valley Wines, a family-run operation specializing in Zinfandel, Chardonnay, Cabernet Sauvignon, and a pear wine. The Johnsons, father and three sons, offer live organ concerts on their Marr and Colton theater organ on selected Sundays during the month. The winery also has limited, no-fee campsites for tent campers, but call several weeks in advance. Day trippers can picnic here. Call 433-2319 (same number as Rancho Sotoyome). Johnson's Alexander Valley Wines is open daily 10-5 for tasting and retail sales, and tours are given by appointment.

The Alexander Valley Vineyards, 8644 Highway 128, houses modern vinicultural equipment in a Spanish-style winery amid oaks and rolling hills. The neighboring Victorian home belonged to Cyrus Alexander, who rests in the Alexander family graveyard on a knoll overlooking the winery. The restored Alexander Valley schoolhouse stands nearby. The large, thick-trunked grapevines in the vineyards also look like holdovers from Cyrus's halcyon days, but they are new, notes Harry Wetzel, Jr., winery owner, and they are flourishing in the rich, gravelly loam of the Alexander Valley.

Wetzel, chairman of the Garrett Corporation, was drawn to this site by Russell Green, once owner of Healdsburg's Simi Winery. Today the Wetzel family's vineyards produce all the grapes used to make Alexander Valley Vineyard's Chardonnay, Johannisberg Riesling, Chenin Blanc, Gewurztraminer, and Cabernet Sauvignon. The winery is open for tasting and sales 10-5 weekdays, 12-5 weekends. Tours are by appointment, 433-7209. Picnic tables are near the winery.

The Thunderbird Ranch, 9455 Highway 128, 433-3729, is a family campground with shaded campsites, pool, hot showers, playground, recreation room, and farm animals.

Don't plan to stay here in July or August; it's a summer camp for kids then.

Field Stone Winery, 10075 Highway 128, has a distinctive stone face, but the rest of this winery is buried in a hillside, part of an underground facility for aging wine. The winery was founded in 1977 by the late Wallace Johnson, former Berkeley mayor, cattle rancher, and inventor of the Upright mechanical harvester (for grapes). Field Stone Winery has a nearly all-female staff, including winemaker Deborah Cutter, who creates Johannisberg Riesling, Chenin Blanc, Cabernet Sauvignon, Petite Sirah, Gewurztraminer, Spring Cabernet (Beaujolais style), and Muscat Canelli. The tasting room is open 9-5 daily; tours by request. There is an area with barbecue facilities available by prior arrangement, 433-7266.

One of the Alexander Valley's most talked about wineries, Jordan, is not open to the public, but you can catch a quick glimpse of it as you drive along Highway 101 near Lytton Springs. Jordan Vineyard and Winery, 1474 Alexander Valley Road, built by Thomas Jordan, Jr., a Denver oil millionaire, is a bit of Bordeaux in the Alexander Valley. Jordan is making a Cabernet Sauvignon and a Chardonnay to match those of France. Architects Richard Keith and Robert Arrigoni fashioned the Jordan family's chateau-style home and winery. Tours are offered if prearranged; call 433-6955.

If you're headed toward Santa Rosa, take Chalk Hill Road off Highway 128. You can buy boysenberries (June and July) and peaches (July and August) daily 8-7 at Chalk Hill Vineyard, 14255 Chalk Hill Road. No grapes sold to the public, however. Call first, 433-5218. At the Rocking WA Ranch, 12000 Chalk Hill Road, Wes Archer sells natural meats (beef, pork, lamb, turkey), fertile eggs, and honey. Archer's Limousin and Markey cattle are raised without hormone-injected feed. Open April 1 to November 28, Saturdays, by appointment; call 433-3261. Chalk Hill Road joins Faught Road, then Old Redwood Highway north of Santa Rosa.

116

Mount St. Helena

The Bay Area's highest peak, Mount St. Helena, is a place of some mystery. Is it a volcano? Did a Russian princess climb it? For whom is it named? Were its rocky heights the inspiration for Robert Louis Stevenson's Spyglass Hill in *Treasure Island?* You may not find all the answers, but you're sure to enjoy the mountain. If you've got a good pair of legs, take a four-mile hike to the summit where, in clear weather, you can see the Sierra and Mount Shasta.

From Healdsburg, take Highway 128 through Alexander Valley and Knights Valley to Calistoga in Napa County, then follow Highway 29 north to the Robert Louis Stevenson State Park. The 4,343-foot summit of Mount St. Helena lies in Sonoma County, but the volcanic folds of the peak straddle Sonoma, Napa, and Lake counties. Despite its conelike appearance, the mountain is not a volcano.

Russian explorers from Fort Ross climbed the peak in 1841 and left a plaque with the names of their party. Although no woman's name appeared on the plaque, legends abound that Helena de Gagarin, wife of the commandant at Fort Ross, also climbed the peak. Early historians believed the mountain was named for Helena, but to this day no one is certain of the name's origin.

Scottish writer Robert Louis Stevenson and his bride, Fanny, honeymooned on the Napa side of the mountain from May to July 1880. Stevenson wrote of his stay in *Silverado Squatters,* and Stevenson buffs believe the rocky crags of Mount St. Helena served as a model for the locale in *Treasure Island.* Today you can park your car and hike to the site of the mine where Robert and Fanny honeymooned in a now-vanished bunkhouse. There's also a monument to Stevenson. A hike up to the summit of the peak recreates Sierra or Rocky Mountain experiences, with pines and wind and grand vistas. And there's no charge.

The Geysers

At The Geysers, natural dry steam is harnessed to produce enough electricity for a city half the size of San Francisco. Here, in the rugged Mayacamas Mountains in northeastern Sonoma and southern Lake counties, is the world's largest and most productive geothermal field.

The Geysers' natural dry steam comes from ground water heated by molten magma beneath the earth's crust and forced to the surface through faults in the mountains. Unlike wet geysers, such as Yellowstone's Old Faithful, this dry steam is vented through hissing openings called fumaroles. Because dry steam is the simplest, cleanest, and cheapest form of geothermal energy known, Pacific Gas and Electric (PG&E) has opened electric generating plants here.

To see The Geysers, take Dry Creek exit off Highway 101, go one-quarter mile to Healdsburg Avenue, proceed north two miles, and turn right onto Alexander Valley Road. Drive three more miles, turn left onto Highway 128, and go north until you find Geysers Road. Follow this winding route sixteen miles, past old mercury mines and the extinct town of Mercuryville to Vista Point. The Cloverdale route to The Geysers, the rougher of the two roads, begins with an exit off Highway 101 one mile north of town onto Geysers Road, then a drive of fourteen miles to Vista Point. At the overlook you can see the steamy geysers and steam-capped cooling towers next to generating units; a diorama explains how steam produces electricity. Nearby a visitor's center will be built.

Local Indians believed spirits inhabited The Geysers, and in 1847, when Bear Flagger William B. Elliot happened upon the hissing hillsides in Big Sulphur Canyon, he thought he'd found the "Gates of Hell." The Geysers became a nineteenth-century tourist attraction, with a resort hotel (site of the planned visitor's center) hosting

The Geysers. (Redwood Empire Association)

dignitaries such as the Prince of Wales, Guiseppe Gari-
baldi, President U. S. Grant, Henry Ford, Mark Twain,
Robert Louis Stevenson, and President Teddy Roosevelt.
The reckless, death-defying stagecoach driving of Charlie
Foss frightened more visitors than did the steamy "Gates
of Hell."

As early as 1922, efforts were made to harness The
Geysers, but not until 1955 was the first well drilled to tap

the underground steam. When PG&E opened its first generating plant in 1960, it signaled the company's—and the nation's—entry into the era of geothermal energy. Today PG&E operates the power plants at The Geysers; other companies provide the steam to PG&E.

More than 200 wells have been drilled at The Geysers, to an average depth of 8,500 feet. When steam reaches the surface, it is first cleaned of tiny particles by "whirling" in centrifugal separators. Insulated pipes then conduct the steam to the generating units. The steam's energy spins the turbine blades, which in turn drive the generators that produce electricity. The steam strikes the turbine blades at about 12,000 feet per minute (more than 135 miles per hour), at a temperature of about 355 degrees Fahrenheit. The cooling towers gather spent steam now condensed to hot water, and some of the cooled water is recycled.

About 2 million pounds of steam per hour are needed to operate a 110,000-kilowatt generating unit. Each 110,000 kilowatts of electricity replaces the need to burn approximately 1 million barrels of oil per year. Currently, fifteen units are scattered over the pine-forested hills, with a total generating capacity of 909,000 kilowatts. No one knows the maximum extent of the geothermal field, but it is believed to be more than 350,000 acres. To date, some 25,000 acres have been explored. In the coming decades PG&E and other operators hope to have over 2,000 megawatts of production at The Geysers. With one megawatt equal to 1,000 kilowatts, this is enough energy to meet 10 percent of PG&E's need. Although geothermal operations produce foul-smelling hydrogen sulfide, they emit no smog and, unlike hydroelectric plants, they don't require damming of a river.

In the past, PG&E has offered free, four-hour public tours of The Geysers, but currently these tours are limited to people directly involved in geothermal production. To arrange for a tour, call Mr. Hourigan at the San Francisco PG&E office, (415) 781-4211. Jack Trotter is the local PG&E geothermal information specialist, P.O. Box 456, Healdsburg, CA 95448, 433-8221.

Dry Creek Valley

The Dry Creek Valley, the most direct and scenic route to Lake Sonoma, can be reached by taking Dry Creek exit off Highway 101, or Healdsburg Avenue to Dry Creek Road in Healdsburg. This valley is a self-contained entity, marked by the now ever-flowing Dry Creek (thanks to runoff from the Warm Springs Dam fronting Lake Sonoma) and bounded on two sides by forested ridges and hills. For more than a century, the Dry Creek Valley has produced fruit and wine grapes, and within the last decade has come into its own as a separate wine appellation district.

The valley's original inhabitants were Pomo Indians. In 1843, the Rancho Tzabaco, which included Dry Creek Valley, was granted to Jose German Pena. One of Pena's adobe homes still stands in the valley.

American settlers (many from Missouri) followed, then German and Italian families flocked here. The fertile valley was soon planted in fruit orchards and dotted with well-tended white frame Victorian farmhouses. The micro-climate of the Dry Creek Valley—where the Russian River fogs curve up into the Dry Creek watershed, only to be baked away by the summer sun—creates warmer days than in neighboring Healdsburg. Zinfandel, Chardonnay, Cabernet Sauvignon, and Petite Sirah grapes love such a climate, as local wines prove. Today there are seven wineries in the valley, but only Dry Creek Vineyards is open daily to receive visitors. (Four are open by appointment; Frei Brothers Winery and Fredson Winery aren't open to the public.)

Dry Creek Valley Winery Tour

Begin your Dry Creek Valley rambling with a stop at one or two neighboring delis, which have all the makings for a picnic. Dry Creek Liquors and Delicatessen, 177 Dry Creek Road, open daily, has sandwiches to go; dozens of varieties of cheese, including California Chevre, a French-style goat cheese made in Sonoma County by Laura Chenel; and spotlights over 500 local and imported wines. The Warm Springs Station and Delicatessen, 520 Dry Creek Road, also open daily, sells sandwiches, homemade chili, beer, and wine.

For a chance to pick your own apples, pears, and walnuts, in season, stop at Mark Hoffschneider's farm, 1524 Dry Creek Road. It's open Friday to Monday between July 20 and Halloween, 433-4146. And if you still need picnic supplies, there's the century-old Dry Creek Store, 3495 Dry Creek Road at Lambert Bridge Road, three miles north of Highway 101. The adjacent Dry Creek Inn has live music, 433-4171. Note that Dry Creek Store is the only grocery store and gas station on the eleven-mile stretch between Highway 101 and Lake Sonoma.

Dry Creek Vineyards, at 3770 Lambert Bridge Road, began in 1972 when ex-Bostonian David Stare turned an old prune orchard into an award-winning winery. Stare feels Dry Creek Valley is similar to the Bordeaux region in France, and he makes Zinfandel, Chardonnay, Chenin Blanc, Fume Blanc, Cabernet Sauvignon, Gamay Beaujolais, and Petite Sirah. Dry Creek Vineyards is open daily for tasting and sales, 10:30-4:30, tours by appointment, 433-1000. Picnic tables also.

At 3805 Lambert Bridge Road lies Robert Stemmler Winery, which produces Chardonnay and Cabernet Sauvignon. Open by appointment only, 433-6334. Lambert Bridge Road intersects West Dry Creek Road, but if you're bound for Lake Sonoma, follow Dry Creek Road.

Hankerin' for a hayride? Hop on over to Palace Hill Ranch, 4701 Dry Creek Road, where Chris and Jean Haugsten offer hayrides through the vineyards to local wineries. You get your choice of hefty Percherons or elegant Tennessee walkers to pull either wagons or buggies. The Haugstens also sell organically grown whole or half hogs (cut, wrapped, and frozen), or you can return home with smoked ham, bacon, and wine grapes. Call 433-3211.

Timber Crest Farms, 4791 Dry Creek Road, is rancher Ron Waltenspiel's locale for processing and selling organically dried fruits—prunes, raisins, apricots, figs, peaches, pears, apples, pineapples, cherries, almonds, and several nut varieties—twenty-one kinds of fruits and nuts in all. You can buy them here, at local health food stores, or via a mail order business. The Waltenspiels give a thirty-minute tour of their fruit processing facility daily, except Sunday. Tours given 8-5 weekdays, 10-2 Saturdays. Call 433-8251 or write Timber Crest Farms, 4791 Dry Creek Road, Healdsburg, CA 95448. Don't miss eyeballing the stalwart old Plasberg home next door.

West Dry Creek Road parallels Dry Creek Road but dead-ends before reaching Lake Sonoma. Its southern end hooks up with Westside Road, a scenic, winery-dotted drive that ends in the Russian River resort area. Along West Dry Creek Road stand several wineries, an orchard, and two Christmas tree farms.

At 4085 West Dry Creek Road is Lambert Bridge Winery, built in 1976 by Gerard Barnes Lambert, scion of the Lambert pharmaceutical firm (Listerine is one product). Lambert makes Cabernet Sauvignon, Chardonnay, and Johannisberg Riesling. Open by appointment only, 433-5855. Nearby is A. Rafanelli Winery, 4685 West Dry Creek Road, representing an old Dry Creek Valley name with a new wine outlook. Americo Rafanelli produces the only estate-bottled Zinfandel from Dry Creek Valley made entirely by hand in a typical Italian style. Open by appointment only, retail sales by the case, 433-1385. Both these wineries are near Dry Creek Vineyards and Robert Stemmler Winery on Lambert Bridge Road.

If you're looking for a Christmas tree, head for the Kitchen Ranch, 2681 West Dry Creek Road, open weekends, November 28 through December 20, 9 until dusk (433-4085); or stop at Heron Lake Tree Farm, 2785 West Dry Creek Road, for Scotch pines, Douglas firs, or Monterey pines, as well as Christmas wreaths. Heron Lake is open 9-5 daily, November 29 until sold out; 433-2356.

At other seasons of the year you can rent your own

fruit tree through the unique rent-a-tree program at Amal
Orchards, 6200 West Dry Creek Road. Marc Leinwand
rents fruit trees for one year at $20 to $35, with 400 pounds
of fruit guaranteed; just bring your own boxes at harvest-
time. Leinwand also has U-pick apple, pear, and plum
trees, plus vegetables, and he sells lamb, pork, turkeys, and
stewing chickens. All products are organic. Amal
Orchards is open 9-5 weekends, June through December,
or by appointment, 433-7174.

Preston Vineyards, 9282 West Dry Creek Road, is one
of the smallest wineries in the area, located in a refurbished prune dehydrator, reputed to be the first built in
Sonoma County. Owner Lou Preston turns out Sauvignon
Blanc, Chenin Blanc, Napa Gamay, and Zinfandel. Tours
by appointment only, 433-4748.

Lake Sonoma

Scheduled for completion by the summer of 1984,
Lake Sonoma will be the North Coast's newest
recreation spot, offering swimming, waterskiing,
fishing, motorboating, canoeing, kayaking, hiking, horseback riding, camping, and, for you less active types, the
opportunity to relax and enjoy nature. Currently, the
visitor's center, the fish hatchery, and the Warm Springs
Dam overlook are open to visitors.

To reach Lake Sonoma from Healdsburg, the best
route is Dry Creek exit off Highway 101 to Dry Creek
Road. Other routes to Dry Creek Road from Highway 101
include Lytton Springs Road, Canyon Road, and Dutcher
Creek Road. Cloverdale visitors can reach Lake Sonoma
via Hot Springs Road.

The Warm Springs Dam, a 319-foot-high earthen
embankment dam, is 3,000 feet wide at its crest from abutment to abutment, 2,600 feet long at its base, and 30 feet
wide at the top. The U.S. Army Corps of Engineers has
literally moved a mountain into the Dry Creek Valley via
a 3,600-foot-long conveyor belt, and the 30 million cubic

yards of earth used to construct the dam make it the largest structure ever built in Sonoma County.

The resultant Lake Sonoma, a 17,600-acre lake with 3,600-acre surface area, will have 53 miles of shoreline zigzagging into the steep-sided canyons of the Mendocino plateau. The surrounding Lake Sonoma Recreation Area will be a federally controlled development with campgrounds, horse trails, a marina, and boat launching facilites, in operation by 1986.

Designed to control Russian River flooding by damming Dry Creek, a river tributary, the Warm Springs Dam and Lake Sonoma will provide recreation in a county area short on parks, but its water supply will also encourage housing developments on some of the county's farmlands. Construction of the dam was accompanied by a bitter, protracted struggle between developers and conservationists, finally settled in 1978. When completed, the $275 million project will drown Warm Springs Creek, forming the South Lake area of Lake Sonoma, and Dry Creek, creating the North Lake area.

The steep hills and ridges around Lake Sonoma contain a mixture of evergreen forests, oak woodlands, and grassy meadows, rich in redwoods, Douglas firs, laurels, buckeyes, madrones, a half-dozen species of oaks, and the bushy sedge plant used by Pomo Indians to make North America's finest woven basketry. The rare peregrine falcon haunts these hills, along with black-tailed deer, the gray fox, and mountain lions.

The Mahilakawna Pomo lived in this area for at least 5,000 years until forcibly removed by the U.S. Army in the 1850s and driven like cattle to Mendocino and Lake counties. Many Indians died along the way, and Pomo today remember this as the "death march." Ranchers and vineyardists then took over the area, and one of California's earliest resorts was opened here. The Skaggs Springs Hotel took in up to 300 visitors a day to bathe and drink the "healthful waters" of nearby mineral springs.

Today's visitors can stop in at the visitor's center to see displays on the region's history and on the construc-

tion of Warm Springs Dam, Pomo Indian exhibits, plus
exhibits of native plants and animals. Hours are 11-4
weekdays, 11-6 weekends.

The adjacent fish hatchery is a pampered spawning
ground for native steelhead trout and silver salmon, and
in the future it will also be a spawning ground for king
salmon, once native to the Russian River. Two 10,000-
gallon tanks hold fish for public viewing, while six holding
ponds in the $8.1 million hatchery nurture infant fish
from birth to fingerling stage, when they are released into
the lake and Dry Creek. The fish hatchery is open daily,
with rangers on duty to answer questions. Group tours,
limited to forty people, can be arranged two weeks in
advance; call 433-9483, 8-4:30 weekdays. Hours for the
visitor's center and fish hatchery are likely to change, so
call ahead.

A mile and a half drive will take you to the Warm
Springs Dam overlook, situated on a 1,000-foot-high bluff
overlooking the construction area of the dam and soon-to-
be-filled Lake Sonoma. Follow Skaggs Springs Road from
the visitor's center to the overlook, which has observation
decks, rest rooms, and picnic tables. The overlook is open
8-4 daily. From here you can take a scenic but winding
thirty-mile drive via Skaggs Springs Road to Stewarts
Point on the Sonoma Coast.

Future facilities in the South Lake area of Lake Sonoma
will include a marina, an RV campground, beaches, and
equestrian trails. Motorboats and waterskiing will be per-
mitted on this part of the lake. The Buzzard Rock campground will contain 100 RV campsites in an open area
with few trees. The Oak Knolls campground will offer
shady oak-covered campsites and others with views of the
lake and the Pritchett Peaks area.

The more rugged and secluded North Lake area will
feature swimming beaches and sheltered coves for bass
angling, a boat launch site, and equestrian trails. The
Cherry Creek campground will have forty-five RV campsites, while the Hot Springs Road day use area will offer
spectacular vistas of the lake and Thompson Ridge.

Westside Road

A scenic, quiet drive down Westside Road will take you from Healdsburg to the Russian River resort area, past award-winning wineries, farms selling fresh-picked apples or peaches, and splendid vistas of vineyards, orchard lands, and redwood forests.

From Healdsburg Avenue in Healdsburg, take Mill Street under Highway 101 to Westside Road. Kinley Drive off Westside Road takes you to the Massoni Ranch, 1558 Magnolia (off Kinley Drive), for sales of a variety of apples. Call 433-6067 for hours.

Where Westside Road meets West Dry Creek Road stands Madrona Knolls, slated to become Healdsburg's next bed and breakfast inn. Built in 1881 for San Francisco banker John Paxton, Madrona Knolls has a seventeen-room house (including six bathrooms), five cottages, and a Victorian horse barn, all situated on ten acres. It's located at 1011 Westside Road; 433-4231.

Continue south to Mill Creek Winery, 1401 Westside Road, operated by the Kreck family, which produces wines from Dry Creek Valley grapes. Their 1979 Merlot won a gold medal at the 1981 wine judging of the Sonoma County Harvest Fair. Other wines include Cabernet Sauvignon, Chardonnay, Cabernet Blush (a rose), Gewurztraminer, Pinot Noir, and Gamay Beaujolais. The Krecks also produce and bottle wines from the nearby vineyard of Claus Neumann for Neumann's Los Robles Lodge in Santa Rosa. Mill Creek Winery is open daily 10-4 for sales. Tours by appointment, 433-5098.

Near historic Felta School (1906) are two Farm Trail stops. Middleton Gardens, 2651 Westside Road, offers peaches, apples, and vegetables from June to October 15, Monday through Saturday, 9-5; Sunday, 1-5; 433-4755. Middleton Gardens has hard-to-find Rio Oso peaches. Across Westside Road is Hill's Headacres, 354 Foreman Lane, with prunes, apples (Gravensteins, Red and Golden

Delicious, Romes, and others), and persimmons. Open weekend afternoons, July 25 to October 20, or by appointment, 433-3258.

The Sonoma Antique Apple Nursery, 4395 Westside Road, is a unique apple orchard planted with almost-extinct varieties of apples (thirty-five so far), either dwarf or semidwarf in size—just right for crowded urban backyards. Owners Carolyn and Terry Harrison graft rare apple scions to rootstock for diminutive orchards. Open as of February on weekends 12-4, or by appointment, 433-6420.

The Bishop's Ranch, 5297 Westside Road, offers meditation and renewal in their serene, Spanish-style chapel. The Society of St. Francis, an Episcopal order of brothers, operates the 67-acre ranch as a retreat for individuals and nonprofit groups. The Bishop's Ranch is open to the public on the first Wednesday of each month, 10 A.M. to 3 P.M., for a mass, luncheon, and time for reflection and relaxation; 433-2440.

Six miles south of Healdsburg stands the Hop Kiln Winery, 6050 Westside Road, a David among wine Goliaths—its 1978 Zinfandel was the sweepstakes winner at the 1980 Sonoma County Harvest Fair, besting hundreds of other wines. Owner Dr. Martin Griffin produces 100 percent varietal wines from grapes grown around the 1905-era hop kiln. Griffin's wines (of Russian River Valley appellation) include French Colombard, Gewurztraminer, Chardonnay, Johannisberg Riesling, Napa Gamay, Zinfandel, Petite Sirah, and "A Thousand Flowers," a blend of Johannisberg Riesling, French Colombard, and Gewurztraminer.

The redwood and stone hop kiln towers (an historic landmark) provide a naturally cool aging environment for the wines. The photogenic hop kiln was built with Angelo "Skinny" Sodini as stonemason. Inside the winery are photo displays of the hop industry when the crop was extensively grown in Sonoma County for beer manufacturers.

Stone hop kilns, now a winery. (Don Edwards)

Hop Kiln Winery is open daily 10-5 for tasting, sales, and tours by appointment, 433-6491. The adjacent red Victorian home and the winery are part of the Sweetwater Springs Historic District. Sweetwater Springs Road runs from Westwood Road to Armstrong Woods Road near Guerneville.

Eight miles south of Healdsburg, at 8075 Westside
Road, is another old hop ranch-cum-winery, Davis Bynum
Winery. Bynum, an ex-journalist, buys about 85 percent
of his grapes from nearby growers. He combines wine from
vineyards in the cooler Russian River Valley regions with
wine from the warmer Alexander and Dry Creek valleys,
and the result has been an award-winning Pinot Noir.
Davis Bynum Winery sells Cabernet Sauvignon, Zinfandel, and Chardonnay also. Open for tasting and sales
daily 9-5, tours by appointment, 433-5852.

Redwood Empire Association

The Sonoma Valley 4

Valley of the Moon

The Sonoma Valley has a history unequaled almost anywhere in California. Mission fathers, latter-day conquistadores, rebellious Americans, and European noblemen are all characters in the Sonoma saga that delights and enthralls history seekers. The Valley offers other pleasures as well: To wine lovers, it means premium wineries, fine restaurants, and scenic spots for a wine-and-cheese picnic. To vacationers, it is a recreational mecca; to retirees, a retreat; and to artists and writers, a haven.

The Sonoma Valley, Jack London's beloved Valley of the Moon, nestles between the long volcanic arms of the Sonoma Mountains to the west and the Mayacamas Mountains to the east, then expands into the fertile flatlands fronting San Pablo Bay. Rich, peppery volcanic soil and mineral hot springs first drew the Coastal Miwok, Pomo, Wappo, and Patwin Indians here. Amid the wild oat- and oak-covered hills, the Indians hunted deer and bear, collected acorns and berries, built huts of tule reeds, and caught sturgeon in San Pablo Bay.

Father Jose Altimira chose this valley as the site of the last of California's twenty-one missions. In 1823, the padre founded the Mission of San Francisco de Solano, the only mission established under Mexican rule. The mission marked the end of El Camino Real, the "royal road" that ran from San Diego northward, connecting California's missions.

Mariano Guadalupe Vallejo, native *Californio* and a Mexican Army officer, rode in eleven years later to secularize the mission and to begin a pueblo ("town") and a presidio ("fort"). Vallejo laid out the pueblo around the Sonoma Plaza, making Sonoma the first non-Indian settlement north of San Francisco Bay. A major business center in Alta California, Sonoma was also the northernmost outpost of the Catholic, Spanish-speaking realm that extended unbroken to the tip of South America.

American settlers, induced by stories of free land in California, crossed the Sierra only to find that the Mexican government forbade them to buy land or hold office. In protest, thirty-three American immigrants seized Sonoma, arrested Vallejo, and on June 14, 1846, raised the Bear Flag in the Sonoma Plaza. This "Bear Flag Party" declared California an independent republic, a nation that lasted twenty-five days, until the American flag went up in Sonoma.

Sonoma prospered as the military units of Col. Jonathan Stevenson's New York Regiment and the U.S. Army moved in; then the town waned when her citizens stampeded to the gold fields. But Sonoma Valley's gold lay in grapes. General Vallejo's pioneer winemaking successes attracted European viniculturists.

First to appear was Hungarian Count Agoston Haraszthy, founder of the Buena Vista Winery. Later Charles Krug of Germany trained under Vallejo before striking out on his own to establish the Napa Valley's wine industry. Sonoma Valley's noted Rhinefarm flourished under Jacob Gundlach, Charles Bundschu, and the Dresel brothers of Germany's famed Dresel champagne family.

By the 1880s, vineyards blanketed the Sonoma Valley hillsides, yielding grapes for the region's thirty-seven wineries. Sonoma County produced two-thirds of the state's red wine. Then phylloxera, a grape-root louse, nearly destroyed the vinelands. Julius Dresel of Sonoma was the first vineyardist to halt the disease, which he did by grafting phylloxera-stricken vines onto resistant rootstock. Today, the grapes of many of California's—and Europe's—vineyards descend from these hardy vines. The

1880s also saw the first wave of Italian winemakers in the Sonoma Valley. Families such as the Sebastianis and the Paganis carried the wineries through the long night of Prohibition.

The Sonoma Valley is now a distinct, premier wine-growing district, often compared to the Burgundy region of France. Local microclimates nurture fine varietal grapes such as Zinfandel, Petite Sirah, Cabernet Sauvignon, Pinot Noir, and Chardonnay. Sonoma Valley vintners can now tout the region as a government-approved appellation of origin, assuring wine drinkers that a majority of the grapes used to make the wine were grown here.

In the last century, the Sonoma Valley thrived as a favorite resort spot for San Franciscans. Tourists rode trains to bathe in natural hot springs and camp beside tree-lined creeks. Resort towns like Boyes Hot Springs, Agua Caliente, El Verano, Glen Ellen, and Kenwood sprang up. Great estates like those of the Spreckels and Hearst families dotted the Valley, while Socialist author-turned-farmer Jack London formed his Beauty Ranch near Glen Ellen.

Most of the resorts have disappeared, but tourists still flock to the Sonoma Valley to sample wines from the region's fifteen wineries and to buy local cheese, bread, and fresh produce. The Sonoma Valley's rich array of restaurants spotlights local food and wines, and there's plenty to do to whet the appetite—horseback riding, swimming, bicycling, golfing, or soaring above the vineyards in a hot air balloon. Lodging in the Valley is limited but distinguished, including country inns and an internationally known resort hotel, as well as standard motels, overnight trailer and RV parks, and campsites in the hills.

Southern Sonoma Valley

The Sonoma Valley's charm is enhanced by the fact that it is off the beaten path. The town of Sonoma is forty-six miles north of the Golden Gate Bridge and eighteen miles from Highway 101 in Novato. Bay

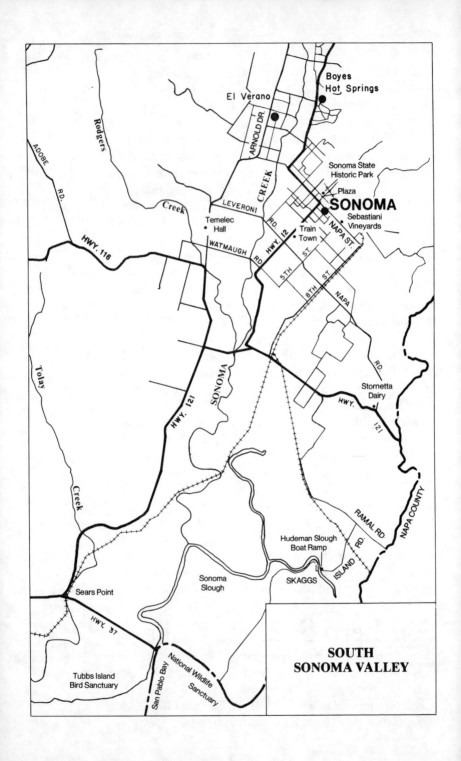

Boyes
Hot Springs

El Verano

Rodgers

ADOBE RD.

Creek

HWY. 116

Temelec
Hall

LEVERONI RD.

ARNOLD DR.

CREEK

Creek

WATMAUGH RD.

HWY. 12

SONOMA

Sonoma State
Historic Park

Plaza

SONOMA

Sebastiani
Vineyards

Train
Town

NAPA ST.

5TH ST.

8TH ST.

NAPA RD.

Stornetta
Dairy

HWY. 121

Tolay

HWY. 121

Creek

HWY.

RAMAL RD.

NAPA COUNTY

Sears Point

HWY. 37

Sonoma
Slough

Hudeman Slough
Boat Ramp

SKAGGS

ISLAND RD.

Tubbs Island
Bird Sanctuary

San Pablo Bay

National Wildlife
Sanctuary

**SOUTH
SONOMA VALLEY**

Area visitors take the Highway 37 exit off Highway 101, then follow Highway 121, Fremont Drive, and Highway 12 to the Sonoma Plaza.

The country roads of the southern Valley lead you past dairies, fruit stands, and fishing spots. Except for occasional vineyards, you'd hardly think you were in the wine country, for the sloughs along the meandering Sonoma Creek are used principally for cattle grazing, fishing, and hunting. Much of this area would appear familiar to Father Jose Altimira, for this is the route he traveled in search of a site for the Mission San Francisco de Solano.

The American settlers who opened up this part of Sonoma included Granville Swift, a member of the Bear Flag Party, and his cousin Franklin Sears, whose ranch is now Sears Point, site of the Golden State International Raceway. Swift, a grandnephew of Daniel Boone and a rough-cut, hard-drinking trapper-turned-miner, made his wealth in gold along the Feather River and returned to the Sonoma Valley to build one of California's grandest country homes.

Swiss and Italian dairymen followed, and many of the Valley's dairy ranches are worked by their descendants. The southern Sonoma Valley is also a fruit-growing region, a reminder of Prohibition days when vintners turned vineyards into orchards.

Sears Point

Sports car and motorcycle racing fans flock to the Golden State International Raceway at the intersection of Highways 37 and 121 to see some of the top names in the racing world compete on the grueling road course, the rugged motocross dirt track, and the drag strip. Mario Andretti, Al Unser, and Bobby Allison have all toured the track at Golden State, along with Hollywood celebrities such as Paul Newman, Clint Eastwood, James Garner, and Candice Bergen.

Twenty thousand spectators jammed the stands in July of 1981 to see Germany's Klaus Ludwig, in his turbo-

charged Mustang, overtake Britain's Brian Redman,
driving a Chevy-powered Lola, to win the International
Motor Sports Association Camel-GT race. Other annual
racing events include NASCAR road races and sports car
racing by the Sports Car Club of America (SCCA) with
TRANS-AM, CAN-AM, Formula Atlantic, and Pro Formula
Ford entrants. Motorsports events include the AMA
motorcycle road races and several motocross races.

Golden State International Raceway's Sears Point
location can get hot in summer, and it is miles from
restaurants and lodging. Prices for events vary; call
938-8448 for prices and further information.

The Raceway is also home to the Bob Bondurant
School of High Performance Driving. Bondurant began
his driving school following a serious accident in 1968,
which ended his competitive racing career. The school
offers instruction in competition road racing, advanced
road racing, high performance driving, and advanced
highway driving. Write the Bob Bondurant School of
High Performance Driving, Golden State International
Raceway at Sears Point, Highways 37 and 121, Sonoma,
CA 95476, or call 938-4741.

Sonoma Valley Farm Trails

Agriculture dominates Sonoma Valley's economy, with an
average annual agricultural income of $12 million pro-
duced from the Valley's 30,000 acres of vineyards, dairy
ranches, and fruit orchards. The Valley's roadside stands
are good spots to load up on produce to go with Sonoma
wine, bread, and cheese.

Thirsty tourists and natives alike stop at Napoli Lenhert's two Cherry Tree stands for 100 percent pure cherry
cider, grape juice, apple-based fruit juices, applesauce, or
fruit spreads (apple butter, blackberry, or boysenberry).
Lenhert uses primarily Sonoma County-grown fruits for
his juices. His Cherry Tree No. 1, on Highway 121
between Highway 37 and Fremont Drive, is open daily in
summer, weekends in winter. Cherry Tree No. 2, along

Highway 121 at 1901 Fremont Drive, is open daily all year; it also features deli items and sandwiches, and there are picnic tables.

The Fruit Basket, 24101 Arnold Drive (Highway 121), is a produce palace with fresh and dried fruits, vegetables, nuts, grains, beans, rice, homemade pasta, eggs, imported olives, and honey. They also have a wide selection of Sonoma, Napa, and other California wines; you save 10 percent if you buy by the case.

A bulwark of Sonoma Valley's dairy industry is Clover-Stornetta Farms, Inc., where guernsey cows are raised for their rich milk. Visitors can see the milking of the guernseys 2-4 P.M. daily, April through October, at the Stornetta Dairy, 4300 Fremont Drive; call 938-2354 for milking times. Romberg's Drive-in Dairy, 19655 Arnold Drive near Sonoma, sells low-priced, high-quality milk—raw and homogenized—in half-gallon glass bottles and gallon plastic containers. Romberg's also distributes cottage cheese, butter, and buttermilk. Current hours for Romberg's are 9-10 A.M. and noon to 6 P.M., weekdays; noon to 6 P.M., Saturdays.

Your Thanksgiving turkey (or its parents) probably began life in the Sonoma Valley, for the Nicholas Turkey Breeding Farms, Inc., headquartered here, produce the eggs and poults (young turkeys) for about 75 percent of all the primary breeding turkeys in the nation. Nicholas Farms sell their egg stock to Swift, Armour, Norbest, and other breeders and packers, and the Sonoma company is believed to be the world's biggest turkey breeder.

The Sonoma Slough

Sonoma Creek and the sloughs that form its tributaries make up the Sonoma Slough, a marshland that attracts hunters, fishermen, and nature lovers. Before the Sonoma Valley had railroads, steamers traversed these waterways as far as the town of Schellville, which was originally called St. Louis after St. Louis, Missouri. Railroad competition and river silt ended travel along Sonoma Creek.

The Tubbs Island Bird Sanctuary, a 332-acre marsh preserve, is the spot for hikers, photographers, and bird-watchers. The sanctuary is part of the San Pablo Bay National Wildlife Refuge and can be reached by taking a dirt road off Highway 37 just past Sears Point. Fall is the best time to visit this habitat for migratory birds. The U.S. Fish and Wildlife Service operates the Tubbs Island Bird Sanctuary. Call (415) 792-0222 for visiting hours.

Hudeman Slough Boat Ramp offers access to sturgeon and striped bass fishing in San Pablo Bay. This county-maintained, free, day-use facility has a boat launch, parking for boat trailers and vehicles, and rest rooms. Hudeman Slough is seven miles southeast of Sonoma on Skaggs Island Road. To get there, take Ramal Road off Highway 121 east of Schellville and follow it to Skaggs Island Road.

Temelec Hall

Temelec Hall, one of the state's finest nineteenth-century mansions, today is the privately owned clubhouse of the adult community called Temelec. Sharp-eyed motorists can spot the mansion's upper floors and cupola to the west as they drive along Arnold Drive between Watmaugh and Leveroni roads.

Granville Perry Swift, the burly Bear Flagger who built this three-story antebellum mansion for his bride in 1858, wanted his home to outshine General Vallejo's Lachryma Montis showplace near Sonoma. Swift kept Indian laborers to build his mansion from locally quarried basalt rock; the Indians worked by day with cannonballs tied to their ankles, and they were chained to the walls at night. Temelec Hall cost between $140,000 and $250,000 to construct (sources vary), but Swift had enough gold leftover to transform nuggets into $50 slugs marked with his own symbol.

Fortunes change, however; Swift's wife divorced him, he lost much of his money, and he died when his mule threw him over an embankment while he was inspecting

his mines. Treasure hunters roamed the grounds of
Temelec Hall, seeking buried gold, and more than one was
successful.

Temelec Hall became a social center when next owned
by Col. William K. Rogers, a member of the Sonoma
County Board of Supervisors who was unmasked as a
fugitive living under an assumed name. Hearst executive
Edmond D. Coblentz and his wife refurbished Temelec
Hall and lived in this historic landmark until the property
was sold to become an adult community.

Train Town

Train Town's two miniature steam engines and handcrafted railroad cars enthrall passengers who take a
quarter-hour trip to Lakeville, a pint-sized, western-
flavored hamlet populated with geese and ducks ready to
delight children. The trains, one-fourth normal size, chug
through ten landscaped acres, over a trestle, and through
a 120-foot-long tunnel.

Train Town, 20664 Broadway, one mile south of the
Sonoma Plaza, is open daily during summer months, weekends, and most holidays (weather permitting) in winter,
from 10:30-5:30. Admission prices: $1.80 for adults, $1.50
for seniors and children two to sixteen years, free for kids
under two years. Call 938-3912.

From here, follow Broadway (Highway 12) to the
Sonoma Plaza, put on your walking shoes, and get ready
to explore the city of Sonoma, a little place with lots of
history.

The City of Sonoma

The Mission San Francisco de Solano, at the heart
of this city of just over 6,000 souls, is one of the
attractions that brings 1 million tourists annually
to the Sonoma Valley. Padre Altimira explored the Petaluma, Sonoma, and Napa valleys before planting the

mission cross at Sonoma in 1823. The Spanish-born priest went over ecclesiastical heads to gain governmental approval of his mission founded to Christianize local Indians and to check the Russians at Fort Ross and Bodega. At its height in the 1830s, the mission had nearly a thousand Indian converts; herds of cattle, sheep, and horses; fields of grain and vegetables; vineyards; and a complex of adobe structures including a church and chapel, a priests' house, and shops for carpentry, weaving, and blacksmithing.

In 1834, the mission was secularized by Mariano G. Vallejo, a strong-willed, proud native of Monterey, related by blood and marriage to many of California's ruling families. Vallejo was commandant-general of the northern frontier (composed of nineteen present-day California counties), and he founded the pueblo of Sonoma as the first planned city north of the San Francisco Bay. His home, La Casa Grande, attracted international visitors, as Russians, Americans, British, and French forces jockeyed for control of Mexican California.

Americans were lured to California by rumors of free land, but they found all the land claimed by the Mexicans. Among the many wagon trains that reached California was the Grisby-Ide party from Illinois and Missouri. Several members of this party, with the left-handed backing of Capt. John C. Fremont, plotted to overthrow the Mexican government.

"About half past five in the morning of Sunday, June 14th, 1846, a group of rough looking desperados surrounded the house of General Vallejo and arrested him," wrote Rosalia Leese, Vallejo's sister, of the Bear Flag Revolt. "General Vallejo, dressed in the uniform of a General of the Mexican Army, was the prisoner of this large group of rough-looking men, some wearing on their heads caps made with the skins of coyotes or wolves . . . worn buckskin pants . . . several had no shirts; shoes were to be seen on the feet of fifteen or twenty among the whole lot."

Vallejo, his brother, his secretary, and his brother-in-law Jacob Leese were taken to Sutter's Fort. The Bear Flaggers, along with trappers and farmers from the Sacramento, Napa, and Sonoma valleys, set up their own government in the style of the Texas Republic. They raised a lone star flag depicting a bear and the words "California Republic" on it. Most of the Bear Flaggers simply wanted land, but the others' reasons for supporting the government were as varied as the men who founded it. Trapper Ezekiel "Stuttering" Merritt held a personal grudge against the Vallejos; William B. Ide, a New England carpenter, envisioned a republic independent of both Mexico and the United States.

Ide was elected president of the new republic. He issued a proclamation guaranteeing civil and religious freedom to all Californians, but that did not soothe tempers. The *Californios* and the Americans in Sonoma County grouped into armed camps. Two Bear Flaggers, George Fowler and Thomas Cowie, were tortured and murdered near Santa Rosa by a group of *Californios*, which then fled south to join General Jose Castro.

The *Californios* and Bear Flaggers clashed at Rancho Olompali, north of present-day Novato in Marin County, and each side retreated to lick their wounds. American families crowded into Sonoma, joined by some of Captain Fremont's men, including Kit Carson, and anxiously awaited the *Californios'* next move. On the night of June 30, the Bear Flaggers were raising their rifles against a group of armed men riding toward Sonoma, when Kit Carson cried out, "Hold on! 'tis Fremont." Sonoma was now firmly American.

On July 9, U.S. Navy Lt. Joseph W. Revere (a grandson of Paul Revere) lowered the Bear Flag and replaced it with the American stars and stripes. Most of the Bear Flaggers then formed the "California Battalion" and joined Fremont to fight with American troops in the Mexican War.

The Bear Flag Revolt was the opening shot in the Mexican War, and it prevented the peaceful annexation of California to the United States. Mariano Vallejo, released from Sutter's Fort jail on August 6, found his horses and cattle stolen, his fields stripped of grain. John C. Fremont returned to Washington to be court-martialed and dismissed from the service for his role in the Mexican War. California's only president, William Ide, moved to Colusa, where he died under mysterious circumstances.

Sonoma then became a military base, first under the privately organized military units of Jonathan Stevenson's New York Volunteer Regiment and later under the U.S. Army. Some of these men stayed to settle in Sonoma. The army's three-year stint brought to Sonoma a number of officers who later served as Union generals in the Civil War; among them were William T. Sherman, George Stoneman, and Joe Hooker. (Hooker's penchant for prostitutes in his Sonoma army days coined a new word for loose women.)

Sonoma soon rivaled San Francisco as a commercial center, but the gold rush killed the pueblo's growth. The railroad arrived in 1879, and commerce revived as the trains carried away Sonoma Valley wine, fruit, and basalt blocks quarried from the hills, while tourists made Sonoma a resort.

Italians came to Sonoma to work the quarries; among them was Samuele Sebastiani, who purchased a portion of the old mission vineyards in 1904 and began a winery. Today Sebastiani Vineyards is Sonoma Valley's largest winery, and the city of Sonoma contains a number of buildings constructed by Samuele.

During World War II, Gen. H. H. "Hap" Arnold, commander of the U.S. Army Air Corps, moved near Sonoma, and while here he formulated the air strategy that subdued Germany and Japan. (Arnold Drive is named for him.) Arnold retired after the war and was followed by a number of other retired military officers. Sonoma and surrounding towns became retirement meccas.

The town of Sonoma grew slowly, which meant that many of her historic structures remained, and, beginning in the 1960s, the efforts of numerous civic groups and private individuals rescued and restored many of the city's unique buildings. Today Sonoma is a charming town, popular with tourists but also frequented by local residents who enjoy shopping and dining here.

Sonoma Plaza Walking Tour

Few spots in Sonoma County evoke such a definite sense of place as the town of Sonoma, and the best spot to drink in this feeling is the Plaza. You can park your car on any side of the Plaza (two-hour parking limit) or park behind the Sonoma Barracks building in the free lot just off First Street East.

The eight-acre Plaza, a state and national landmark, is the largest in California. It is an ideal picnic spot, with numerous tables under the nearly two hundred trees; many annual events are held here, from art shows and barbecues to the popular Vintage Festival. The Sonoma Plaza also has a children's playground, a duck pond, an amphitheater, and a rose garden with many varieties, including the salmon-colored "Sonoma Rose." A monument honors the raising of the Bear Flag here in 1846, while a European fountain memorializes the Italian heritage of Sonoma.

Sonoma's City Hall, a basalt stone structure begun in 1906, is here in the Plaza. The building is identical on all sides so that no Plaza merchants would feel slighted. The old, brick Carnegie Library today is the home of the Sonoma Valley Chamber of Commerce, open weekdays, 9 A.M. to noon and 1 to 5 P.M.; 996-1033. Stop here to get the Sonoma Valley Wine and Road Map ($1), the Sonoma Walking Tour guide ($1), current Sonoma County Farm Trails maps, and information on local wineries, restaurants, lodging, shops, parks, and other attractions. A bulletin board in front of the chamber office also has helpful information. The chamber's address is 453 First Street East, Sonoma, CA 95476.

Surrounding Sonoma's Plaza are Mexican-era adobes (the biggest collection north of Monterey), false front

Bear Flag Monument, Sonoma Plaza. (Redwood Empire Association)

western-style buildings, and rusticated, basalt structures crafted by Italian stonemasons. The shops, restaurants, and delicatessens ringing the Plaza reflect the vitality of the many peoples who settled Sonoma—Mexicans, Anglos, Italians, French, Germans, Chinese, and Jews. European and Latin American visitors often say they feel at home when they first glimpse the Sonoma Plaza.

Mariano Vallejo laid out the Plaza in 1835 as the nucleus of the city of Sonoma. Using a pocket compass, Vallejo and William A. Richardson, an English sea captain, measured the Plaza boundaries and the pueblo's streets. Soil from the Plaza was made into bricks for Sonoma's adobes.

The Plaza was the center of life in the pueblo; Vallejo's Mexican soldiers drilled here, and it was the site of an aborted Indian uprising, several duels, horse races, and dog and 'coon fights. The Bear Flag was probably raised in the Plaza. In the 1880s, about half of the Plaza grounds were taken up by a depot and roundhouse for the Sonoma Valley Railroad. After the railroad buildings were moved to their present site at Depot Park, the Ladies Improvement Club started the landscaping efforts that resulted in the parklike setting of the Plaza.

Sonoma Plaza is bound by Spain Street on the north, Napa Street on the south, and First Street West and First Street East. Several historic structures—Mission San Francisco de Solano, the Sonoma Barracks, the Toscano Hotel, La Casa Grande, and the Blue Wing Inn—comprise the Sonoma State Historic Park. Mariano Vallejo's last home, Lachryma Montis, also a part of the Sonoma State Historic Park, is located one-half mile west of the Plaza on West Spain Street. The admission ticket you purchase at the Mission San Francisco de Solano is also good for the Sonoma Barracks, Lachryma Montis, and Vallejo's Petaluma Adobe.

The mission, on the corner of East Spain Street and First Street East, is a good spot to begin your walking tour. It's commonly called the Sonoma Mission to avoid confusion with Mission San Francisco de Assisi in San Francisco. Named for a Peruvian saint, the mission complex began in 1823, but most of what you now see is a restoration, with only the priests' quarters dating from mission days.

A large church building that served mission Indians is completely gone, and the austere chapel erected by Mariano Vallejo in 1840 as a parish church later became a hay barn, winery, and blacksmith shop before the mission buildings became state property in 1903. Sixty-two paintings of California missions by local artist Chris Jorgensen decorate the padres' quarters. Sonoma Mission is open daily 10-5; admission is 25 cents for kids six to seventeen, 50 cents for adults. Don't miss ringing the original mission bell in front of the chapel.

Next door is the Barracks, a restored two-story adobe built by Indian laborers between 1836 and 1840 to house General Vallejo's troops. From here, Vallejo launched more than a hundred military expeditions against northern California Indians. Among Vallejo's Indian allies was six-foot-tall Chief Solano of the Suisun Indians. Solano County is named for this mischievous leader, who once nearly caused an international incident by trying to kidnap the wife of the Russian commander of Fort Ross. Vallejo discharged most of his soldiers in 1844.

The Barracks have been occupied by the Bear Flaggers, Stevenson's New York Regiment, and the U.S. Army. Jewish merchant Solomon Schocken later had a store here. Former Sonoma *Index-Tribune* publishers Walter and Celeste Murphy bought the Barracks in 1934, before it was to be leveled for a gas station. Owned and restored by the state, the Barracks now contains exhibits of Sonoma's Indian, Mexican, and American pioneer epochs, plus an audio-visual presentation on the Barracks' restoration. Behind the Barracks are *hornos* (adobe bread ovens); Sonomans once gathered in this courtyard to bet on bear and bull fights. The Sonoma Barracks is open daily 10-5; admission is 25 cents for children six to seventeen, 50 cents for adults.

In Sonoma Plaza directly across from the Barracks is the Bear Flag monument, a bronze figure with the unfurled flag. Various stories surround the making of this flag: Mrs. John Sears donated white cloth for the banner; "Dirty Mathews" stole his wife's red petticoat from the clothesline to make a stripe; and William Todd, a nephew of Abraham Lincoln, painted a bear, a star, and the words "California Republic" on the cloth. The *Californios* laughingly said the bear more closely resembled a pig. The original flag was destroyed in the 1906 earthquake and fire in San Francisco, but in 1911 the state legislature adopted its design as the state flag.

Adjacent to the Barracks is the Toscano Hotel, 20 East Spain Street, begun in the 1850s as a general store and later turned into a hotel for Italian immigrant workers. (Toscano means "man from Tuscany," home province of the proprietors.) It's furnished in period furniture by the League for Historic Preservation, which hosts docent tours of the building on weekends, 1-4:30 P.M., and on Tuesdays, 11 A.M.-1 P.M. No charge.

The parklike space next to the Toscano Hotel, with public rest rooms, walkways to the public parking lot, and picnic tables behind the Barracks, is the site of Mariano Vallejo's La Casa Grande ("the big house"). Only the adobe Indian servants' quarters remain, part of the imposing two-story home where eleven of Vallejo's fifteen children were born. La Casa Grande's three-story tower allowed Vallejo to survey the countryside. A constant stream of visitors—Sir George Simpson of Britain's Hudson Bay Company, French attache Eugene Duflot de Mofras, U.S. Navy Com. Thomas Jones, and Capt. John Sutter among them—flocked to Vallejo's home as American and European powers plotted to control California. The Bear Flag Party arrested Vallejo here. In 1867, a few years after the Vallejo family had moved to Lachryma Montis, La Casa Grande burned to the ground. Part of this site is occupied by buildings of the state Department of Parks and Recreation office, which has a free, historical exhibit in one of the structures.

The neighboring Sonoma Cheese Factory, 2 West Spain Street, and the Vella Cheese Company, three blocks east at 315 Second Street East, are two of seven northern California cheese factories that make Jack cheese, a mild, white, moist, porous cheese that's a perfect match for

Sonoma County wine and sourdough bread. It's a versatile cooking cheese (great for omelets, souffles, or over meats and vegetables), and dry Jack makes a sweet-tasting grating cheese. Jack cheese is the West's only native cheese, named for Monterey County dairy owner David Jacks.

Jack cheese is made by scooping curds into muslin squares that are knotted at the top to make a bag, leaving a distinctive mark on the cheese. The cheese is shaped into wheels and aged thirty days. Dry Jack is also shaped into wheels, but cooked at a higher temperature and aged longer. Small wheels weigh about three pounds, large ones ten pounds (the Sonoma Cheese Factory offers a 10 percent discount on large wheels). Jack cheese flavor improves with age, but once cut the cheese should be refrigerated.

Sonoma's two cheese factories began in 1931, when the Vella and Viviani families converted an old, stone brewery into a cheese operation. The Vella Cheese Company still makes and sells cheese in the ex-brewery, while the Viviani family opened the Sonoma Cheese Factory in the 1940s, after the two families dissolved their partnership.

The Sonoma Cheese Factory has a five- to ten-minute slide show on cheese making, after which you can look through a window at the actual process. They sell Sonoma Jack cheese along with fifty imported and domestic cheeses (you can get free samples of some), sandwiches, wine, gifts, and delicatessen items. There's indoor/outdoor dining too, and you can mail some Sonoma Jack to the folks back home through their mailing service. Open 9-6 daily, 938-JACK.

At Vella Cheese Company you can see cheese making between 10 A.M. and noon most weekdays, then buy their Monterey Jack, Cheddar, blue, and Swiss cheeses. Vella's also mails their cheeses. Open Monday through Saturday, 9-6; Sunday, 9-5. Call 938-3232.

Marioni's Restaurant, 8 West Spain Street, offers seafood, steaks, and spirits. In the same block is a Sonoma institution, the Swiss Hotel, 18 West Spain Street, where chef Fred Wing delights diners with Italian/American *and* Chinese cuisine. The adjacent Gray Fox Saloon features

Sonoma Valley wines. The Swiss Hotel and Gray Fox
Saloon are located in the historic Salvador Vallejo Adobe,
built in 1840 by a brother of Mariano Vallejo; it became
the Swiss Hotel in the 1880s.

The Sonoma Valley Art Center, 14 West Spain Street,
spotlights the works of many local artists and contains
Charles Gill's lapidary shop. Art Center members sponsor
the annual free June art show in Sonoma Plaza. The
Center is open daily 1 to 5 P.M.; call 996-1466 for visits at
other hours.

The Sonoma Hotel, 110 West Spain Street, offers the
only lodging on the Plaza. Built about 1872, the Sonoma
Hotel is now a restored and antique-furnished country inn
(one room has furniture originally owned by General
Vallejo) with seventeen rooms, five private baths. Black
authoress and actress Maya Angelou holed up here to
write her third novel. Call 996-2996 for reservations.

A few doors down on the opposite side of West Spain
Street is "La Casa" Adobe, 143 West Spain Street, built in
1836 for Don Juan Castaneda, a Mexican captain whose
Rancho Cotate is today the cities of Rohnert Park and
Cotati. The adobe is privately owned.

Walk back to the Plaza and start down First Street
West, a fine street for antique and gift shopping. The first
building is the Salvador Vallejo Adobe, 405-427 First
Street West, constructed between 1836 and 1846 by Indian
laborers, possibly as the pueblo's governmental offices.
The southern portion of the adobe is more authentic; the
northern portion of the edifice was destroyed in the 1906
earthquake and today is the El Dorado Hotel, featuring
Italian and American cuisine in the glass-paneled garden
court or in the dining room. Within and behind this adobe
is The Garden Gate, 415 First Street West, a pleasant spot
for plants and garden accessories. It is open Wednesday
through Saturday, 10-5; Sunday, 12-4.

Herb Hoeser's Sonoma Sausage Company, 411 First
Street West, is a sausage lover's heaven, with over sixty
Sonoma-made sausage varieties, many based on German
recipes Hoeser gathered in Europe. Customers' favorites

include north country, Hawaiian-Portuguese, and hot beer sausages, and English bangers. You can also bite into herb loaves, smoked turkeys and hams, German potato salad, or sauerkraut. Currently, the Sonoma Sausage Company is open Monday through Saturday, 9-6; call 996-5211.

Two antique, false front western-style buildings, at 437-439 and 447 First Street West, date from the mid-nineteenth century and once belonged to French wine-maker Camille Aguillon. Antiques for your home are found at Accents, 433 First Street West; the Antique Guild of Sonoma, 497 First Street West; and at Roger Barber, 383 First Street West, home of Asian antiques.

The Leese-Fitch Adobe, 487 First Street West, dates from 1836. On three sides, it once had two-story verandas which were supported by columns fashioned from ships' masts. Jacob P. Leese, married to Mariano Vallejo's sister Rosalia, was another Sonoman arrested and imprisoned by the Bear Flaggers. Henry D. Fitch bought the adobe in 1848, a number of years after he and Josefa Carrillo shocked Mexican California by eloping to Chile. This adobe served as U.S. Army headquarters from 1849 to 1851 under Gen. Persifor Smith. Today it contains commercial establishments.

Some of Sonoma's newest shopping stops are along Napa Street, facing the Plaza. The Feed Store, 103 West Napa Street, once sold hay and grain; now you can find clothes, jewelry, toys, and gifts in its specialty shops. Also here is La Placita ("small produce market") with all kinds of fresh fruit and vegetables, dried fruit, nuts, and farm eggs, many from Sonoma Valley farms. The Sonoma Marketplace, 201 West Napa Street, is another shoppers' bazaar. Here you can pick up Italian deli treats and sand-wiches, or sit down to hot homemade luncheon specials— all at Berto's Deli. If you're looking for Chinese cuisine, the Lok Sing Restaurant in the Sonoma Marketplace serves lunch and dinner. The Feed Store and the Sonoma Marketplace are both open daily.

Three blocks south of the Sonoma Plaza is the Au Relais Restaurant, 691 Broadway, featuring fine French cuisine that draws diners from all over the Bay Area. Owner-chef Harry Marsden has put his European training to good use with palate-pleasing results. Call 996-1031 for reservations.

If you're walking off a meal or waking up an appetite, follow First Street East south of the Plaza to see some historic sights. At 542 First Street East is the Gothic revival church built by Sonoma Methodists and today the city's First Baptist Church. It was one of the first Protestant churches organized and built north of San Francisco. The Julius Poppe House, 564 First Street, is a Gothic cottage decorated with intricate trim.

The Nash-Patton Adobe, 579 First Street East, is a compact dwelling where Sonoma's first American *alcalde* ("mayor"), John H. Nash, was arrested in 1847 by Lt. William Tecumseh Sherman. Nash had refused to relinquish his office to the next *alcalde*, Lilburn W. Boggs, a former Missouri governor and a protege of General Vallejo.

Walk back to the Plaza, where you will see a series of stone buildings beginning at First Street East and East Napa Street. These basalt structures were erected at the turn of the century by Italian stonemasons hired by Sonoma businessman Augustino Pinelli to work the quarries north of Sonoma.

The Boccoli Building (ca. 1896), 101 East Napa Street, now is the locale for the Capri Restaurant, while the neighboring Dal Poggetto Building (ca. 1908) sports the Sonoma Station Espresso Cafe. In 1904, Frenchman Andre Castex opened Sonoma's first bakery, the Pioneer; his ovens now are part of the dining room of the Eastside Grill, 133 East Napa Street, which features an indoor Mexican mesquite charcoal grill and an art nouveau bar made of Hawaiian koa wood. Keith and Joanne Filipello, owners of the Capri and co-owners of the Eastside Grill, pride themselves on using fresh, often locally grown ingredients. The Capri offers continental cuisine, while the Eastside Grill serves seafood, pasta, and meats.

A beautifully restored Victorian stick-style home lures shoppers with a bookstore, a boutique, and Peterberry's, an espresso coffee haven with indoor and outdoor dining. The home is adjacent to the Eastside Grill at 139 East Napa Street.

Retrace your steps to the Plaza and walk down First Street East. The east side of the Plaza is dominated by the Sebastiani Theatre, 476 First Street East, one of the many building projects completed by Samuele Sebastiani during Sonoma's depression years. The theater stands on the site of Christian Brunner's Sonoma house. Swiss-born Brunner and his wife adopted orphaned Eliza and Georgia Donner, whose parents died in the Donner Party's cannibalism-ridden Sierra winter ordeal of 1846 and 1847. (General Vallejo was one of many Californians who sent a relief party to the Donner Party survivors. Eventually, five survivors settled in Sonoma County.)

In 1911, a disastrous fire destroyed most of the buildings along this side of the Plaza. Local merchant Augustino Pinelli directed fire fighters to use his 1,000-gallon tank of red wine to quench the flames, thus saving several structures.

The Sonoma French Bakery, 468 First Street East, is a mecca for lovers of croissants and bread (sweet or sourdough). Patrons jam the tiny bakery, take a number, and patiently wait in line. Owners Gratien and Lili Guerra, natives of French Pyrenees, and their assistants hand-make the bread and bake it in ovens imported from France. The Guerras also sell rolls and pastries. The Sonoma French Bakery is open Wednesday through Saturday, 8-6; Sunday, 8 A.M. to noon. Phone 996-2691. If the bakery is closed during your Sonoma visit, check the Sonoma Cheese Factory, which occasionally has loaves.

A few steps north from the bakery is the Place des Pyrenees, 464 First Street East, an off-street cobblestone mall. Francoise Guerra, daughter of Sonoma French Bakery's owners, runs the Cafe Pilou, a country-style French restaurant with indoor and outdoor seating for breakfast, lunch, and dinner. Guerra, trained in European cooking schools, spotlights local foods including, of course, Sonoma French bread. The large plaster relief on the restaurant depicts animal chefs en route to a banquet hall; it once decorated San Francisco's famed Poodle Dog Restaurant. Call 996-2757 for reservations.

Gift shops and boutiques compose other Place des Pyrenees shops, while the adjacent Arts Guild of Sonoma, 460 First Street East, highlights paintings, pottery, and other art treasures from the hands of local artists.

El Paseo de Sonoma, 414 First Street East, is another tucked-away shoppers' delight, combining history, dining, and shopping. You enter through the doorway of the century-old Pinelli Building, crafted from burgundy-hued "plum" stone by Augustino Pinelli, to reach most of the shops and the Vasquez House, a pioneer home with constantly changing historical exhibits.

El Paseo's Pip's Wines and Accessories features tasting (for a nominal fee) of Sonoma County wines plus the sale of wines, glassware, wine racks, and books. The Old City Pottery shop is housed in an old bakery, where you can see the original ovens. Diners can drop in at Gino's of Sonoma, a popular lunch and dinner spot with a bar facing the Plaza, or at La Casa Mexican Restaurant, around the corner from the Plaza opposite the Sonoma Mission. Delicatessen devotees head for two First Street East spots: the Old Sonoma Creamery, number 400; or Brundage's, number 492, which serves Chinese foods. Both have sit-down ice cream fountains.

The Vasquez House, operated by the Sonoma League for Historic Preservation, is open 1-5, Wednesday through Saturday. The simple, frame home was one of several shipped from Sweden around Cape Horn to California in 1851. The original owner was U.S. Army Col. Joseph Hooker, later a Civil War general. Pedro Vasquez, Sonoma councilman and part owner of a large Marin County ranch, later owned the home. The historic house became the property of the League in 1974 through the generosity of Robert M. Lynch, current owner/publisher of the Sonoma *Index-Tribune*, and his wife. The League's docents host the exhibits and staff a coffee and gift shop. The docents also offer periodic, scheduled guided tours of

historic Sonoma sites. Tour reservations are necessary; call
938-4193.

Sonoma holds still more surprises for those willing to
take a three-block walk from the Plaza to Sebastiani Vineyards, home of the Sonoma Valley's largest winery. Start
on East Spain Street, opposite the Sonoma Mission, where
the wisteria-covered, two-story adobe Blue Wing Inn
stands. Some say it's haunted, and well it could be; this
venerable site was once a rowdy gold rush-era saloon,
where U. S. Grant, William T. Sherman, Kit Carson, and
the notorious bandit Joaquin Murietta gathered. Grizzled
miners tossed gold nuggets into the aprons of the owner's
sons as tips, and lucky cleaning women made pin money
from the gold dust swept off the barroom floor. Today the
adobe's first floor is occupied by shops.

A block away is the Ray/Adler Adobe, 206 East Spain
Street, a two-story Monterey colonial-style privately
owned home built between 1846 and 1851. It was once a
mess hall for Colonel Stevenson's New York Regiment;
later, one of California's earliest Masonic lodges met here.
Among its owners was Lewis Adler, a German immigrant
who brought his business partner, Heinrich Schliemann,
to Sonoma. Adler's sister jilted Schliemann, who left
Sonoma for a career in archaeology and later discovered
the ancient city of Troy.

Sebastiani Vineyards

Tradition and innovation are hallmarks of Sebastiani
Vineyards, 389 Fourth Street East, a top attraction in
Sonoma, where visitors enjoy the instructive tours; the
friendly, informal tasting room; and the chance to see
numerous hand-carved wine barrels and an outstanding
collection of Indian artifacts. The Sebastianis maintain an
inventory of twenty-two premium wines, along with a
number of bulk wines. In 1981, the winery introduced low-
calorie, low-alcohol Light Country White wines.

It all began when Samuele Sebastiani left his native

Tuscany, in northern Italy, and immigrated to California, where he worked the stone quarries on Schocken Hill near Sonoma. By 1904, he'd bought the old Milani winery, plus vineyards that once had been harvested by mission padres and by Mariano Vallejo. Samuele Sebastiani, who sold his wine door to door from a horse-drawn wagon, survived Prohibition by making sacramental and medicinal wines. His son, August, joined him in 1934, and the Sebastianis became a sustaining force of Sonoma Valley winemaking from Repeal until the mid-1960s. August—a familiar Sonoma figure in his striped overalls, straw hat, and pickup truck—transformed the winery from a bulk wine facility to a major wine producer with an output of over 3 million cases annually by the late 1970s.

August Sebastiani was the first vintner to mass-produce low-priced premium varietal jug wines, and in 1972 he pioneered the making of Beaujolais in the French *nouveau* style. The Sebastiani family's forte has been red wines aged in redwood vats and small oak barrels. Following August's death in 1980, his son Sam took over the winery's management. Presently, Sebastiani Vineyards is constructing bulk wine facilities at Schellville, while the Sonoma location will continue premium wine production and construct new facilities for visitors.

Sebastiani Vineyards' better known wines include Barbera, Green Hungarian, Cabernet Sauvignon, Zinfandel, and Amore Cream Sherry. A highlight of the winery tours are the hundreds of hand-carved casks created by octogenarian Earle Brown, who began wood-carving after his retirement. The Indian Artifacts Museum contains Indian basketry, Navajo textiles, and other objects gathered by August Sebastiani, including the purchased collection of the late Rose Gaffney of Bodega Bay.

The winery is open daily 10-5. Tours run from 10 A.M. to 4:20 P.M.; tour appointments are provided for groups of twenty or more. The Indian Artifacts Museum is also open daily 10-5. Visitors should plan to get to the winery early on weekends to avoid crowds. Picnic area included. Call 938-5532.

Sonoma Bike Path

You can bicycle, jog, or walk from the Sebastiani Vineyards to Robinson Road near Highway 12, on the western edge of the city of Sonoma. Along the way you'll pass the Vella Cheese Company, the Depot Museum, and Vallejo's home, Lachryma Montis. A parcourse has been built along the path for simple exercises. Eventually, the Sonoma bike path will run 8,000 feet from Lovall Valley Road, east of Sebastiani Vineyards, to Highway 12. No motorized vehicles or horses are allowed on the 6,000 feet of the path already completed.

Depot Park Historical Museum

One (long) block north of the Plaza is the Depot Park Historical Museum, 285 First Street West. The original Sonoma Depot (1880) was being considered for a museum site by the Sonoma Valley Historical Society when an unsolved arson fire destroyed the structure in 1976. Society members, the city of Sonoma, and the county of Sonoma raised funds to build a replica of the depot. Today visitors can explore the depot building and the adjacent railroad cars, reliving train travel the way it was a century ago. The Society operates the depot and presents an ever-changing series of exhibits on the Old West. The Depot Park Historical Museum is open Wednesday through Sunday, 1-4:30 P.M. Admission prices: adults, 50 cents; seniors and children ten to eighteen, 25 cents; children nine and under free. Tours can be arranged by calling 938-9765. The gift shop sells antiques and local history books.

The grassy park surrounding the depot is a nice, quiet picnic spot, with tables, a small children's playground, public rest rooms, and free parking. The nearby Depot Hotel 1870, 241 First Street West, 938-2980, once was a hotel for railroad travelers, but today lures travelers for delicious meals. The "chef specials" featured with regular menu items make this indoor/outdoor dining spot a memorable one.

Three blocks north of the Plaza off First Street West is Sonoma's Mountain Cemetery, at the foot of 658-foot-high Schocken Hill, site of one of the region's many rock quarries. This pioneer cemetery contains the graves of General Vallejo, the Sebastianis, and the site of the only Revolutionary War soldier buried in California, Capt. William Smith, who joined the Virginia Navy at age eleven in 1779 and died in Sonoma in 1846. The Daughters of the American Revolution have erected a marker to commemorate Smith.

Lachryma Montis

Lachryma Montis was General Vallejo's home for the last thirty-five years of his life, the "American" period in his career. After his imprisonment and release during the Bear Flag Revolt, Mariano Vallejo the *Californio* made a successful transformation into an Anglo-oriented Californian and turned from living in an adobe home to residing in a Victorian carpenter's Gothic house. He was a delegate to California's constitutional convention and a state senator, and he invested heavily in an attempt to make the town of Vallejo California's capital. After the legislature moved to Sacramento, Vallejo turned to winemaking and writing, limiting his political activities to serving as Sonoma's mayor. California historian Hubert Bancroft used much of Vallejo's research for his historical works.

To visit Lachryma Montis, follow Spain Street west to Third Street West and proceed down a tree-lined road. The well-maintained home and landscaped grounds were held by Vallejo's heirs until they sold the property to the state in 1933; currently it is a part of the Sonoma State Historic Park. Vallejo built his redwood home in 1851 and 1852, then christened it Lachryma Montis (Latin for "mountain tear") after mineral springs on the property. A duplicate of this house was built for Joseph Bonaparte, exiled King of Naples, in Bordentown, New Jersey.

Next to the home is the Swiss Chalet, a warehouse built to store Vallejo's wine, fruit, and other produce; now the distinctive, half-timbered structure is a museum. The

The Swiss Chalet at General Vallejo's Sonoma home, Lachryma Montis.
(Redwood Empire Association)

grounds of Lachryma Montis contained Vallejo's orchards and vineyards. (His prize-winning wines were an incentive for other vintners to settle in the Sonoma Valley.) Today the landscaped grounds are a pleasant picnic spot for visitors. Lachryma Montis is open daily 10-5. Admission 50 cents adults, 25 cents kids.

Sonoma's Festivals

History, hilarity, art, wine, and even the fine art of calf roping are highlighted in a number of summer and fall events. June's festivities include the Sonoma Valley Art Center's annual arts and craft show, a free, weekend event held in the Plaza. The chamber of commerce sponsors an ox roast on the second day of the art festival, with live entertainment to accompany the beef dinner. The Sonoma Kiwanis Club has a turkey barbecue in the Plaza at the end of June.

The Bear Flag Revolt is remembered with the Native Sons' Flag Day barbecue, June 14, in the Plaza. Wine and history, along with the rich culinary diversity of the Sonoma Valley are part of the wine appreciation day sponsored by the League of Historic Preservation. This biannual event offers a number of scheduled tours to the Sonoma Valley's wineries, including several that normally do not open their facilities to visitors.

Sonoma's Wine Country Rodeo, held on rodeo grounds south of Sonoma at Watmaugh Road and Arnold Drive, spotlights Professional Rodeo Cowboys Association broncobusters in bulldogging, bareback riding, calf roping, and bull riding competition—a full June weekend of Wild West happenings.

The Old-Fashioned Fourth of July celebration focuses on a parade around the Plaza and an art show in the Plaza, courtesy of the Sonoma Valley Art Center. There's live entertainment, a chicken barbecue, and, of course, fireworks at Arnold Field, two blocks north of the Plaza.

Sonoma's biggest fete is the Vintage Festival, held each September in and around the Plaza. The celebration of the grape harvest features pageantry with the blessing of the grapes, historical vignettes, grape stomping, wine tasting, food and game booths, a variety of musical groups, art shows, a parade, and the hilarious firemen's waterfight.

Information about Sonoma's annual events is yours by calling the Sonoma Valley Chamber of Commerce, 996-1033.

Sonoma Winery Tour

East of the city of Sonoma stand four wineries— Hacienda Wine Cellars, Buena Vista Winery, Gundlach-Bundschu Winery, and Haywood Winery. You can begin in town at Sebastiani's and then taste your way through the other wineries, with time out for picnics and Farm Trail stops.

Hacienda Wine Cellars and Buena Vista Winery are forever linked with the names of two world-roamers: Hungarian Count Agoston Haraszthy, and Frank H. Bartholomew, board chairman emeritus of United Press International. Haraszthy founded Buena Vista, while Bartholomew revived it and later established neighboring Hacienda.

Haraszthy was a flamboyant, dark-eyed, full-bearded man, equally at home within the palace of Germany's Prince Metternich or on horseback along the Santa Fe Trail. A political exile from his native Hungary, he roamed across America, living first in New York, then in Wisconsin (where he founded Sauk City), and finally in California, where he was sheriff of San Diego and assayer of the U.S. Mint in San Francisco before he was drawn to the Sonoma Valley by General Vallejo's vinicultural successes. Haraszthy had tried his hand at grape growing wherever he traveled, and in 1857 he started Buena Vista ("good view") Winery, complete with stalwart stone buildings and cellars dug into the hillsides. He built a Pompeian-style villa nearby. Haraszthy traveled to European vinelands to bring back hundreds of grape varieties and 2,000 years of vinicultural knowledge.

Haraszthy has sometimes been called the "father of the California wine industry," and while this title is disputed, he was instrumental in bringing many European vintners to California, including Charles Krug, founder of the Napa Valley's wine industry, and the Dresel brothers, who introduced German wine-making techniques to Sonoma County. Although he was for many years credited with bringing the mysterious Zinfandel grape to California, wine researchers now agree Haraszthy probably did not introduce this popular varietal grape to the state. Zinfandel, now identified as Italy's Primitivo grape, flourishes as one of California's most productive wine grapes.

In 1869, Haraszthy took off again, this time to found a sugar plantation in Nicaragua. He vanished in the jungles,

reputedly eaten by alligators. The Buena Vista Vinicultural Society, centered around the winery, survived
until the 1906 earthquake, then folded.

In 1941, Frank Bartholomew, a war correspondent for
United Press International (and later its president), bought
the defunct winery, restoring both the buildings and the
winery's reputation for premium wine production. Bartholomew sold Buena Vista Winery in 1968, but returned
to the wine business in 1973 when he established Hacienda
Wine Cellars.

To reach the wineries, start at the Plaza or at Sebastiani
Vineyards and watch for winery signs along the way
marking your route. Hacienda is our first stop, so drive
along East Napa Street and turn left onto Seventh Street
East; go to Castle Road, turn right, and drive one mile to
Vineyard Lane. Hacienda Cellars, 1000 Vineyard Lane, is
housed in a Spanish-style structure that once was a hospital, and it's near the site of Haraszthy's long-vanished
villa.

Although a new winery, Hacienda has deep Sonoma
roots. The "Clos de Agoston" vineyards commemorate
Haraszthy's plantings of European grape varieties here in
1862, and principal owner and president Crawford Cooley
is a descendant of William B. Elliot, a Bear Flagger and
discoverer of The Geysers. Hacienda's wine roster includes
Chardonnay, Gewurztraminer, Johannisberg Riesling,
Chenin Blanc, Pinot Noir Blanc, Cabernet Sauvignon,
Zinfandel, and Pinot Noir. The winery is open for tasting
and sales daily 10-5; tours by appointment only, 938-3220.
Bus tours and other large groups are also welcomed, but
call for an appointment. The oak-dotted Wine Garden is a
restful picnic spot with tables for more than a hundred
guests.

To reach Buena Vista Winery, retrace your steps on
Castle Road, turn onto Lovall Valley Road, and take Old
Winery Road. If coming from the Plaza, take East Napa
Street to Old Winery Road. Buena Vista, the state's oldest
bonded winery, lies in a eucalyptus-shaded valley at
18000 Old Winery Road. The massive stone buildings

stand as fitting tributes to Count Haraszthy and to his
sons, Attila and Arpad (both married daughters of General Vallejo), who made champagne here.

Buena Vista Winery, a state historical landmark, is
today owned by the A. Racke, a German wine and liquor
company. The actual wine-making processes take place
elsewhere in the Sonoma Valley, but you can taste and
buy the results, or enjoy a self-guided historical tour
through Haraszthy's cellars daily 10-5. Buena Vista's wine
offerings include Chardonnay, Gewurztraminer, Fume
Blanc, Green Hungarian, Cabernet Sauvignon, Burgundy,
Pinot Noir, Ultra Dry Sherry, Golden Sherry, and Vintage Port, plus special red and white wine selections sold as
Buena Vista Cask Wines and Buena Vista Cabinet Wines
(from an old European custom of locking rare wines in a
cabinet). The winery's shady, terraced picnic spots are
popular with wine country visitors.

The Buena Vista Winery sponsors two cultural events
on its grounds, the midsummer Mozart concert series and
scenes from Shakespearean plays each fall. The Mozart
concerts, held on Sunday afternoons, include complimentary wine on arrival and wine tasting after the concert. A
shuttlebus conveys concertgoers from the parking lot of
the Sonoma Veterans Memorial Building, 126 First Street
West, to the winery. Tickets are $12; call 938-8504, or
write Buena Vista MOZART, Sonoma, CA 95476. Tickets
can be bought at the winery or at Buena Vista's Tasting
Room, Pier 39, San Francisco. Each Saturday in September and October, Shakespearean comedy scenes are performed by players of the Sonoma Vintage Theatre. Tickets
($4, $3 seniors and children) are sold at the winery.

Gundlach-Bundschu Winery, 3775 Thornsberry Road,
is your next stop. From Buena Vista Winery or from town,
take Old Winery Road to Lovall Valley Road, and make a
right turn onto Thornsberry Road. Gundlach-Bundschu
Winery, once a well-known name in pre-Prohibition
California, is again establishing a fine reputation under
the direction of Jim Bundschu, great-great-grandson of the
founder, and his brother-in-law, John Merritt.

Jacob Gundlach was the first of several German emigres who located in this wooded area at the foot of Arrowhead Mountain. Gundlach arrived in 1854 and was joined by his son-in-law, Charles Bundschu, and by the Dresel brothers, Emil and Julius, of the Dresel champagne family of Germany. Here, at the Rhinefarm, they introduced German wine-making techniques to the region, perfected dry white wines, and developed successful wholesale and retail wine markets in San Francisco and New York. Julius Dresel discovered the technique that stopped phylloxera (a grape-root louse) by grafting disease-prone vines onto phylloxera-resistant rootstock, thus saving the vineyards of America and Europe.

During Prohibition the winery and vineyards fell into disuse, but they were revived by Jim Bundschu and John Merritt, who used a portion of the old winery building for the new winery. Today's Gundlach-Bundschu wines are Cabernet Sauvignon, Pinot Noir, Merlot, Zinfandel, Chardonnay, Johannisberg Riesling, Gewurztraminer, Sonoma Riesling, Sonoma Rose, and Kleinberger, a unique grape that's a clone of Johannisberg Riesling. Gundlach-Bundschu Winery is open daily 12-4:30 for tasting and sales. Also available are informal tours, including displays of their rich viticultural history, and a picnic area; 938-5277.

The last winery on the Sonoma Winery Tour is Haywood Winery, 18701 Gehricke Road off Lovall Valley Road between Fourth Street East and Seventh Street East. The winery's slope-clinging vines—planted on the Chamizal (Spanish for "thicket of hardwood") Ranch in the rugged, mountainous country above Sonoma—have already produced an award-winning White Riesling, although Haywood's first releases were in 1981. Haywood is open for tours by appointment only, no sales or tasting, 996-4298.

A wine country mini-brewery, New Albion, produces traditional British-style ale, porter, and stout—all good companions to Sonoma's cheese, bread, and sausage. New Albion Brewery, with a current production of 120 cases per week, plans to open a new brewery and associated tasting room at 800 West Napa Street, Sonoma. Founded in 1976 by ex-navyman Jack McAuliffe, who acquired a taste for British beers while stationed in Scotland, New Albion's brewers make their beers in an old-fashioned top fermentation method rather than in the lager style used by larger breweries. You can buy New Albion at the Sonoma Cheese Factory or at Plaza Liquors on the Plaza.

Hot Springs Resorts

Northwest of the city of Sonoma lie the old resort towns of El Verano, Boyes Hot Springs, Fetters Springs, and Agua Caliente. From Sonoma, Highway 12 (Sonoma Highway) and Arnold Drive run parallel routes through the towns and the Sonoma Valley until they join northeast of Glen Ellen. Highway 12 is the busier, more commercial route, while Arnold Drive is the more direct way to reach Glen Ellen.

Sonoma Valley Indians first discovered the healing powers of the hot springs in this area, and in the nineteenth century several unsuccessful attempts were made to develop them. Capt. Henry E. Boyes, an expatriate English naval officer, brought his wife to the Sonoma Valley for her health; acting upon the advice of General Vallejo, he started a resort in today's Boyes Hot Springs. Just after the turn of the century, several other resort towns, some with hot springs, also sprang up, including El Verano (Spanish for "the summer place"), Fetters Springs, and Agua Caliente.

San Francisco families came by train, and later by car, for a "summer rendezvous." It was a constant round of swimming, concerts, dances, teas, and vaudeville and motion picture shows. Prohibition completely changed the resort towns; they became strictly adult playgrounds, with "hot" jazz spots, speakeasies, and "oases" operated by madams such as Spanish Kitty Lombard. In the early

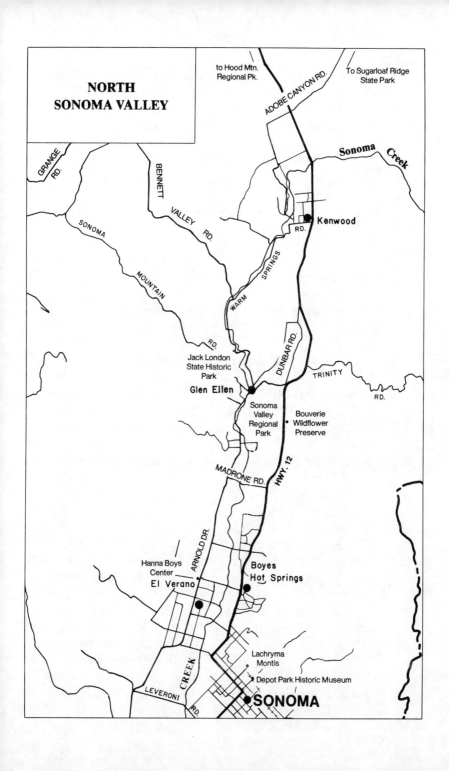

1930s, pint-sized Baby Face Nelson caused a stir in El Verano when he passed through town.

The towns quieted down following Repeal, although in the late 1960s and early 1970s, Fetters Springs boasted an eclectic eatery, Juanita's Gallery, captained by flamboyant Juanita Musson, reputedly a former madam, whose colorful language matched her muumuus. Her restaurant was well known for its cuisine and for the host of animals, including the monkey Beauregard, who were kept about the place.

Today the area's main attraction is the refurbished Sonoma Mission Inn, a self-contained resort. But there are two wineries—Hanzell and Valley of the Moon—on the outskirts of the region, plus restaurants, craft shops, and the last of the mineral spas, Agua Caliente Mineral Springs.

Sonoma Mission Inn

The Sonoma Mission Inn is a statement of wine country elegance. Its pink, Spanish-style buildings are on seven landscaped acres just two and a half miles north of the Plaza on Highway 12. The Inn treats its guests to first-class luxury, with everything from canopied beds, Olympic-sized swimming pool, three lighted tennis courts, and spa to fine French and northern Italian cuisine. The Inn's luxuriously appointed rooms, 100 in all, are located in two wings off the huge lobby.

The atmosphere recalls the days of the Roaring Twenties and the Big Band era, when Hollywood celebrities, California entrepreneurs, and sports figures all gathered at the Sonoma Mission Inn. (The San Francisco Seals and Oakland Oaks baseball teams held their spring training camps in Boyes Hot Springs.) Businessman Ed Sadfie, who divides his time between New York and San Francisco, in 1979 bought the aging resort for $2.5 million, then pumped another $7 million into restoring it. Among the Inn's recent guests have been Telly Savalas, Faye Dunaway, Rod Stewart, and Bianca Jagger.

The Provencal is the Inn's elegant dining spot for lunch or dinner, or you can go casual in the Grill area. Evening entertainment includes the Sonoma Mission Inn Trio, playing nostalgic music of Glen Miller and Frank Sinatra, and the Inn's lounge is a popular stop for relaxation. The concierge can arrange equestrian outings, hot air balloon flights, or bicycling adventures for guests.

The Spa at Sonoma Mission Inn revitalizes guests with a six-day, $1,500 program of quality body conditioning, beauty care, massage, herbal cleansing, and hydrotherapy in the same mineral waters that first brought people to Boyes Hot Springs. For inn and restaurant reservations, and spa information, call 996-1041, or write Sonoma Mission Inn, Boyes Hot Springs, CA 95416.

Mid-Valley Wineries

Nestled almost in the heart of the Sonoma Valley are two distinctly different wineries: tiny, prestigious Hanzell Vineyards and folksy, unpretentious Valley of the Moon Winery.

Located at the end of Lomita Avenue, off Verano Avenue and Highway 12, Hanzell Vineyards is open for tours by appointment only (996-3860). Founded in 1956 by the late James D. Zellerbach—originator of the paper company of the same name, former U.S. ambassador to Italy, and chief administrator for the Marshall Plan in Europe—Hanzell Vineyards is known for two innovations in viticulture: the use of French Limousin oak barrels to age American white wine and the use of stainless steel tanks for fermentation. After Zellerbach introduced these changes, scores of vintners followed suit. By using French oak barrels, American vintages of Chardonnay could for the first time compete favorably with Burgundian white wines.

Hanzell Vineyards (the name is a combination of Zellerbach's wife's first name, Hannah, and his own surname) produces limited quantities (2,000 cases annually) of Chardonnay and Pinot Noir at the winery modeled after the Chateau Clos de Vougeot. The current owners are Countess Barbara de Brye, a native of Australia, and her French husband, Jacques de Brye.

The Parducci family's Valley of the Moon Winery, 777 Madrone Road, between Highway 12 and Arnold Drive north of Agua Caliente, is a family-operated winery in the same vein as Sebastiani and Gundlach-Bundschu. Enrico Parducci, a native of Bagni di Lucca, Italy, bought the defunct winery in 1941; today his son Harry and grandson, Harry, Jr. manage it.

Situated beside Sonoma Creek, Valley of the Moon Winery originally was a part of the Agua Caliente Rancho granted to Lazaro Pena, a Mexican soldier. General Vallejo later bought the property and deeded 640 acres to the Vallejo children's music teacher in exchange for their piano lessons. In 1851, Col. "Fighting Joe" Hooker took over the ranch and planted a vineyard. Later owners included Eli Shepard, former American consul to Tient-sin, China (he named the property Madrone Vineyards), and Senator George Hearst (father of William Randolph Hearst), wealthy mine owner and newspaper publisher. Hearst planted French grape varieties at Madrone Vineyards and served his own wines in Washington, D.C. In 1891, he sold the winery, which passed through many hands before the Parducci family purchased it.

Today, Valley of the Moon Winery is known for both its jug wines and its 100 percent Sonoma Valley varietals: French Colombard, Semillon, Zinfandel, Pinot Noir, and Zinfandel Rose. Valley of the Moon Winery is open for tasting and sales 10-5 daily except Thursday. Also available are a gift shop and picnic tables. Call 996-6941.

Dining, Dancing, and Other Diversions

Scattered along Highway 12 (Sonoma Highway), Arnold Drive, and the side streets of the hot springs resort area are several eating and recreational spots. Hanging literally on the coattails of the Sonoma Mission Inn is the Big 3 Fountain, 18130 Sonoma Highway in Boyes Hot Springs,

serving hearty, inexpensive breakfasts, lunches, and
dinners, plus ice cream creations at the soda fountain.
Nearby is Mancuso's, 18020 Sonoma Highway, with continental and southern Italian cuisine.

Calories don't count when you drop in at Moosetta's,
18976 Sonoma Highway, where everything is made from
scratch—piroshki, soups, hors d'oeuvres, and delectable
pastries (take-out only). Open Tuesday through Saturday,
10-6; 996-1313.

The Little Switzerland, Grove and Riverside Drive,
El Verano, is the place to wear your lederhosen, to polka
or waltz to a German-style band, to drink beer, and to eat
sausages and dumplings. The handpainted Swiss murals on
the walls make European visitors feel right at home; Little
Switzerland is popular with folk dancing groups too. Open
every weekend, Friday through Sunday; 938-9990.

Agua Caliente Mineral Springs, 17310 Vailetti Drive
off Highway 12, is a popular place for aquatic families to
spend the day. It has a spacious, 86-degree warm mineral
water pool (water changed daily), cold water diving pool,
baby pool, extensive picnic grounds with barbecue pits,
and a group dancing facility. It's open from Memorial Day
until early September. Hours are 10:30-6, weekdays;
9:30-7, weekends. Current prices: $3 adults, $2.50 for
those under sixteen, $1.50 for children under eleven. Call
996-6822.

Golfers gather at the Sonoma National Golf Club,
17700 Arnold Drive, a public, 18-hole championship
course, par 72, sporting a pro shop, clubhouse, swimming
pool, dining room, plus cart and club rentals. Daily green
fees are $6.50; weekends are $9.50. Call 996-0300.

Although the hot springs resort region retains a num-
ber of historical buildings, few are as well known as the
former home of Spanish Kitty Lombard, 400 Solano
Avenue, between Riverside Drive and Linden Avenue in
El Verano. A Barbary Coast madam who transplanted her
establishment to the Sonoma Valley before Prohibition,
Spanish Kitty was suspected of harboring Baby Face
Nelson, the Prohibition mobster who rode shotgun for the

infamous John Dillinger. Today the home is privately owned, but it opens each year for Spanish Kitty's Erotic Art Show. This event is complete with a live band, belly dancers, and the erotic food contest, where local cuisine notables create eye-popping edibles which are awarded prizes, then eaten. For date and admission prices, write the Sonoma Valley Arts Guild, 460 First Street East, Sonoma, CA 95476, or phone 996-3115.

The Scenic Highway

Highway 12 (Sonoma Highway) between Agua Caliente and Oakmont is a state-designated scenic road, marked with signs depicting an orange poppy on a blue background. Much of this was the old stage and railroad route between Sonoma and Santa Rosa. You'll see vineyards, oak forests, and stands of eucalyptus trees; historic, white-frame farmhouses and barns; and the heavily wooded slopes of the Sonoma and Mayacamas mountains. There's no passing lane between the city of Sonoma and Melita Road near Santa Rosa, so plan on a half-hour drive when traveling the eighteen miles between the towns.

Six miles northwest of Sonoma on Highway 12 is the Sonoma Valley Regional Park. The parking area is adjacent to the California Division of Forestry fire station. This 162-acre park, with rolling, grassy hills and oak forests, offers two miles of hiking and riding trails, and picnic tables with barbecue grills. No motorized vehicles allowed. The free-admission park is open daily from dawn to dusk. Opposite the park, on the east side of Highway 12, is the Bouverie Wildflower Preserve, a twenty-two-acre meadow set aside for viewing native Sonoma County flowers such as the California poppy, lupine, and wild iris.

At 13255 Sonoma Highway stands Glen Oaks, a privately owned two-story stone mansion built in 1860 by Col. Charles Stuart, a pioneer vintner who named his vineyards Glen Ellen after his wife, Ellen. The nearby town of Glen Ellen was also named for her, so the Stuarts changed the name of their ranch to Glen Oaks to avoid confusion. Just beyond Glen Oaks is the Arnold Drive cutoff to the town of Glen Ellen and to Jack London State Historic Park. A few hundred yards farther north on Highway 12 is the Trinity Road cutoff, a scenic, twisting route over the Mayacamas Mountains to Oakville in the Napa Valley. The twelve-mile route between Highway 12 and Oakville isn't recommended for trucks.

Just past Nuns Canyon Road on Highway 12 is Beltane, a country inn. The double-story, southern-style ranch home was owned by Mary Ellen "Mammy" Pleasant, a plantation-born slave who was a voodoo queen, madam, abolitionist, cook, and one of nineteenth-century San Francisco's most powerful women. Mammy used voodoo, blackmail, violence, even murder to manipulate the rich and powerful of gold rush San Francisco. An early and active advocate of civil rights for blacks, Mammy furnished money and guns for John Brown's raid on Harpers Ferry, Virginia.

Mammy's ranch home, Beltane, was built in 1892 by William Bell, a British soldier of fortune and financial wizard worth $30 million. Mammy, his mistress, was later accused of his murder in their San Francisco "House of Mystery," but she never stood trial. In her later years Mammy lived a sedate life at Beltane; she died at age 92, virtually penniless. The inn features three upstairs rooms, all with private baths; 996-6501.

North of Beltane lie the vines of Wildwood Vineyards. This is an excellent spot to view the Valley's spectacular autumn colors—a rainbow of gold, scarlet, purple, and orange.

Jack London Country

The restless spirit of Jack London pervades the town of Glen Ellen and the park cradled in the hills above. At the Jack London State Historic Park, you can see the simple cottage where London wrote and died, his grave, the ruins of his Wolf House, and the House of Happy Walls, built by his widow and now a museum.

To reach Glen Ellen and the park, follow Highway 12 four miles north from Sonoma, turn left on Madrone Road, drive past the Valley of the Moon Winery, turn right on Arnold Drive, and continue two miles north. Signs in downtown Glen Ellen direct you a mile into the hills along Jack London Ranch Road to Jack London State Historic Park.

Before you reach Glen Ellen, you'll pass Sonoma State Hospital, the first hospital west of the Mississippi founded for the care of the mentally retarded. Fronting the hospital are the "Butler oaks," pin and scarlet oaks shipped here from New England by the late Dr. Fred O. Butler, a director of the hospital. Each fall the blazing oak leaves attract many for a visual feast.

Jack London, the illegitimate son of an astrologer, adopted his stepfather's name, and fought and sweated his way out of San Francisco and Oakland ghettos to roam the world. He left a legacy of 51 books, 193 short stories, and numerous articles. A tough-fisted, hard-drinking dreamer with a love for books and a passion for writing, London had been a newsboy, oyster pirate, railroad tramp, serious socialist, and Klondike miner before he sold his first story at age twenty-two. Eight years later he was America's highest paid author. He died at age forty.

In 1903, London came to Glen Ellen on vacation. He stayed to divorce his wife and marry the vivacious Charmian Kittredge. Jack and Charmian lived at Wake Robin Lodge while acquiring a series of hill country properties to create their 1,400-acre Beauty Ranch.

After the Londons took a twenty-seven-month cruise in the South Pacific aboard their custom-built sailing ship, the *Snark*, they returned to Glen Ellen, where Jack took up scientific farming with the aid of Luther Burbank. London's success as a farmer was uneven, but the Beauty Ranch attracted a stream of guests—an average dinner party could include socialists, socialites, scientists, hoboes, actresses, writers, and a lunatic or two.

Jack and Charmian London at their Beauty Ranch. (Courtesy Mary Eileen Cass)

In 1911, London began construction of Wolf House. Built of native stone and designed by San Francisco architect Albert Farr, it was to be one of the world's unique homes. But on an August night in 1913, an arson fire destroyed the nearly completed house. To this day the

174

arsonist's identity is unknown. Three years later London was dead, some say by suicide, some believe by uremic poisoning.

Strikingly handsome, courageous, dynamic, London epitomized the grit and *machismo* of pre-World War I America. His socialist writings made him popular worldwide, even to this day, while his rugged adventure stories enthrall millions.

Jack London State Historic Park is a paradise for hikers and horseback riders. Entrance fee is $2 per vehicle, $1 for seniors, $8 per bus, 50 cents per dog, with tickets also good for Sugarloaf Ridge State Park, Armstrong Redwoods State Reserve, and Boothe-Napa Valley State Park. Park hours are 8-5 daily. The parking lot nearest the House of Happy Walls is for cars, while a special parking place for horse trailers is off a right-hand turn immediately inside the park. There are picnic tables near the equestrian parking lot, but overnight camping is not allowed in the park. Pick up a free copy of the Ranch Trail Guide and follow the numbered trail markers.

The series of stone structures adjacent to London's white frame cottage were used to house his prized English shire horses. The smooth-walled buildings were constructed by Chinese laborers for the Kohler and Frohling Winery in the 1880s, while the edifices with protruding stone walls were built for London by Italians from Tuscany under the direction of stonemason Natale Forni. London's cottage dates from 1862, built by Jackson Temple, a state supreme court judge. The author lived here from 1911 until his death in 1916. During these years he churned out 1,000 words daily, completing *John Barleycorn* and *The Valley of the Moon*.

A short hike away is London's "Pig Palace." This unique piggery was designed in a circle for efficiency, and each family of Duroc Jersey pigs had its own quarters. Unfortunately, the pigs contracted pneumonia from the concrete floors and all died. The nearby twin, concrete silos were the first in the state.

A mile hike will bring you to an artificial lake with a log

Ruins of Jack London's Wolf House. (Redwood Empire Association)

cabin London built to recreate his Klondike days. Hikers and horseback riders can follow trails from the lake for a two-mile trip to the summit of 2,200-foot-high Sonoma Mountain. The entire loop from parking lot to summit and back is 6.6 miles.

Return to the parking lot and walk a few hundred yards to the House of Happy Walls, built between 1919 and 1922 by Charmian London. It is like the Wolf House, although built on a smaller scale. Today it's a museum of London's worldwide travels and of his works. Open 10-5.

The trail to the Wolf House ruins takes you through a forest of oak, madrone, redwood, and buckeye trees. London used locally quarried stone and redwood timbers from the Sonoma mountains to create his palace, which had a two-story living room, a banquet hall for fifty guests and a reflecting pool for simple solar heating. The half-mile walk back to the House of Happy Walls takes a detour to London's grave, situated in a grove of oaks and marked by a boulder rejected by the Wolf House workmen.

Glen Ellen

The town of Glen Ellen had its beginnings when Mariano Vallejo constructed his sawmill beside Sonoma Creek over 140 years ago. Frenchman Joshua Chavet developed this area into a premier wine-growing region that attracted French, German, British, and Italian vintners. The wooded hillsides were cleared to make way for vineyards.

The narrow-gauge railroad reached Glen Ellen in 1879; weekend visitors from San Francisco paid $1 to $1.50 round trip. A second rail line soon reached the town, and thousands of visitors came to camp in tents or cottages, or to stay in hotels. Glen Ellen was a lively place with eight saloons, dancehalls, and brothels. San Francisco's Barbary Coast toughs brawled with local cowhands in the streets.

Jack London came to Glen Ellen in 1903, shortly after

the publication of his first big novel, *The Call of the Wild*.
The majority of his works were written here, first at Wake
Robin Lodge and later at his Beauty Ranch cottage. Glen
Ellen, a mecca for London lovers, is now a pleasant stop
for dining and shopping, or for a vacation stay.

Most of Glen Ellen's attractions are located along
Arnold Drive, the main route through town. At 14301
Arnold Drive is Mama's Royal Cafe, a Mexican restaurant
and a cabaret housed in an ancient structure with a water-
wheel, part of General Vallejo's sawmill. The restaurant
was formerly Juanita's Galley, one of several eateries
operated by the flamboyant Juanita Musson.

The adjacent building, part of the London Glen Village, originally was built by French baker Chavet as his
winery. It was later operated by the Pagani family as a
winery, and some say the ghost of Charles Pagani haunts
the place. Today it's J. J. Haraszthy & Son Wine Cellars,
operated by the great- and great-great-grandsons of Count
Haraszthy. The small winery produces Zinfandel, Pinot
Noir Blanc, Gewurztraminer, and Johannisberg Riesling.
It's open for tours by appointment only; phone 996-3040.

Across Arnold Drive, at number 14300, stands Russ
Kingman's Jack London Bookstore, featuring books on
Jack London plus rare, used, and out-of-print books. Kingman is the author of *A Pictorial Life of Jack London*. His
bookstore is open Wednesday through Sunday. (Among
Glen Ellen's present-day writers is culinary authoress
M. F. K. Fisher, praised as America's foremost philosopher
of food. *The Gastronomical Me* and *An Alphabet for Gour-
mets* are two of her many works.)

At 13750 Arnold Drive is Shone's Country Store,
housed in a stone and wooden building dating from Glen
Ellen's pioneer days. Shone's is a popular deli stop, as is
the Glen Ellen Square, a deli and market at 13647 Arnold
Drive.

The London Lodge, 13740 Arnold Drive, is an unusual
combination of lodge, restaurant, tavern, and Jack London Museum. Diners can eat inside or on the deck above

Sonoma Creek. The Jack London Museum contains Russ Kingman's collection, recently sold to the new owners of the lodge. Call 996-6306 for restaurant reservations.

Good Day Sunshine, 13647 Arnold Drive, is a show-place for local artists and craftspeople, with stained glass, wine goblets, textiles, jewelry, and handcrafted toys. Open Monday through Saturday, 10-5:30; Sunday, 12-4. Nearby is a Dip into the Past, 13690 Arnold Drive, an antique store open Wednesday through Sunday, 11-5.

Follow Arnold Drive to Highway 12 to reach Kenwood and Santa Rosa, or take the back way to Kenwood via Warm Springs Road, off Arnold Drive. Warm Springs Road is a quiet, shady route; along the way, at 4100 Wake Robin Road, you'll pass the Wake Robin Lodge, a privately owned, octagonal, shingle home where Jack London lived from 1905 to 1911. You can glimpse the home from Warm Springs Road. London wrote *The Sea Wolf* and planned his voyage on the *Snark* while at Wake Robin Lodge.

Glen Ellen Winery Tour

Except for J. J. Haraszthy & Sons, which is in the town of Glen Ellen, the area's other wineries are scattered in country locales: Grand Cru Vineyards near Highway 12, H. Coturri & Sons in the Sonoma Mountains, and Kistler Vineyard in the Mayacamas Mountains.

Grand Cru Vineyards, One Vintage Lane, is reached by taking Dunbar Road off Highway 12 or Arnold Drive to the winery's sign and following a dirt road past Dunbar School. Francois Lemoine, a native of the French Alps, established the winery in 1886. The Felix Mancuso family later owned it, and the winery was one of a handful of Sonoma Valley wineries to reopen after Prohibition. The dormant winery was reopened in 1970 by Robert Magnani and Allen Ferrera; they built the A-frame winery building on the stone foundations of Lemoine's winery. Present owners are Walter and Tina Dryer.

Grand Cru Vineyards' wines include Zinfandel, Chenin Blanc, Pinot Blanc, Gewurztraminer, Cabernet

Sauvignon, and "Induced Botrytis" Gewurztraminer, created by using an induced botrytis mold on the Gewurztraminer grapes to make a fragrant and sweet dessert wine. The winery is open for tasting on weekends and for sales daily, 9-5; tours by appointment, 996-8100. A picnic area next to the winery affords a fine view of the Sonoma Valley.

H. Coturri & Sons Winery, 6725 Enterprise Road, off Warm Springs Road and Sonoma Mountain Road, is a new winery open for tours by appointment only; call 996-6247. The Coturri clan presently makes Semillon, Johannisberg Riesling, and Pinot Noir wines in a traditional style.

Between the Mayacamas mountain ridges that separate Sonoma and Napa counties lies Kistler Vineyards, 2995 Nelligan Road. This winery, not open for tasting or tours, produces Chardonnay, Pinot Noir, and Cabernet Sauvignon, using time-tested methods.

Kenwood

The town of Kenwood, her wineries, the Oakmont adult community, and Annadel State Park near Santa Rosa all lie within the boundaries of the old Rancho Los Guilicos, an 18,833-acre spread once owned by William Hood, a Scottish shipwright rich from trading, mining, and construction. Los Guilicos, a Spanish corruption of the name of the Wappo Indian village of Wilikos, was originally granted to Capt. Juan Wilson, a brother-in-law of General Vallejo and stepfather to Romualdo Pacheco, California's only governor of *Californio* descent to serve after statehood. Wilson sold his ranch to Hood and his partner for $13,000. Hood had his winery on the ranch, along with herds of cattle.

Much of the ranch was marshland, but once it was drained and the railroad arrived, new communities sprang up. Among these were Los Guilicos, later named Kenwood after the town of Kenwood, Illinois, and Melita Station, today part of Santa Rosa but once a shipping point for stone quarried from the hillsides of what is now Annadel State Park.

Kenwood was laid out in the 1880s around a small plaza, today the setting for the Gothic Kenwood Community Church. Nearby is the Kenwood Depot, built in 1887 of locally quarried stone; it is the only stone depot in the Sonoma Valley. Kenwood grew as a major ranching, grape, and orchard region, with tourists flocking to the town to enjoy the hot mineral springs. The trains stopped running in 1936, and Kenwood has remained small.

Today Kenwood boasts three wineries and several nurseries, and it serves as the gateway to Sugarloaf Ridge State Park, Hood Mountain Regional Park, and Annadel State Park. The town lies four miles north of Glen Ellen via Highway 12 or Warm Springs Road.

Wildwood Farm, 10300 Sonoma Highway, is a nursery and garden center which many visitors compare to a park. Owners Ricardo and Sara Monte offer three acres of plants, including California native flora and perennials, and they've constructed an eleven-sided greenhouse for their Australian and Tasmanian tree ferns. Wildwood Farm is open daily 9-5, closed Mondays; 833-1161.

At 9900 Sonoma Highway is Ray's Rancho, serving family-style dinners of seafood, meat, and fowl, and featuring live entertainment with a country and western band. The Vineyards Inn, at the corner of Sonoma Highway and Adobe Canyon Road, is a popular spot for Mexican cuisine devotees.

Kenwood's best-known restaurant is probably the Golden Bear Lodge, 1717 Adobe Canyon Road, off Sonoma Highway, offering continental cuisine at a creekside setting. It's closed in winter.

Morton's Warm Springs Resort, 1651 Warm Springs Road, sports three swimming pools, all heated by natural warm springs, seven picnic grounds, baseball and volleyball fields, a snack bar, a dance floor, and grassy lawns or wooded sites for picnics. Morton's is popular for group and company picnics; the spacious grounds can accommodate up to 2,400 people at once. It's open May to September; hours are 10-7, weekdays except Monday; 9-8, weekends. The pools are generally open from 10 to 6. Current rates are $2 adults on weekdays, $2.75 on Saturdays, $3 on Sundays; children two to eleven, $1.50 any day; children under two, free. Season passes are also available to families and individuals. Call 833-5511 for more information.

The Fourth of July is a big day in Kenwood, for the festivities include the annual Kenwood Pillowfight Championships. This event attracts men and women who pay to entwine themselves around a greased, stainless steel pipe (dubbed "The Shaft") above a mud pit, where they flail away at their opponent with a pillow. Past participants have included comedians Tom and Dick Smothers. Entrants should pick up their entry forms at the Kenwood Country Store, 405 Warm Springs Road, and return them before the Fourth. Other Fourth festivities include a chili tasting and judging contest, a footrace, and a parade.

Kenwood Winery Tour

Kenwood's three wineries—Kenwood Vineyards, Chateau St. Jean Winery, and St. Francis Vineyards—are dramatically different in their wines and ambience. Soon to join them, but not yet open to the public, will be Smothers Winery, operated by entertainers Tom and Dick Smothers.

Kenwood Vineyards, a rustic winery at 9592 Sonoma Highway, opposite Warm Springs Road, combines a nostalgic approach to winemaking with vigorous growth. Founded in 1906 by two Italian immigrant brothers, John and Amadeo Pagani, Pagani Brothers Winery (as it was then called) for years was a Sonoma Valley landmark. Visitors stopped to sample the jug wines made by John's son, Julio Pagani. After Julio's death, the winery was sold to Martin Lee, Sr., and others and was renamed Kenwood.

Since 1970, Kenwood Vineyards has employed the *cuvée* (French for "cask" or "lot") method of making small batches of a specific wine variety, individually fermented, then put in a cask. In the small, amicable tasting room you can sample Chenin Blanc, Zinfandel, Cabernet Sauvignon, Chardonnay, Johannisberg Riesling, and Pinot Noir, and you can buy some to take home. Open daily 10-4:30; tours by appointment only, 833-5891.

A mile north on Sonoma Highway lies Chateau St. Jean Winery, impressive both in its Mediterranean-style architecture and its award-winning Chardonnays and Johannisberg Rieslings. Despite its French name, only Chateau is pronounced in the French manner, with St. said as in St. Nick and Jean pronounced like the denim fabric, for the winery is named after Jean Merzoian, wife of one of the winery's founders.

Chateau St. Jean's landmark mansion, built by the Goff family in the 1920s, has been recently joined by new, similarly styled structures that include a two-story viewing tower. After a self-guided tour through the winery, you can taste their Chardonnay, Johannisberg Riesling, Fume Blanc, Cabernet Sauvignon, and other varietals. Winemaker Richard Arrowood maintains the separate identities of the growers, both in production and in labeling, so that visitors can buy Chardonnays and other wines from such premium growers as Robert Young of Alexander Valley.

The winery has branched into champagne production in a separate facility in Graton, but no sparkling wines have yet been released. Chateau St. Jean, 8555 Sonoma Highway, is open daily 10-4:30, and its vineyards and lovingly landscaped grounds make it a prime picnic spot; 833-4134.

Directly across Sonoma Highway is St. Francis Vineyards, 8450 Sonoma Highway, a modern building on the site of vineyards planted in 1911 by viticulturist Will Behler. This new winery produces Chardonnay, Gewurztraminer, Johannisberg Riesling, Merlot, and Pinot Noir from its nearby vineyards. St. Francis Vineyards is open daily for tasting and sales, with picnic tables on the grounds. Tours by appointment only, 833-4666.

Hillside vineyards near Glen Ellen. (Wine Institute)

Sugarloaf Ridge State Park

Immediately north of Chateau St. Jean Winery is Adobe Canyon Road. A three-mile drive will take you into the volcanic hills that form the Mayacamas Range (Mayacamas is an Indian word meaning "the howling of mountain lions") and to Sugarloaf Ridge State Park. Sugarloaf Ridge is a lopsided, conical peak that forms a dramatic backdrop for the Chateau St. Jean Winery; it is a source for the headwaters of Sonoma Creek.

The park's twenty-five miles of trails range in elevation from 600 to 2,700 feet. You can hike or horseback ride through forests of laurel, buckeye, and redwood, and over chaparral ridges covered with wild flowers and manzanita. Native animals include black-tailed deer, raccoons, gray foxes, and skunks. The only plants and animals to avoid are poison oak and rattlesnakes.

184

Family campgrounds in the park offer fifty campsites, each with a table and bench, charcoal barbecue stove with grill, tent sites, and parking spur. An organized group camp for up to forty people is available by reserving directly through the park; the group camp is popular with horsepeople.

Spring and fall are the best seasons to visit Sugarloaf; summer days can get very hot. The roads to the park are steep and narrow, and vehicles over twenty feet in length shouldn't use them. Fees are $2 for day use, $3 for overnight. Campsites are available on a first-come, first-served basis; the group campsite can be reserved by contacting the park office several weeks in advance. Write to Sugarloaf Ridge State Park, 2605 Adobe Canyon Road, Kenwood, CA 95452, or call 833-5712. Your day-use ticket is also good at Jack London State Historic Park.

The Hood Mansion

Back on Sonoma Highway, the Hood Mansion lies one mile north of Sugarloaf Park at Los Guilicos, formerly a school for girls, now a law enforcement training center and a juvenile hall. The Hood Mansion, a California Historical Landmark that stands behind the center and hall buildings, can be seen from the highway. Visitors can drive up to it via Pythian Road off Sonoma Highway, but the mansion is open only on special occasions.

Scotsman William Hood, owner of Los Guilicos Rancho, built the two-story, brick, twenty-room mansion in 1858 for his bride, Eliza Shaw. He was thirty-nine; she, fourteen. The Hoods raised cattle, made up to 200,000 gallons of wine in their winery buildings, and entertained lavishly on their estate. Hood rode about his property on a saddle trimmed with South American silver, his long white hair and beard, like Buffalo Bill's, flowing behind him.

Hood died almost broke, but Eliza rebounded, and by 1888 she was California's leading winemaker. Eliza eventually sold the mansion to Sen. Thomas Kearns, a Utah

mining millionaire; then the property became a home for
the aged, a correctional school for girls, and, since the
early 1970s, Santa Rosa Junior College's law enforcement
training center and Sonoma County's juvenile hall.

Hood Mountain Regional Park

I n this wilderness retreat on the edge of Santa Rosa,
you can hike an easy, two-mile trail along Santa Rosa
Creek, or you can test your lungs and legs on the trail
to the summit of 2,730-foot-high Hood Mountain, highest
peak in this section of the Valley of the Moon. From Gun-
sight Rock, highest point in the park, you can see thousands of square miles of northern California, from the
Sierra foothills and the Pacific Coast to San Francisco's
skyline, but be in shape for the nine-mile round-trip hike
from the park entrance.

The volcanic slopes of Hood Mountain originally bore
the title Mount Wilikos, for the Indian village of the same
name, but Los Guilicos Rancho owner William Hood
renamed the peak for himself.

Hood Mountain Regional Park offers a variety of land-
scapes, from grassy meadows to forests of manzanita,
madrone, pine, and Douglas fir, with fields of wildflowers
in spring and a rich array of colors in fall. A small picnic
area is one-quarter of a mile from the parking lot, and
there's limited overnight camping. Day-use fee is $2,
camping is $5. The park is open 8-5 in winter, longer in
spring, and is closed in summer due to fire danger. Call
539-7798 for more information.

Hood Mountain Regional Park lies seven miles up Los
Alamos Road off Sonoma Highway. Camping reservations
should be made one week in advance; write to Sonoma
County Regional Parks, 2403 Professional Drive,
Suite 100, Santa Rosa, CA 95401, or phone 527-2041.

Redwood Empire Association

Western Sonoma

5

Apple Country

C hilly, Pacific-born morning fogs and sunny afternoons provide the perfect climate for western
Sonoma County's apple orchards, berry farms,
vineyards, dairies, and redwood forests. Apples, especially
the juicy, tart, versatile Gravenstein, are the number one
crop, but locals and visitors alike enjoy a cornucopia of
homegrown delights—strawberries, raspberries, and
blueberries in May and June; field-ripened tomatoes and
corn in midsummer; apples, from the Gravenstein picked
in July to the Rome Beauty harvested in November;
pumpkins in October; Christmas trees in December; and,
of course, local wines all year 'round. No other single
region of Sonoma County contains as many roadside
produce stands and Farm Trails stops as Sebastopol,
capital of the apple country.

Sebastopol, the area's largest town with nearly 6,000
people, shares western Sonoma County with smaller
towns and villages: Graton and Forestville to the north;
Bloomfield to the south; and Valley Ford, Freestone,
Occidental, and Camp Meeker to the west. Sebastopol lies
on the western fringe of the Santa Rosa plain, just beyond
the marshy Laguna de Santa Rosa, formed by the waters
of Santa Rosa and Mark West creeks. Behind the town is
the Gold Ridge region, so named for the orchard-covered
hills and valleys that rise from just under one hundred feet
at Sebastopol to almost six hundred feet in elevation near

Occidental. The Gold Ridge has cooler summers than many other parts of the state and winters cold enough to provide the dormancy necessary to grow Gravenstein, Jonathan, Delicious, and Rome Beauty apples. The Sebastopol region is California's top apple-producing area and a major force in making California the nation's fifth largest apple-producing state.

Forestville is in the apple country, too, although it is also considered a Russian River resort town. There are vineyards here, growing grape varieties that love the cooler coastal climes—Chardonnay, Gewurztraminer, Johannisberg Riesling, and Pinot Noir—plus nearly a dozen small wineries and numerous berry farms.

The semi-isolated, dairy country towns of Bloomfield, Valley Ford, and Freestone today are smaller than a century ago when they were among the earliest settlements in western Sonoma County. The towns of Occidental and Camp Meeker began as logging camps and railroad stops. Today Occidental's fame lies at the end of a fork, with a trio of Italian family-style restaurants attracting thousands each year, while local artisans and craftspeople display their wares in refurbished, century-old logging camp buildings.

Pomo and Coastal Miwok Indians first inhabited this country, much of it dark and damp from the redwood forests that extended from one ridge to the next. Russians from Fort Ross, Bodega Bay, and Bodega were the first European settlers, but their stay was cut short by Mexico's entry into the region. In 1844, Joaquin Carrillo, a brother-in-law to General Vallejo, was granted the 13,400-acre Llano de Santa Rosa Rancho ("Santa Rosa plain ranch"), which includes present-day Sebastopol. Carrillo built the town's first home, an adobe once located at the intersection of Petaluma and Sebastopol avenues, now long gone. During the Bear Flag Revolt, Carrillo was taken prisoner by the Americans, and after American squatters overran his lands, he opened his home as the Analy Hotel in Sebastopol. Sebastopol is one of three Sonoma County

towns established by the Carrillo family; the others are
Santa Rosa and Healdsburg.

Another brother-in-law of General Vallejo, John
Rogers (Juan Bautista) Cooper, was granted Rancho El
Molino, around present-day Forestville, in 1836. The
English-born Cooper, a half-brother of Thomas Larkin,
American consul during Monterey's Mexican period,
erected California's first power-operated commercial
sawmill along the banks of Mark West Creek near the
Russian River.

General Vallejo's desire to settle western Sonoma
County as a buffer against Russian encroachment spawned
several more land grants, which eventually became settlements. John Rogers Cooper, a sea captain by trade,
encouraged three of his sailors to apply for land grants
here; two of them, Scotsman Edward McIntosh and James
Dawson, an Irishman, built a home and claimed the
Rancho Estero Americano. McIntosh rode to Monterey to
file for the land but returned with only his name on the
deed. The enraged Dawson soundly thrashed McIntosh,
then sawed their cabin in two, moving his portion to
today's Freestone. Dawson then filed for and received the
Rancho Canada de Pololimi.

A spunky, hospitable Irishman, Jasper O'Farrell,
surveyed much of early California for both the Mexican
and American governments, and eventually owned
Rancho Estero Americano and Rancho Jonive, west of
Sebastopol. In 1847, he fled to Sonoma County to escape a
lynching party, upset over his map of San Francisco which
made Market Street a wide, commercial thoroughfare,
much to the chagrin of Market Street property owners.
All's forgiven now; O'Farrell Street in San Francisco
memorializes him.

O'Farrell named his Freestone ranch Analy after his
Irish birthplace; the name was adopted for the township
surrounding Sebastopol and the town's high school.
Fellow Irish immigrants followed O'Farrell to the west
county region to work the sawmills and plant the first

commercial crop, potatoes. O'Farrell and his wife, Mary, daughter of Bear Flagger Patrick McChristian, were congenial hosts but poor business people, and O'Farrell, once the county's second wealthiest man after General Vallejo, was reduced to near poverty at his death.

The forests in western Sonoma soon gave way to orchards, with the first Gravenstein apple trees planted in 1883 by Nathaniel Griffith, aided by a young naturalist, Luther Burbank. The Sonoma County origins of the Gravenstein, earliest-ripening apple to reach consumers, are unclear, but the seeds probably came from the Russians at Fort Ross or crossed the plains with pioneer William J. Hunt, whose sons founded the Hunt Brothers food processing company in Sonoma County. Today 90 percent of the nation's Gravenstein apples are grown in Sonoma County.

Luther Burbank bought eighteen acres west of Sebastopol in 1885 and conducted many of his experiments here. He named his holding the Gold Ridge Farm after the bountiful orchards of the same name. Burbank's cottage and many of his plants still stand on privately held land on Bodega Avenue.

The Sebastopol/Forestville region became the center of a vast apple, berry, grape, canning cherry, and produce area, with Chinese, Italian, Portuguese, and Japanese immigrants to work the orchards. Farther west, extensive lumbering of the redwood forests between 1870 and 1910 fueled the growth of railroad towns and logging camps, including Freestone, Occidental, and Camp Meeker.

Today the logging camps and railroad are gone, and only limited logging is done in the second-growth redwood forests. The fruit industry remains strong, however, and the apple is still king. In recent years, western Sonoma County has also been associated with a "back to the land" movement. In the late sixties and early seventies, two communes were begun near Occidental; old-time Sonoma residents strongly objected and, after prolonged legal battles, these experiments in living were ended. But the area still attracts people wanting to escape city or suburb and live a simpler life. Scattered among western Sonoma's orchards, you'll see their country homes, many with wood-burning stoves inside and livestock out back.

Gravenstein Highway

Sebastopol and the apple country can be reached in several directions, but the best route for northbound travelers is Highway 116 or Gravenstein Highway South, from Cotati to Sebastopol. Highway 116 continues through Sebastopol to Graton and Forestville, and then to Guerneville in the Russian River resort region. From the Rohnert Park/Sebastopol/Highway 116 exit off Highway 101 to downtown Sebastopol is 8.5 miles.

The scenery along Highway 116 is a mosaic of turn-of-the-century farmhouses and modern ranch-style dwellings, produce stands, antique stores, even a flea market. Side roads will lead you to nurseries, apple farms, and a cheese factory. This is a popular route to the Russian River, with only one passing lane on the way, so plan on a leisurely trip and allow plenty of time to stop and explore.

Heading west from Cotati, near Stony Point Road you'll find Jimmy's Fruit Basket, 7188 Gravenstein Highway South, a produce stop for fresh fruit, vegetables, juice, and olives; they offer discounts on Gravensteins in the early fall. If you're in search of a Christmas tree, turn right off Gravenstein Highway South to Stony Point Road and 1492 Lowell Road, where you'll find Ibleto Tree Farm. You can cut a Monterey pine any day from Thanksgiving to December 24, open 9-5. Owner Art Ibleto is Sonoma County's "spaghetti king," for he and his family members operate a delicious spaghetti stand each summer at the Sonoma County Fair.

Each fall, hundreds of schoolchildren head for Petersen Pumpkin Farm, 6110 Petersen Road, off Gravenstein Highway South, to pick their own pumpkins off the vine. Call 795-5785 for hours and prices.

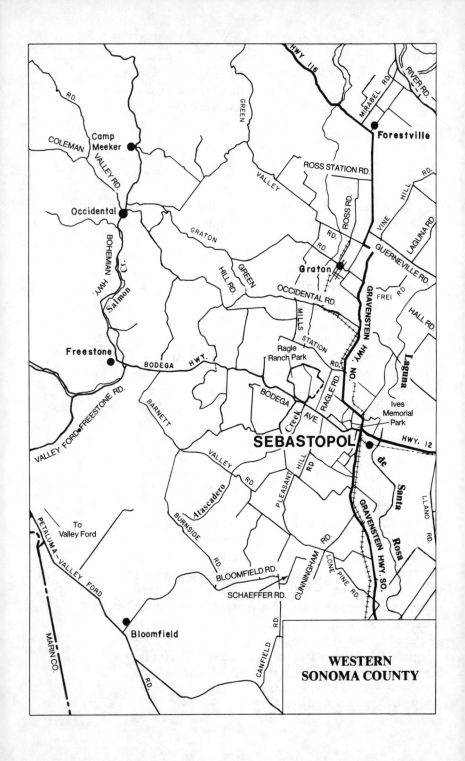

WESTERN
SONOMA COUNTY

Hungry? Then stop at Vast's Art Gallery and Restaurant, 5186 Gravenstein Highway South, or at Neshai's Barbeque, at number 3963. Silvie and Fred Vast offer brunch, lunch, and dinner with a French touch, plus smoked turkey at their Hickory Smokehouse Shoppe and the creations of local artists in the gallery; 795-4747. Vast's also sells California Chevre, Sonoma County's French-style goat cheese. Diminutive Neshai's is a countertop diner with barbecued beef, pork, and lamb ribs, plus hot links, to eat here or to take out; 823-9884.

At Llano Road and Gravenstein Highway South stands one of the county's oldest wooden structures, the recently restored, freshly painted Llano House, a road-house that served pioneer travelers between Petaluma and Sebastopol starting in the early 1850s. At present the Llano House isn't open to the public.

Follow the cheese factory signs on Llano Road to the Joe Matos Cheese Company, 3669 Llano Road, where Joe and Mary Matos make a semisoft Portuguese-style cheese with raw milk from their own cows. You can sample the cheese and buy by the pound or wheel. Open daily 9-5; 584-5283.

The tiny community of Cunningham is centered around Gravenstein Highway South and Lone Pine Road. You can stop here to shop for antiques, plants, apples, and pears, or to take a fishing break. The Lone Pine Trading Post, 3598 Gravenstein Highway South, carries furniture, glass, and a huge selection of vintage clothing from gowns and tuxedos to furs. They're open daily 10:30-6; 823-6768. Nearby is Watershed Antiques, at number 3790, with furniture, glass, and collectibles. Open Wednesday through Sunday, 10-5. Turn left onto Lone Pine Road to Bob and Shaun's Fish Farm, 5570 Lone Pine Road, for public trout and catfish fishing all year, a special treat for kids. Prices vary for the fish caught; open daily 8-6. The Fish Farm also sells strawberries from April 15 to October 15. Call 823-9483 for information.

Two nursery stops are Lone Pine Gardens, 6450 Lone Pine Road, and Sonoma Horticultural Nursery, 3970

Azalea Avenue (Gravenstein Highway South to Hessel Road to McFarlane Road to Azalea Avenue). Lone Pine Gardens specializes in bonsai plants such as dwarf pines, oaks, maples, and redwoods, plus cacti and succulents. They're open all year, Thursday through Sunday, 10-5, or by appointment, 823-5024. Azaleas and rhododendrons are the specialties at Sonoma Horticultural Nursery, where myriads of hybrid, standard, and dwarf rhododendrons and luxurious azaleas are sold in a parklike setting. Open all year, Thursday through Monday, 9-5; 823-6832.

At 1200 Cunningham Road, off Lone Pine Road, is Michael Martin's Buena Vista Orchard, selling cider and ten apple varieties. If you want to pick your own apples, bring containers and stop by between July 25 and October 25, weekends and holidays, 10-4; 823-9613. The Stokes Ranch at 1910 Schaeffer Road (take Schaeffer Road off Cunningham Road) has pears and apples between August 2 and August 15, plums from August 15 on. Open daily 9-6; 823-8285. The Snyder Ranch at 1890 Schaeffer Road has U-pick cherries from June 16 to July 12, Satsuma plums and Gravenstein apples, August 1 and 2, and other apple varieties on September weekends. Open 9-6 on dates listed; 823-9300.

Midgley's Sebastopol Country Flea Market, 2200 Gravenstein Highway South, is the county's largest and most active flea market, held outdoors year 'round on weekends, starting at 7 A.M. The flea market grounds get crowded, so come early.

You'll find more apples at Frank's Apple Stand, 1794 Gravenstein Highway South, a tree-shaded landmark. In addition, they offer a wide variety of other produce—pumpkins, squash, Indian corn, eggs, walnuts, and cider in season. Open daily 9-6, from May 1 to December 20.

Motorists heading into Sebastopol are often startled by the sight of an ornate Buddhist temple on the outskirts of town. The Enmanji Temple is a symbol of Sebastopol's well-established Japanese population. Originally built by the Manchurian Railroad Company for exhibition at the

Enmanji Buddhist Temple, Sebastopol. (Don Edwards)

1933 Chicago World Fair, the temple is a Kamakura-style building, with a tiered roof and extended beam supports, representative of Japan's Kamakura period (1180-1333 A.D.). It was brought to Sebastopol and opened for worship in 1934.

The practitioners are Jodo Shinshu Buddhists, who are instructed in Buddhist teachings by a minister, unlike Zen Buddhists who emphasize meditation. The temple's current minister is the Reverend Don Castro, the first non-Asian to head a temple in the history of the Buddhist churches of America; he holds weekly services and meditation sessions.

Each July, Enmanji Temple hosts a Chicken Teriyaki Barbecue and Bazaar, featuring sushi, kushiyaki, and imagawa-yaki pastry; a bonsai plant exhibition; viewing of the elaborate, bronze-plated shrine within the temple; plus booths for games and collectibles. Call the Sebastopol Chamber of Commerce for more details, 823-3032.

Sebastopol

ebastopol's compact downtown area, where freight trains still chug along Main Street, is deceptively unhurried and low-keyed. Actually, this west county town and its environs rank among the fastest growing and most popular residential regions in Sonoma County. And Sebastopol owes it all to apples, especially the Gravenstein which, along with other apple varieties, funnels $50 million annually into the county's economy, employing hundreds of apple farmers and thousands of farm laborers, apple packers, and processors.

In the beginning Sebastopol was simply a rest stop on the Indian trail between Santa Rosa and Petaluma, then on the Mexican oxcart route (Joaquin Carrillo had his adobe here). Soon it had grown into a pioneer village, called Pine Grove, with a few general stores and a post office. In the early 1850s, the town's name changed. While British forces were besieging the Russians at the Crimean port town of Sebastopol, a feud occurred between two Pine Grove residents. It turned into a prolonged fistfight, which ended when the loser, a man named Hibbs, fled to Dougherty's store; his pursuer, denied entrance by the store's owner, laid siege to the store. The Pine Grove boys referred to the incident as "Hibb's Sebastopol," and the name stuck. Evidently Sebastopol was a popular name for pioneer California towns; several wore the title, but only Sonoma County's Sebastopol retains the name.

Three decades later, many of the forests had been cleared, and by then Sebastopol's chief crops, potatoes and grain, were suffering from overproduction and poor prices. Farmers looked for other crops to plant in the sandy loam soil. The Gravenstein apple held the answer. Like Sonoma County's Zinfandel grape, the origins of the Gravenstein (probably of Danish or German ancestry) and how it got to Sonoma County (from Fort Ross's Russians or from the Midwest and South via American pioneers) are shaded in mystery, but its productivity was anything but enigmatic. Nathaniel Griffith, the "grandfather of the Gravenstein," planted the first commercial orchards in 1883, and apple grower William J. Hunt perfected an apple dehydrator a few years later.

After the arrival of the Northwestern Pacific Railroad in 1890, townspeople built apple-packing plants, canneries, apple dryers, even apple vinegar and apple brandy distilleries. Sebastopolians made Gravensteins into juice, cider, and even dairy feed, and they pioneered the development of applesauce. Luther Burbank, who worked extensively on Gravensteins at his Gold Ridge Farm, summed it all up: "The Gravenstein apple has proven to be the money-maker in Sonoma County."

Alongside the Gravenstein orchards were planted thousands of acres of other crops—berries, pears, peaches, prunes, grapes, and hops. Sebastopol's Royal Anne canning cherry crops ranked second in the nation.

In 1904, a local electric railroad line was laid from Petaluma to Sebastopol, Forestville, and Santa Rosa; it was dubbed the "Cow's and Chicken's Line" for its farm freight and frequent stops. Two years later, Sebastopol was severely damaged by the big '06 earthquake, but the town was rebuilt and continued as the commercial center of this fruit-growing region.

Today Sebastopol's 8,000 acres of apple orchards are planted predominately in Gravensteins, but other apple varieties, including Jonathan, McIntosh, Rhode Island Greening, Red and Golden Delicious, and Rome Beauty, along with less well-known apple types like Winter Banana or Baldwin, are raised. About 85 percent of the apples are processed as juice, cider, or applesauce; the remainder are packed for the fresh fruit market, with some shipped all the way to the East Coast.

The century-old apple industry (many of the growers have been on the land for two or three generations) is now facing an uphill battle to preserve Sebastopol's Gravenstein orchards. Competition from out-of-state and out-of-country apples, many kept in cold storage and released just as fresh Gravensteins hit the produce shelves, has cut into Sonoma County's apple sales. Some growers had survived by selling a few acres to someone who sought "a house in the country and enough room to keep a horse," but restrictive zoning laws now prohibit lot splits. Rather than replant old, unproductive orchards, these growers have opted to sell out, and the orchards are then replaced by "ranchettes" and country estates. The remaining apple growers have organized and are actively promoting Gravensteins locally and nationally.

You can buy Gravensteins at any of the apple country stops mentioned in this chapter, or follow the Farm Trails map or the Sebastopol "apple map" (available at local farm outlets or at the Sebastopol Chamber of Commerce). If you haven't tried a Gravenstein apple, you're in for a treat! When green and tart, the Gravenstein makes excellent pies and applesauce; when it ripens with its characteristic red stripes, it is a wonderful eating apple. Local bakeries and restaurants incorporate the apple into everything from pies, cakes, and cookies to bread and meat dishes.

Tour of Sebastopol

Sebastopol is a walkers' and browsers' town, with country-living shops, delis and restaurants, several interesting bookstores, plus picnicking and swimming at nearby Ives Memorial Park. Sebastopol has no lodging; best bets are Santa Rosa motels, Russian River resorts, or motels in Occidental.

Highway 116 (Gravenstein Highway) is called Main Street and Healdsburg Avenue within the city limits. Highway 12 (Luther Burbank Highway) connects Sebastopol to Santa Rosa; under the name of Bodega Avenue and Bodega Highway, this same route continues west of Sebastopol to Bodega Bay and the Sonoma Coast.

The intersection of Highways 116 and 12 is Sebastopol's center. One block north to McKinley Street and one block east to Weeks Way is the Sebastopol Chamber of Commerce, 144 Weeks Way. Office manager Harriet Kimes has local maps, Sonoma County Farm Trails maps, Sebastopol apple maps, Christmas tree farm maps, plus information on local events. Open weekdays 9-12 and 1-4:30; 823-3032. Mailing address is P.O. Box 178, Sebastopol, CA 95472.

Longtime rural residents and folks new to the area enjoy Sebastopol's "country living" shops: Mostly Kitchen, 176 North Main Street; and Frizelle-Enos Co., Inc., 265 Petaluma Avenue. Mostly Kitchen features cooking utensils of all kinds, including canning supplies. Frizelle-Enos stocks one of Sonoma County's largest collections of wood-burning stoves, plus solar heaters, feed and pet supplies, gardening tools and seeds, hardware, and books about country life. Across the street, at 258 Petaluma Avenue, stands a buff-colored stone building that was once the powerhouse for the Petaluma and Santa Rosa Railroad, an electric rail line.

For those wintry, rainy nights, why not pick up a book to read next to your fireplace or wood-burning stove? There are three bookstores in downtown Sebastopol: Merit Book Center, 6960 McKinley, for paperbacks and magazines; Sebastopol Book Shop, 133 North Main, for hard-to-find new and used books; and Copperfield's, 146 North Main.

An in-town location with outdoor noshing is Coffee Company, 6930 Burnett Street, serving breakfast, vegetarian and seafood lunches, and espresso coffee, with over forty coffee bean varieties for sale. Open daily. Fresh fish fanciers head for The Dapper Snapper, 305 North Main Street, with outdoor seating for enjoying a seafood lunch with wine or beer. For dessert, or just to satisfy your sweet tooth, stop at the Sebastopol Bakery, 7225 Healdsburg Avenue, for goodies like apple pie and Swedish apple cake.

At 327 North Main, near The Dapper Snapper, stands a large, red, 1907-era Queen Anne home, one of Sebastopol's most impressive Victorians. Sebastopol's early residents were farmers, farm workers, and tradesmen, and the homes they built tended to be simple and functional, unlike the more elegant Victorians of Petaluma and Santa Rosa.

Sebastopol has two French restaurants, both located about a half mile south of town. Newly opened Le Pommier, 1015 Gravenstein Highway South, includes among its offerings the *caneton roti Gravenstein* (duckling roasted with apples and calvados sauce). Phone 823-9865 for reservations. Close by is Chef Pierre Laguorgue's Chez Peyo, 2295 Gravenstein Highway South, with such dishes as *vol au vent au champignon* (pastry shell with sauteed mushrooms and mornay sauce). Phone 823-1262 for reservations.

The spot for nightlife is Zerbino's, 234 South Main, where there's pizza and beer, live music, occasional plays, and comedians. Open nightly.

Picnickers headed for the Russian River, the coast or one of Sebastopol's two parks can buy their supplies at one of the delis in town. Giovanni's Delicatessen and Wine Shop, 171 Pleasant Avenue North, spotlights pasta, frittatas, meats, and cheese, while The Town's Deli, 6970 McKinley Street, is the place for soups, sandwiches, and desserts. The Apple Blossom Express, 6961 Sebastopol Avenue, is a cafe and deli dishing up Italian, German, and Russian specialties.

If you happen to be in town when fresh apples aren't in season, then stop at the Sebastopol Cooperative Cannery, 6782 Sebastopol Avenue, a grower-owned concern that processes some of the 110,000 tons of apples produced each year in Sonoma County. The cannery just completed a new processing plant, and here you can buy applesauce, apple juice, dehydrated apples, and apple concentrate. Open all year, weekdays, 8-12 and 1-5. Call 823-6421.

Three blocks from the center of town at Bodega and Jewell avenues, lies Ives Memorial Park and Swimming Pool, a shady, grassy picnic spot with a children's playground, a duck pond, and a solar-heated, outdoor pool

SEBASTOPOL

201

with large sun deck. The pool is open summer months only; call 823-8693 for hours and prices.

Luther Burbank's Gold Ridge Farm

One-half mile from Ives Memorial Park, at 7777 Bodega Avenue, is the privately owned acreage of Gold Ridge Farm, where from 1885 until his death in 1926, Luther Burbank experimented with fruit trees, vegetables, and ornamental plants. Burbank commuted almost daily from his home in Santa Rosa, and his route, Highway 12, is now called the Luther Burbank Highway.

On his eighteen-acre experimental farm, Burbank built a cottage and worked to perfect Gravenstein apples, plums, cherries, grapes, and lilies. His large "nurse" trees contained multiple grafts—an apple tree held 526 varieties in its branches, while a cherry tree carried over 400 kinds. Thousands of visitors came to see Burbank here and in Santa Rosa, and the naturalist was forced to charge admission to curb the crowds.

The Stark Brothers nursery company managed the farm following Burbank's death, and his widow sold fourteen acres for development as a low-cost, senior housing center. After many years of neglect, civic and historically minded Sebastopolians formed the Burbank Experimental Farm Committee to save the remaining 3.2 acres of the Gold Ridge Farm. Visitors may see the farm on a limited basis by writing the Western Sonoma County Historical Society, P.O. Box 816, Sebastopol, CA 95472.

Ragle Ranch Park

Ragle Ranch Park, a 156-acre, day-use regional site, is located one mile off Bodega Avenue on Ragle Road. Once the ranch of a pioneer Sebastopol family, the county-owned rolling hills and oak/fir woodlands contain hiking and horseback riding trails, barbecue facilities, picnic areas, and rest rooms. The Sebastopol Rotary Club has

donated a workout course for pre-jogging limbering-up
exercises, and future park plans call for three multiuse
sports fields, two baseball diamonds, running trails, and
volleyball and basketball courts.

Sebastopol's Festivals and Fairs

Sebastopol salutes the apple with two seasonal festivals, a
blossom festival in spring and a harvest fair in autumn.
Each April, near Easter, the Sebastopol Chamber of Commerce hosts the Apple Blossom Festival, a weekend full of
events, including coronation of the Apple Blossom Queen,
a parade down Main Street, a footrace, live entertainment,
apple displays, plus historical exhibits and an art show at
the Sebastopol Veterans Memorial Building, next to Ives
Memorial Park. A highlight of the festival is in the self-
guided, thirty-five-mile tour of blossoming apple orchards
in the Gold Ridge district, with road signs posted by the
Sebastopol Realtor Associates. For information and
tickets to events, call the chamber office, 823-3032.

The Apple Fair is held in mid-August at Ragle Ranch
Park, sponsored by Sonoma County Farm Trails to mark
the Gravenstein apple harvest. The fair is a revival of
those held at the turn of the century and features agricultural products produced by Farm Trails members, a
turkey barbecue (with apple pies, cakes, and cookies),
bluegrass bands and belly dancers, and locally made crafts
and artworks. Current admission prices: $2 adults,
$1 seniors and youths ten to eighteen, children under ten
free. For ticket information about the two-day event,
contact the Sonoma County Farm Bureau, 544-5575.

On the Fourth of July, the annual Sebastopol Rodeo is
held at the Indian Valley Ranch, 2900 Llano Road, east of
Sebastopol. Competitors, many from pro-rodeo circuits,
come from as far away as Texas to compete against local
talent, including Sebastopol resident Lee Farris, one of the
country's top calf ropers. Contact the Sebastopol Chamber of Commerce about tickets and events, 823-3032.

Sebastopol Farm Trails

A round Sebastopol are many produce stands and Farm Trails outlets, offering a myriad of fresh fruit, vegetables, and meat. The Gold Ridge district west of town is orchard country, and here you can choose from many varieties of apples, harvested from midsummer to late fall. If you want to pick your own apples, be sure to bring bags and boxes (and you might be glad to have a lunch and some water or other drinks). The Santa Rosa plain to the east is the place to find poultry and eggs; and along Highway 116, north toward Forestville, are numerous berry farms and wineries.

Gold Ridge

The Gold Ridge district is hilly farmland covered with apple orchards; also found here are nurseries, Christmas tree farms, and egg and produce ranches. From the higher ridges you will find uncluttered views of the Santa Rosa valley, Mount St. Helena, and Mount Jackson.

In spring, Gold Ridge is a visual treat, with pale pink apple blossoms and multicolored wildflowers blanketing the hillsides. In late summer and early autumn, the apple trees hang heavy with fruit, so heavy that boards are frequently used to prop up the branches. In late fall, the air is crisp and apple scented; this is the time to don bulky sweaters and head out to cut your own Christmas tree, with a stop to sip hot cider.

As you drive through the Gold Ridge orchards, note the different varieties of apple trees: Gravensteins are the tallest trees; Rome Beauty trees have a weeping and arching design; Golden Delicious trees have light gray bark. Scattered among the orchards are apple processing and packing plants, an occasional obsolete apple dryer or an old hop kiln, as well as country homes and "ranchettes."

The main routes through the Gold Ridge region are Bodega Highway between Sebastopol and Freestone, and Occidental Road, which runs west off Highway 116 to Occidental. First we'll take Bodega Highway and follow it west.

Just on the edge of town, at 953 Ragle Road near Ragle Ranch Park (off Bodega Highway), lies Hall's Hen-ry. They sell brown and white eggs, frying chickens, and roasting and stewing hens. Open all year, Thursday through Saturday and Monday, 8-5; Sunday, 8-1. Phone 823-0688. Among the many Farm Trails outlets near Ragle Ranch Park is Redwood Grove Nursery, 8306 Bodega Avenue, sporting one of the West's largest fuchsia collections. Around the nursery's appealing patio stand fountains, fuchsias, and ferns, while the potting shed holds garden supplies and fuchsia literature. Senior citizens get a 10 percent discount, and there's a picnic area available. Open all year, daily except Tuesday; 823-9465.

All varieties of apples and sweet corn are available at George LeBallister's, 9180 Bodega Highway; open daily 9-6 from July 15 to October 15. The Apple Tree-Christmas Tree, 10055 Bodega Highway, features just what the name suggests: Gravenstein, Delicious, and Rome Beauty apples, plus apple cider, from August 1 to December 21; and Christmas trees, green or flocked, from November 27 to December 21. Open daily 9-5. Picnic area too.

Farther along Bodega Highway, at 10315, is a popular roadside produce stop, Bill's Farm Basket. Bill and Cara Anstead sell a wide selection of locally grown (and often organic) produce—everything from corn, tomatoes, and peaches to apples and melons. Open every day all year, 9-7 in summer, 9-6 in winter.

On Occidental or Graton roads from Highway 116 to Occidental are more Farm Trails stops. At 8190 Mill Station Road, off Occidental Road, lies Edwards Orchid House, with orchids, flowers, and floral supplies. Open all year by appointment, 10-5; call 823-9550. Off Mill Station Road, at 965 Martin Lane, is Me Gusta Organic Farm, with pork, veal, and goat on order, plus plums, peaches,

Blossoming boysenberry vines on trellises, near Sebastopol. (Don Edwards)

nectarines, and apples. Open by appointment only; call 823-1322.

Bill Hatch's Ranch, 12154 Occidental Road, has Gravensteins and other apple varieties. Hatch also makes a hard cider (7 percent alcohol) blended equally from Gravensteins and Jonathans. No cider is sold at the ranch, but local delis carry it. Call before your visit, 874-2287. Just up Occidental Road, off Green Hill Road, is the Green Hill Berry Farm, 2401 Green Hill Road. Herman Goertz raises blueberries, boysenberries, and olallieberries on five acres close to the redwood forests. Berry season is May 15 to June 20; call ahead to order berries, 823-4357 or (415) 459-1759.

You can treat your palate at Walker Apples, where there's apple tasting before you buy. Lee and Shirley Walker offer samples of apple types you normally don't encounter in the grocery store—Winter Banana, Baldwin, Greening, Bellflower—fifteen varieties in all. Walker Apples is at the end of Upp Road, a scenic, one-half-mile ride over a dirt road off Graton Road. Open daily 10-5, August 1 through November 15; 823-4310.

The Santa Rosa Plain

Several farm basket stops lie directly east of Sebastopol on or near Highway 12 between Sebastopol and Santa Rosa.

Willie Bird Turkeys No. 1, 5350 Highway 12, specializing in Sonoma-grown meat and poultry, is one of three outlets owned by the Benedetti family. They sell fresh turkey (order early for the holidays), chicken, rabbit, and duck; smoked chicken, turkey, and duck; plus Gelbveih (organic) beef. Open all year, Monday through Friday, 9-6; Saturday, 9-5. Phone 545-2832.

D. Grossi Egg Ranch, 4993 Occidental Road, carries eggs, live chickens, walnuts, honey, and jam. Open 8-6, Monday through Saturday; 542-2604. At 1115 Irwin Lane, off Highway 12, is the Sanchietti Ranch, featuring plums, apples, pears, prunes, and walnuts, along with apple juice and cider. Open daily 9-5 from July 15 to December 15; 544-5999. Follow Irwin Lane to Hall Road; at number 5686 is the home of the Woodridge Berry Farm, where boysenberries are offered in the month of June, daily 9-7.

Highway 116 to Forestville

Highway 116 (Gravenstein Highway North) runs through hilly, scenic country dominated by apple orchards that give way to berry farms and vineyards around Forestville. This region was originally granted to Capt. John Rogers Cooper as the Rancho El Molino for the sawmill he erected near the Russian River. Cooper's left arm was withered as the result of a childhood injury, and the *Californios* called him Juan el Manco ("John the maimed"). When excited or vexed, Cooper bit at his maimed hand.

His original ranch home is gone, but motorists on Highway 116 south of Forestville can see the privately owned El Molino Ranch, marked by a sign and a Victorian-era home, where Cooper first settled. The name El Molino has been adopted by Forestville's high school and a number of local businesses.

As you begin traveling up Highway 116, there are two stops to fuel your trip: Andy's Fruit Basket, 1691 Gravenstein Highway North, for produce, eggs, and juices; and Molino Delicatessen, corner of Occidental Road and Gravenstein Highway North, for sandwiches, homemade pastries, beer, and wine.

A short detour off Gravenstein Highway North takes you to the Georgetown Country Store, 4015 Frei Road, where Harvey Smith operates the North Bay's only custom poultry service, busiest during the holiday season. You can bring your home-raised bird to be killed and dressed, or take home one of Harvey's pheasants, turkeys, geese, or other fowl. Open all year, daily 9-5; 823-3142. Near the Georgetown Country Store stands Georgetown, a recreated western village housing a unique collection of Old West and Hollywood memorabilia gathered by George Smith, once an employee of major Hollywood studios. Georgetown is open by invitation only, on weekends. Call 823-6645 after 5 P.M.

Another way to relive the Old West is to jaunt through vineyards, orchards, and country lanes in a fringe-topped surrey or in a Concord stagecoach, part of the collection of twenty-five horse-drawn vehicles John Jenkel has preserved and refurbished. Besides offering one- to four-hour trips in the surrounding countryside, Jenkel rents his vehicles and horses for weddings, group tours, company picnics, or a night on the town in San Francisco. Jenkel's firm, Carriage Charter, also operates at San Francisco's Pier 39. Carriage Charter, at 3325 Gravenstein Highway North, is open by reservation only; prices vary according to vehicle used and length of trip. Carriage Charter operates all year; call 823-7083.

Nearby is Paul Orchards, 3561 Gravenstein Highway North, home of fresh-pressed, unpasteurized apple juice, sold fresh or frozen. If left too long unrefrigerated, the juice will ferment. Art and Barbara Paul also sell five apple varieties from August to December, and fresh garden vegetables from August to September. Open daily 9-5; call ahead for volume buying, 823-7907.

A detour off Gravenstein Highway North at Graton Road takes you to the hamlet of Graton, noted for its spring and fall flower shows at the Graton Community Hall. Going out of Graton, follow Ross Road north to Marcucci Farms, at number 4940. The Marcucci family sells fresh-packed apples (Gravenstein, Greening, Golden and Red Delicious, Jonathan, Rome, and Pippin) from August 1 through November, and Christmas gift packs of apples, dried fruit, jams, jellies, chutney, and Phil Marcucci's homemade grape wine vinegar. Open by appointment; call 823-0794.

Ross Road ends at Ross Station Road, where you can stop for apples and berries in season and wine all year 'round. First stop is El Molino Apple Farm, 9144 Ross Station Road, where W. R. Rasmussen offers sweet corn in August and Gravensteins soon after. Open July 25 to December 31, daily except Sunday, 8-6; 887-2532. Next door is the Green Valley Blueberry Farm, 9345 Ross Station Road, for blueberries and boysenberries picked fresh in season, or made into berry-rich jams, pies, muffins, and tarts. Bruce and Carol Goetz's blueberry bushes resemble trees; the acid soil near Forestville is ideal for the berries. Seventeen blueberry varieties are raised here. Come by during berry season, June 15 to July 31. Open daily 9-6; 887-7496.

The new kid on Ross Station Road is Iron Horse Vineyards, number 9786 at the end of Ross Station Road. The same acid soil, foggy mornings, and sunny afternoons that produce outstanding apples and berries also yield excellent wine grapes. Iron Horse's estate-grown grapes make several varietals: Chardonnay, Sauvignon Blanc, Blanc de Noir (white Pinot Noir), Cabernet Sauvignon, and Fume Blanc.

FORESTVILLE

209

Open 10-4 daily for retail sales; tasting and tours by appointment, 887-2913. Picnic grounds available.

Take Ross Station Road back to Gravenstein Highway North to the Kozlowski's Raspberry Farm, 5566 Gravenstein Highway North. Their on-the-farm salesroom is filled with goodies—fresh raspberries in June, raspberry jam (including a sugarless variety), raspberry vinegar, and raspberry ice cream; frozen berries and jams made from blackberries, loganberries, and blueberries; plus apple-sauce, juice, and cider, and fresh apples in season. Open daily 9-5, June to December; 887-2104.

Close by is Russian River Vineyards and Restaurant, 5700 Gravenstein Highway North, housed in a hybrid Russian-style/hop kiln winery building, where you can taste wine and stay for dinner. Winemaker Mike Topolos makes Cabernet Sauvignon, Zinfandel, Petite Sirah, and Chardonnay, plus a unique apple wine, Gravenstein Blanc. Open for tasting and sales Tuesday through Sunday, 10-5; gifts available too. The restaurant's offerings include beef or mushroom stroganoff, fresh fish, and chef Robert Taylor's "bounty of the county" made from the best, and freshest, locally grown produce. Dine inside, or outdoors under the wisteria and redwoods. Open for lunch, dinner, and Sunday brunch; reservations advised, 887-1562.

Forestville

Despite its hilly locale, rich with groves of redwoods and Douglas fir, Forestville wasn't named for its trees, but after an early settler, A. J. Forrester. The Green Valley region west of town was one of the earliest settled areas in western Sonoma County. Over the years local farmers have raised apples, berries, hops, and grapes. The raspberry farms around Forestville make Sonoma County the state's third largest producer of the berry; of the twenty acres of blueberries raised in California, fourteen are found near this town. But wine is now making agricultural news; the hill country near the hamlet of Trenton and the western Santa Rosa plain close to Forestville contain several wineries and extensive vineyards.

Forestville's lodging is found near the Russian River, while the town proper has several notable restaurants, including L'Omelette, 6685 Front Street (Highway 116), for French cuisine (887-9945); and the Forestville Inn, 6625 Front Street, for Mexican dinners (887-1242). From Forestville, Russian River visitors can follow Highway 116 to Guerneville, 7.5 miles away, or take Mirabel Road 1.5 miles out of Forestville to Mirabel Park on River Road.

Forestville Winery Tour

Although the wineries and vineyards around Forestville are considered part of the wine lands of the Russian River Valley, the grapes grown here love the cool, maritime climate, unlike their heat-loving cousins of the upper Russian River, Dry Creek, and Alexander valleys. Each March, the Forestville wineries join other Russian River Valley wineries in wine barrel tastings; visitors have a chance to sample new releases while learning about winemaking. For a map of the participating wineries, send twenty-five cents and a self-addressed, stamped envelope to Russian Wine Road, P.O. Box 127, Geyserville, CA 95441.

Begin your Forestville wine country rambles by taking Highway 116 south of Forestville to Guerneville Road. At 6300 Guerneville Road stands Dehlinger Winery, close to Vine Hill Road. The Dehlingers, who founded the winery in 1976, make Zinfandel, Cabernet Sauvignon, Pinot Noir, and Chardonnay. Open by appointment only; call 823-2378.

Continue down Guerneville Road almost a mile to Laguna Road; turn left and look for a water tower, below which lies Martini and Prati Wines, Inc., high atop Vine Hill. The original winery on this site dates from 1881. After the turn of the century, Rafaelo Martini bought the property; his descendants were later joined by Enrico Prati, former owner of Italian Swiss Colony. Martini and Prati became Sonoma County's second largest winery and survived Prohibition by making sacramental wines. Today the winery is run by Jim and Tom Martini and Edward (Pete) Prati, Jr. Most of the winery's output is in bulk wines, but it also bottles dry table wines under its own label and maintains the old Fountain Grove label (from Santa Rosa's wine-making commune) for its Cabernet Sauvignon. Martini and Prati is open 9-4 daily for tasting and retail sales; 823-2404.

Follow Laguna Road to Joseph Swan Vineyards, at number 2916. Although not open to the public, the tiny winery is well known to connoisseurs for Swan's Zinfandel and Pinot Noir. Joseph Swan Vineyards contains some of the old buildings of the hamlet of Trenton.

From here take Trenton Road across River Road to Trenton-Healdsburg Road, the location of Mark West Vineyards. Airline pilot Robert Ellis and his wife, Joan, are among the Sonoma County winemakers who originally were captivated by the region's charms and only later turned their love of the good life into winemaking. With a current annual production of 10,000 cases, the Ellises turn out Chardonnay, Gewurztraminer, Johannisberg Riesling, Pinot Noir Blanc, and Pinot Noir. Mark West Vineyards (named for pioneer Mark West) is at 7000 Trenton-Healdsburg Road. Open daily 10-4 for retail sales, tastings, tours, and picnics; 544-4813.

Return to River Road and drive east to Olivet Road, a fertile area west of Santa Rosa that once boasted four wineries. Today this legacy continues with the newly born DeLoach Vineyards, 1791 Olivet Road, where a family of vineyardists turned to making their own wine. You can drop by daily from 10 to 4 for retail sales of their Zinfandel, Gewurztraminer, Chardonnay, Pinot Noir, Fume Blanc, and White Zinfandel. Picnic area also available. Phone 526-9111.

From here, you follow Olivet Road to Guerneville Road to return to Forestville or Sebastopol. If you are following Highway 116 from Forestville to Guerneville, take Martinelli Road to Domaine Laurier, 8075 Martinelli Road, a new winery making Chardonnay, Johannisberg Riesling, Sauvignon Blanc, Pinot Noir, and Cabernet Sauvignon, almost exclusively from their own grapes. Tours and retail sales by appointment only, 887-2176.

Country Roads to Occidental

The map will show you more direct ways to get to Occidental, but if you're not in a hurry and would enjoy a day full of country activity, take the route suggested here, which follows winding country lanes where you'll find antique stores, rural restaurants and delicatessens, picnic spots, ranches and farms—with enchanting scenery all around.

From Sebastopol, take Bodega Avenue to Pleasant Hill Road; turn left and proceed to Twin Hill Ranch. Here, at 1689 Pleasant Hill Road, the Darrel Hurst family has one of the region's largest apple farms, raising over fifty varieties. Inside their vast barn, you can pick up fresh apples in season, or applesauce, apple juice, apple bread, apple pies, and apple cookies, accompanied by honey, jam, cherries, almonds, and walnuts. Children enjoy the animal farm and playground; there are picnic tables too. Campfires, hot cider, and Christmas gift packs are available during Christmas tree cutting time. Hurst's Twin Hill Ranch apples won all the special awards at the 1981 Harvest Fair apple exhibition in Santa Rosa. Visitors can take a forty-five-minute tour of the ranch to see that more than polishing goes into producing outstanding apples. Call ahead for tours, 823-2815. The Twin Hill Ranch is open daily 8-5.

Follow Pleasant Hill Road to Bloomfield Road. The Garlock Tree Farm, 2275 Bloomfield Road, is one of

seventeen Sebastopol-area Christmas tree farms that sell
Douglas fir, Monterey pine, Sierra redwood, white fir, and
other trees. Nearby Canfield Road memorializes the
William Canfield family, which survived the Whitman
Massacre, an Indian uprising in Oregon in 1847, and later
settled in Sonoma County.

Bloomfield Road leaves the apple country for dairy-
lands with herds of holsteins grazing on eucalyptus-
crowned hills. A ten-minute drive will bring you to the
forgotten town of Bloomfield. Once one of the county's
largest communities, it died when the railroads reached
Valley Ford and Two Rock. Today the town's main street
still retains some late nineteenth-century commercial
structures, which seem almost out of place in the vast
countryside. Two town stops include the Emma Herbert
Memorial Park, a good spot for a picnic (rest rooms too),
and Stormy's Tavern, which serves basic American cuisine
such as prime rib and steak. Stormy's is open Thursday
through Sunday. You can't miss either place on Bloomfield Road.

Bloomfield Road joins Petaluma/Valley Ford Road just
south of town. Turn left if you want to go to Petaluma;
take a right to continue to Valley Ford. You can pick up
picnic supplies at Winkleman Bros. Meats and Old Dutch
Deli, 12830 Valley Ford Road, where cured and smoked
meats, and Dutch specialty sausages are sold. Open all
year, daily 9-6; 795-3420. A mile farther on, Highway 1
joins the Valley Ford Road; then it's two miles to the dairy
town of Valley Ford.

Valley Ford

Valley Ford began where Indian and Spanish trails crossed
the Estero Americano Creek; the town grew when it
became the first Sonoma County stop on the North Pacific
Coast Narrow Gauge Railroad, which ran from Sausalito
to Cazadero. The drive north from Valley Ford to Freestone, Occidental, and Camp Meeker follows much of the
old railroad route. (The rails are gone, but you can still

view the narrow-gauge, wood-burning engine "Sonoma"—
$8,000 new—at the California State Railroad Museum in
Sacramento.)

The little town of Valley Ford is known to many people
who came in 1976 to see Christo's Running Fence. Valley
Ford was a central location, and thousands came here to
view the seemingly endless line of suspended cloth that ran
across southern Sonoma and northern Marin counties to
the sea.

Valley Ford is a dairy, beef cattle, sheep, and poultry
town, but it also has some unusual livestock—a llama
herd. You can visit Big Trees Llama Farm, 14430 Coast
Highway 1, to see the animals, or to buy wool or even a
baby llama. Llamas love the brisk, breezy countryside
around Valley Ford. The farm is open all year by appointment; call 795-5726.

A chief institution in this tiny town is Dinucci's Restaurant, famed for its Italian family-style dinners. You can't
miss it on Highway 1. Reservations recommended; call
876-3260. The Valley Ford/Freestone Road takes you into
a sculptured valley and to Freestone, Sonoma County's
first historic district.

Freestone

Named for the easily quarried sandstone in nearby hills,
Freestone had a history before it had a name: Russian
settlers from Fort Ross and Bodega had a farm here; the
enraged James Dawson dragged his half-house here after a
quarrel with his friend Edward McIntosh over their land
grant; and Jasper O'Farrell built his Sonoma County
ranch near Dawson's home. All these pioneer structures
are gone, but the historic Freestone Hotel still stands,
almost in mint condition.

The Freestone Hotel began as Hinds Hotel, built in
1873 to house workers on the North Pacific Coast Railroad. A series of mysterious railroad trestle fires were
traced to the hotel's owner, who feared losing business
once the railroad was finished. Today the hotel houses

Trudie's Antiques, open daily except Monday, 10-5. The adjacent Wishing Well Nursery sports a Victorian gazebo and a hand-carved wishing well.

You can stop for a snack or for picnic supplies at the Freestone Country Store, 500 Bohemian Highway. If you want to spend the night in Freestone, try Green Apple Inn, 520 Bohemian Highway, where Rogers and Rosemary Hoffman have converted a Victorian home into a four-bedroom bed and breakfast inn. Call 874-2526 for reservations. Freestone lies six miles west of Sebastopol and five miles east of Bodega. Occidental is four miles to the north.

Occidental

This small, unincorporated community, nestled in a protected, redwood-shrouded valley, serves as the commercial and social center for perhaps 10,000 west county residents. But Occidental's three, family-style Italian restaurants feed many times that number each year.

The town's first settlers included "Dutch Bill" Howard, a Danish sailor who had nearly lost his life in a New York shipwreck, almost died of fever in west Africa, and survived a Brazilian revolution before coming to Occidental. Howard and sawmill operator M. C. Meeker lured the railroad to town and developed Occidental as a railroad boom town. The entire town was built in four months and took its name from an early-day school district. Along nearby Salmon Creek stood the highest timber railroad bridge west of the Mississippi—300 feet long, 137 feet high.

Italian woodcutters came to Occidental from Tuscany to work in the redwood forests, and a few of them opened boardinghouses that served substantial meals for twenty-four cents. Today the bridge and the railroad are gone, but the tradition of the old boardinghouse remains. Occidental's main industry is now food.

The town's trio of restaurants—the old, informal Union Hotel; lively Fiori's; and modern, roomy Negri's—

all dish up hearty, filling, multicourse meals of antipasto, minestrone soup, salad, and ravioli, with an entree of chicken, steak, or duck (also veal or seafood at Fiori's), plus vegetables, bread, banana or apple fritters, wine, and coffee. The moderate prices have drawn families for three generations. All three restaurants have full bar and live entertainment on weekends, from country-rock bands at Negri's to old-time Italian music at the Union Hotel.

Giovanni Gobetti started Occidental's Paul Bunyan-sized dinners at what today is the Union Hotel, and under the firm, talented hands of Mary Panizerra, Union Hotel dinners have become a tradition for visitors to the redwoods. Fiori's and Negri's later opened in what was christened Calorie Gulch. Occidental's Italian restaurants serve as many as 10,000 dinners each Mother's Day. If you're in town on Easter Sunday, the Union Hotel features *capretto* (kid goat stew) along with its regular meal. The Union Hotel and Negri's are open daily for lunch and dinner; Fiori's is open daily for dinner. All three restaurants are within a block of each other; park in the center of town.

If you're working up an appetite or working off a meal, take a walk around Occidental and look at the delicatessens, and gift and craft shops, all located either on Main Street or Bohemian Highway, near the Italian restaurants. Or take a country drive on the quiet, redwood-shaded roads outside of town.

Occidental's other eating spots include the Occidental Seafood and Cheese Company, at the south end of Main Street, for quiche, bagels, sushi, salads, and seafood. Open weekdays at noon, weekends at 10 A.M. Directly behind Fiori's is Yellow Lizard Ice Cream and Deli, a spot for homemade soups and sandwiches. Open daily at 11 A.M.

Housed in the historic Taylor building adjacent to the Occidental Seafood and Cheese Company is the Land House Bakery, with fresh-baked bread and pastries made daily. The Land House Bakery is one of several local businesses operated by the followers of G. I. Gurdjieff, a Russian philosopher who promoted self-improvement through a system embracing philosophy, religion, and

Calories don't count when you're in Occidental. (Redwood Empire Association)

psychology. Gurdjieff's followers also run nearby Hand Goods on Main Street, a shoppers' bazaar of locally crafted items such as furniture, pottery, quilts, and clothing. Hand Goods is open daily 10-6; 874-2161.

The Fine Art Gallery, also on Main Street, features watercolors, oils, and graphics; open weekends only. Another Main Street store is Local Girls Make Good, for kitchenware and ornamentals, mugs and crockery.

The Occidental Farmer's Market sells fresh, organically grown produce every Saturday, 9 to 1, from June to late autumn, in the downtown parking area of Occidental. An unlikely spot for other natural foods is the Occidental Family Pharmacy, 3690 Bohemian Highway. You'll find shelves filled with herbs, stoneground wheat, and whole wheat pasta, plus round bins of trail mix and carob candies. The pharmacy has a licensed pharmacist but also carries natural health care remedies. There's a lending library of books on holistic health, nutrition, and herbs, too. Open 9-7 weekdays, 10-6 on Saturdays.

Lodging in Occidental is limited to the Union Motel (874-3635), adjacent to the Union Hotel restaurant; and Negri's Occidental Lodge (874-3623), on Bohemian Highway as you enter town from the south.

Coleman Valley Road leads from Occidental to Highway 1 on the Sonoma Coast; on the way it passes through both thick redwood forests and open, grassy hill country with stunning vistas. Along this route are two "New Age" communities, the Farallones Institute and the Ocean Song Institute. The Farallones Institute, 15290 Coleman Valley Road, is an eighty-acre agricultural and alternative energy center emphasizing self-sufficiency in living, including low-cost solar housing, alternative wastewater systems, and collective gardening. In Berkeley, the Institute's urban counterpart is the well-known Integral Urban House. Visitors are welcome to the Institute for a Saturday afternoon tour; call 874-3060. Two-day workshops in alternative technology are held at the Institute, and each fall many of the community's plants are offered for sale. For information, write the Farallones Institute Rural Center, 15290 Coleman Valley Road, Occidental, CA 95465.

The Ocean Song Institute, 19999 Coleman Valley Road, is an educational community based on the teachings of Paramhansa Yogananda, who came from India to America in the 1920s to teach the unity of all religions. Ocean Song members hold a Sunday service at 9 A.M., followed by brunch and a tour of their 900-acre farm. The Institute hosts summer apprentice programs in gardening, dairying, and weaving, and organically grown produce and raw milk are available at the Occidental Farmer's

Market. For additional facts, write to Ocean Song Institute, P.O. Box 659, Occidental, CA 95465, or call 874-2274.

Alternative living has not always been well accepted in western Sonoma. Two Occidental-area communes, the Wheeler Ranch on Coleman Valley Road and the Morningstar Ranch on Graton Road east of town, became storm centers of some of the strongest confrontations to occur between "hip" and "straight" people in the 1960s and 1970s. In 1962, Lou Gottlieb of the Limelighters folk-singing group purchased the land that became Morningstar Ranch; a year later, Bill Wheeler used an inheritance to buy his 315-acre spread. Both ranches became unstructured communal centers; members—many of them vegetarians—participated in what was considered unconventional behavior, including drug use.

Longtime Occidental residents branded the ranches "hippie havens," and county officials sought to close the communes as health hazards. Lengthy court battles followed, and at one point Gottlieb deeded his property to God to avoid complying with an order to tear down ranch buildings. The judge ruled that God did not exist as a legal entity and that Gottlieb was still the responsible party.

In 1971, seventy-five deputies, drug agents, military police, and correctional officers converged on Wheeler Ranch, looking for drugs and runaways; they arrested twenty-five people, including Wheeler (for outstanding traffic warrants). By 1973, both communes were closed, their structures bulldozed to the ground.

Don Edwards

The Russian River

6

Headwaters to Ocean

T he coldest winter I ever spent was a summer in San Francisco," Mark Twain once remarked, and a century-old San Franciscan antidote to chilly summer fog has been a sojourn along the Russian River, with its sandy beaches and warm water. The Russian River, simply called the River, is a barefoot, sand-between-the-sheets place. You can swim, canoe, and fish in the River; hike and horseback ride in the redwood-forested hills; or simply soak up the sun alongside a resort pool or relax in a hot tub. Evenings can be spent by a quiet campfire or dancing the night away to disco or country and western sounds.

On the upper reaches of the Russian River are dozens of small wineries, many campgrounds, and some of the best waters for canoeing. Along the lower stretches of the River, from Forestville to Duncans Mills, you'll find a wide variety of resorts—from rustic to elegant—plus numerous restaurants and topflight entertainment.

The Russian River watershed covers part of Mendocino County and much of Sonoma County. From Cloverdale, the River runs southward through rolling hills and wide, fertile valleys filled with vineyards and orchards. Near Mirabel Park, the River turns west, passing through dark, Germanic forests of redwood and Douglas fir until it enters the Pacific Ocean at Jenner. Some geologists believe the Russian River once flowed directly southward into San

Francisco Bay until ancient earthquakes battered the River into the twisting, tortured route it now follows through the coastal mountains to the sea.

Around present-day Guerneville, the convolutions of the River fashioned an oxbow bend. In this area, called the Big Bottom, some of the earth's loftiest redwood trees grew, safe from Pacific winds in the sheltered, fog-rich valleys. The Pomo Indians avoided these dark, damp redwood groves, building their villages along the upper stretches of the River near present-day Healdsburg and Geyserville.

Russian fur traders were the first explorers on the River. They had come from Alaska to the Sonoma Coast seeking sea otters, and by 1812 were entrenched at Fort Ross. They followed the course of the winding Russian River inland and named it Slavianka ("pretty Russian girl"). The Mexican settlers who followed the Russians called it El Rio Russo, which became anglicized as the Russian River.

The rich, gravelly loam soil of the upper Russian River region attracted midwestern and southern farmers, who planted wheat and raised cattle. In the 1870s, their farms were planted in grapes, prunes, pears, and apples. German, French, and Italian immigrants perfected winemaking techniques in the area, making Healdsburg, Geyserville, and Cloverdale viticultural centers. Later, hops, used in making beer, were planted between Guerneville and Healdsburg; the distinctive, cupola-topped hop kilns can still be seen along Westside and River roads.

In the 1850s, Missouri homesteaders followed the Russian River down from Healdsburg into the Big Bottom region, where mammoth trees reigned and salmon were taken from creeks with pitchforks. Tom Heald (brother of Healdsburg's founder) and his Swiss-born brother-in-law, George Guerne, erected one of the first sawmills on the River near Fife's Creek.

Maine woodsmen, "bluenoses" from lower Canada, and Scottish, Irish, French, and Scandinavian loggers systematically felled these forests they believed would last forever. Chinese laborers tended the logging camps; Italian *carbonieri* gathered wood from downed trees to make charcoal, while they planted vineyards along River hillsides.

In some groves, a single acre of Sonoma redwood forest yielded a million board feet of lumber. An ancient redwood toppled at Austin Creek measured 23 feet in diameter; one man hacked away at it for two years to make 600,000 shingles. A redwood higher than 367 feet, rivaling the tallest redwood now alive, was cut at Fife's Creek. In 1877, the estimated total number of feet of timber in Sonoma County was listed as 1,846,000,000—this after nearly two decades of logging.

Redwoods were hauled to mills by ox teams or floated down the Russian River. Later narrow- and broad-gauge railroads carried lumber away. At "doghole" ports along the northern Sonoma Coast (coves so tiny "only a dog could turn around in them," said sailors), chutes were used to load logs onto two-masted schooners.

The redwood's resistance to warping, splitting, or swelling made it the builders' choice for San Francisco Victorians. The wood's fire and insect resistance made it perfect for railroad ties on the transcontinental railroad. And redwood's inability to give odor or taste to any liquid it touches made it the ideal wood for water tanks, wine vats, and chemical containers.

By 1901, the mills closed in Guerneville; the area was logged out. But vacationers had discovered the Russian River. They rode luxury trains and came here to camp in the second-growth redwood forests and to build vacation homes. Dance halls, roller-skating rinks, and hotels sprang up. The rich and powerful of San Francisco's Bohemian Club carved out their own summer enclave in a virgin redwood grove near Monte Rio.

The Roaring Twenties and the Depression years were the River's halcyon decades. Vacationers sampled booze from nearby backcountry stills and danced cheek-to-cheek to the Big Band sounds of Harry James, Glen Miller, and Tommy Dorsey. Resort business tumbled after World

War II. The River became a low-cost housing area and a center for counterculture activities.

But just as Guerneville, Rio Nido, and Monte Rio have always bounced back from flooding and disastrous fires, so these resort towns survived and eventually revived. In the late 1970s, a Russian River renaissance began. Resorts were renovated, summer homes became permanent residences, restaurants resurrected fine dining—all due to an influx of gas-crunched vacationers, commuters working in Santa Rosa, and gays from San Francisco.

Today, the River is again a favorite vacation spot. The River's water quality has been improved, and growth is expected in the area, especially in Guerneville when the town's sewer lines are completed. Canoeists make the Russian the most popular river run in western America, while steelhead, salmon, and bass fishermen seek out their favorite pools.

Campgrounds, resorts, and inns along the River, from Cloverdale to Duncans Mills, fill up fast in the summer months, especially during three-day holiday weekends. And more and more vacationers are discovering the pleasures of the Russian River in fall and winter: excellent fishing, hiking in misty redwood forests, sampling local wines in uncrowded wineries, quiet dinners in nearby restaurants, evenings by wood-burning stoves in cozy cabins. Nearly all resorts and restaurants are open year-round, many with reduced winter rates. Day-trippers to the River find most resorts provide day rates, with use of facilities from beaches and grounds to pools and hot tubs.

Canoeing the Russian River

The Russian River's close proximity to the Bay Area makes it a popular river run for both novice canoers and white water seekers. The River has a steady summer flow due to water released upstream from Lake Pillsbury and Lake Mendocino; a generally southerly flow and a downstream wind ease along even the most inexperienced canoeist. The Russian River moves slowly, about three nautical miles per hour, and it offers a rich variety of scenery, from farmlands to redwoods. Great blue herons, turtles, and raccoons are among the animals you may see, and the River's many beaches and warm swimming holes are welcome stops. Generally, the river is warm enough for swimming between April and October.

There are seventy miles of canoeing waters between Squaw Rock, seven miles north of Cloverdale, and Jenner, where the River enters the Pacific Ocean; the entire length can be covered by canoe in three or four days. Most visitors opt for a one-day canoe trip of about ten miles, with time out for swimming and picnicking. (Most of the land along the river is privately owned, so please respect property rights.)

Novice and veteran canoeists alike should expect to tip over in their canoes, so don't bring anything that you can't afford to lose. Use a plastic garbage bag to pack your belongings and tie it securely to your canoe. On midsummer days the sun can be intense and temperatures often soar to above 100 degrees Fahrenheit, so protect yourself with sunscreen, a hat, sunglasses, long-sleeved shirt, and jeans rather than shorts. Wear tennis shoes, for the riverbed has rocks and broken bottles. Don't forget water in a plastic container and a change of clothes to leave in your car.

Although the River looks placid, caution is advised. More people probably drown here than in the rough white waters of the Stanislaus and Tuolumne rivers combined, simply because they don't wear life jackets. And each summer several people are permanently paralyzed as a result of injuries suffered when jumping off bridges or banks into the deceptively shallow river.

River-trippers use canoes, kayaks, rubber rafts, and inner tubes. There are three canoe rental outlets—California Rivers in Geyserville, Trowbridge Recreation Inc. in Healdsburg, and Burke's Canoe Trips in Forestville—and many resorts, campgrounds, and country inns also rent canoes.

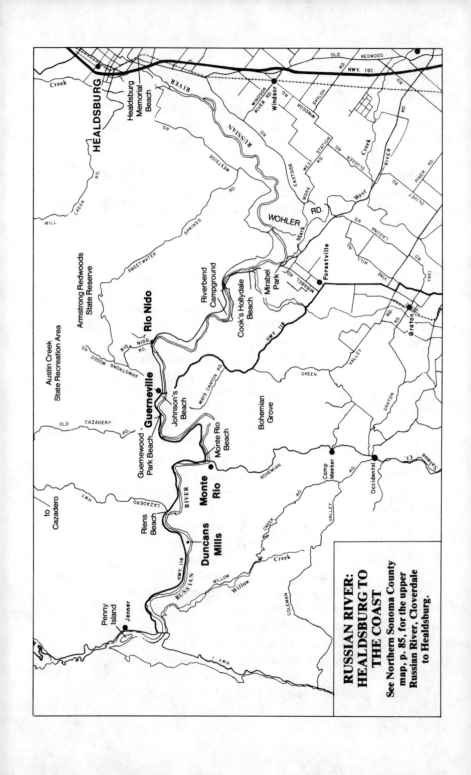

RUSSIAN RIVER:
HEALDSBURG TO
THE COAST

See Northern Sonoma County
map, p. 85, for the upper
Russian River, Cloverdale
to Healdsburg.

California Rivers, 21001 Geyserville Avenue, rents and sells canoes, kayaks, and rafts; offers guided river trips and canoe classes; and has a wide selection of river running equipment. The 1981 prices were $16 per day per canoe, $12 per day for a kayak. Rentals include paddles and life jackets, but no shuttle service. They're open 9-5 daily in summer; 9-5, Monday through Saturday other times of the year. For their catalog, write California Rivers, P.O. Box 468, Geyserville, CA 95441, or call 857-3872.

Trowbridge Recreation Inc., 20 Healdsburg Avenue in Healdsburg, is the king of canoe rentals, with hundreds of Grumman canoes. Trowbridge rents canoes for one- to five-day trips between March and October. Prices are $25 per canoe per day, $35 per canoe for two days, $45 per canoe for three to five days. Rentals include life jackets, paddles, and canoe transport fee. It's wise to make advance reservations by writing to the above address (zip code is 95448) or calling 433-7247. Trowbridge also offers a barbecue buffet dinner on weekends after canoeing; advance reservation required. Trowbridge Recreation opens daily at 8 A.M.

Burke's Canoe Trips, 8600 River Road, has three hundred seventeen-foot canoes for rent at $20 per day, $34 for two days; life jackets, paddles, and transport back included. Their Forestville site also has overnight camping, private beach, and cocktail lounge. Barbecue dinners are available for groups of fifty or more. For details call 887-1222 or write Burke's Canoe Trips, P.O. Box 602, Forestville, CA 95436. Burke's is open daily.

The best canoeing times are between March and October; the water is highest in May, but many prefer the quiet of Indian summer to travel the River. For river flow information, call the River Flow Information Service's Flow "Fone" at (916) 445-3555 or (707) 443-9305.

Squaw Rock to Cloverdale Run

Squaw Rock (so named for the Indian legend of a maiden who jumped off this cliff because her lover was untrue) is a

steep hill hundreds of feet high. It marks the beginning of a
river run that offers some of the best, and nearest, white
water rapids in the Bay Area. Squaw Rock is next to Highway 101; a dirt road one-fourth mile south of the rock
leads to a beach that is the canoe put-in point. This run is
not for novices; from here it's a day-long, seven-mile run to
Cloverdale.

Cloverdale to Asti Run

This run is open and easy, but the river channel changes
with each flood season. The put-in point (also the take-out
point for the run from Squaw Rock) is reached by taking
the First Street exit off Cloverdale Boulevard and driving
to Crocker Road. At a small beach owned by the city of
Cloverdale is Crocker Bridge, the canoe starting point.
This five-mile run takes two to three hours. The take-out
point at Asti is marked by the buildings of Italian Swiss
Colony Winery.

Asti to Geyserville Bridge Run

The run from Asti to the Geyserville Bridge and then on
to the Alexander Valley Campground are the River's most
popular, due to the high water in this section of the
Russian River. From Highway 101, take the Asti exit to
Washington School Road and continue to the Asti summer bridge, where the canoes are launched. Watch for
snags in this section of the river. The six-mile Asti to
Geyserville Bridge Run takes two to three hours.

Geyserville Bridge to
Alexander Valley Campground Run

This is the second half of the most popular river run. From
Highway 101, take the Geyserville Avenue exit to Highway 128. Just before the Geyserville Bridge is the canoe

put-in spot. This six-mile stretch, which takes two to three hours, offers good swimming and picnicking spots. The Alexander Valley Campground charges $2 per canoe for camping; water, rest rooms and fire pits are available. To reach the campground by land, take Dry Creek exit off Highway 101, then follow Healdsburg Avenue to Alexander Valley Road. The campground is off Alexander Valley Road just before you reach the Alexander Valley Bridge.

Alexander Valley Campground to Healdsburg Run

This is the most scenic of all the Russian River runs. Before the Alexander Valley was planted in grapes, you could see the prune orchards in blossom each spring. Today's vistas include vineyards on the nearby hills, plus conical Fitch Mountain as you near Healdsburg. There are fine fishing and swimming spots along this run which ends at the seasonal summer dam at Del Rio Woods Beach. This fifteen-mile trip takes five to seven hours. To reach Del Rio Woods Beach by land, follow Matheson Street from the Healdsburg Plaza until it becomes Fitch Mountain Road. Parking and picnicking are available at the Del Rio Woods Beach.

Del Rio Woods Beach to Healdsburg Memorial Beach Run

This short, three-mile run is often windy. Healdsburg Memorial Beach, one of the finest beaches on the River, has a dam, swimming and boating, and shady spots for picnics. Admission fee is $2. From Highway 101, take the Healdsburg Avenue exit.

The river section between Alexander Valley Campground and Healdsburg Memorial Beach is the site of the annual Russian River Rat Race, held each June. Prizes are

awarded for the best decorated canoes and for canoe race
winners. Festivities include a barbecue and live music.
Call Trowbridge Recreation for details, 433-4116.

Healdsburg Memorial Beach
to Mirabel Park Run

This twelve-mile run, lasting five to six hours, takes you
past Dry Creek (with the Warm Springs Dam at its source
to control Russian River flooding) and into the redwood
forest country. Several nude beaches are along this stretch
of the River, including a popular spot at the seasonal summer dam near Wohler Bridge. (Note that nudity is officially
outlawed by county ordinance.) There's river access at
Mirabel Beach or a mile downstream at Cook's Hollydale
Beach and Campground, a nine-acre site with rest rooms.
Day use is $2, $5 for overnight camping.

Mirabel Park to Hilton Run

The Russian River begins its twisting route through the
coastal mountains along this stretch of the river. This is a
short, four-mile, half-day run, with some nude beaches
along the way. At the take-out spot, Hilton Park, and at
adjacent River Bend Campground there are campsites.

Hilton to Guerneville Run

The willows and other trees overhanging the River create
"The Jungle" section of this run. There's a summer dam
near Rio Nido; take-out points are at Reinhart's Campground (Roland's Sandy Beach) in Rio Nido and at Johnson's Beach in Guerneville. Parking fee for Reinhart's
Campground is $1.50, and the camping fee is nominal;
Trowbridge Recreation hopes to open a campground here,
too. Johnson's Guerneville Beach, just past the Highway 116 Bridge in Guerneville, has free swimming and
parking. This five-mile, half-day run brings you right to
the heart of the Russian River resort area at Guerneville.

Redwood Empire Association

Guerneville to Monte Rio Run

Put-in point is just past the summer dam at Johnson's Beach. This five-mile, half-day run goes past summer homes and old resorts, and the Guernewood Park Beach (Ginger's Rancho) which can be reached by land off Highway 116. Free parking and swimming are available at this popular beach. You may have to portage one or two of the summer dams, and there's a tricky turn to the right near the Bohemian Grove. Monte Rio Beach, just before the Monte Rio Bridge, has free swimming and parking. It's reached by land by following Highway 116 to Monte Rio, then turning left. The Monte Rio Parks and Recreation District has a boat launching ramp and fishing area on the west side of the Monte Rio Bridge.

Monte Rio to Riens Beach Run

This is a short, three-mile, half-day run. To reach Riens Beach by car, take Highway 116 to the sign four-tenths of a mile past Austin Creek Road. It is not recommended that you go farther than Riens Beach by canoe, and the planned river trips end at this point.

If you have the urge to follow the River all the way to Jenner, leave the canoes behind and try a ride on a "super-sled" jet boat. This twenty-mile round trip begins at Monte Rio and lasts about three hours. Fares are $15; children under twelve half price. For reservations, call Russian River Boat Tours, 869-2859 (from 8 to 5 P.M.) or 887-1496 (after 7 P.M.), or write P.O. Box 813, Forestville, CA 95436.

Fishing the Russian River

The Russian River, popular with steelhead trout fishermen, also has black bass, bluegill, catfish, American shad, and smallmouth bass. Even when the Russian River is muddy, its tributaries often run clear.

Summer anglers catch smallmouth bass, while steelhead seekers hit the River in November and December. Check with local bait shops on flood conditions in the winter. Copies of the current California Sport Fishing Regulations on fishing seasons and limits are available at the bait shops.

Smallmouth bass can be caught from rubber rafts between Alexander Valley Bridge and the Healdsburg Memorial Beach. South of Healdsburg lie dozens of pools where steelhead feed. Try Mirabel pool, near Cook's Beach; Guernewood Park pool, near Ginger's Rancho; Northwood pool, near Monte Rio; Monte Rio pool, just beyond the Monte Rio Bridge; and pools around the Hacienda Bridge, Schoolhouse Canyon Campground, and Duncans Mills. Penny Island at the River's mouth is also good for steelhead.

For more information, stop by Healdsburg Sporting Goods, 452-B Healdsburg Avenue, Healdsburg; King's News and Tackle, Main Street, Guerneville; or Lyle's Tackle, 2690 Santa Rosa Avenue, Santa Rosa.

A Country Drive to River Resorts

Five miles north of Santa Rosa is the River Road exit off Highway 101; from here it's about an eight-mile drive to the lower Russian River resort area. The first stretch of road takes you past vineyards that formerly were planted in orchards and hops. There are several stops along the way for fresh farm produce.

A popular stop for day-trippers going to and from the River is the Egg Basket Food Market at Fulton and River roads. At Halloween time pumpkin-pickers head for the Cameron Ranch, 3200 River Road, for U-pick pumpkins, plus apples, squash, and Indian corn. Cameron Ranch is open 9-6 daily during the month of October.

Fall and winter are also the seasons to stop at the Martinelli Ranch, 3360 River Road, where you can buy apples inside an old, red, hop-drying kiln. The Martinellis sell Golden Delicious, Gravenstein, Jonathan, and Rome apples, plus pears, walnuts, and vegetables in season. The apples are sold in twenty- or forty-pound boxes at roughly one-half supermarket price, and you can pick up apple gift boxes before the holiday season, when the Martinellis feature "Christmas in the Barn." Christmas decorations and trees are available, too. Open daily 10-6, August through December. Call 525-0570 or 887-1281.

Past Trenton Road, River Road enters a small valley with two very different country retreats, the Russian River Lodge and the Raford House. The Russian River Lodge, on River Road at Wohler Road, is a predominately gay resort with rooms in the Victorian farmhouse lodge, housekeeping cabins, campsites, pool, and wooded grounds. There's a day use of the facilities, too. For further information, write Russian River Lodge, 7871 River Road, Forestville, CA 95448; or call 887-1524.

A mile north on Wohler Road is a huge, three-story Victorian house, built in the 1880s by Raford W. Peterson, part of a 400-acre hop ranch. Perched on a hillside over-looking vineyards, orchards, and forested hills, the Raford House has eight bedrooms, six with private bath. Con-tinental breakfast is served. For reservations, call Beth Foster or Alan Baitinger, innkeepers, 887-9573; or write 10630 Wohler Road, Healdsburg, CA 95448. No pets or small children are allowed.

Back on River Road, the scenery near Mirabel Park turns from sunny to shady as you enter the redwood forest. Near here, John Rogers Cooper, a brother-in-law to General Vallejo, built the first known power-operated commercial sawmill on Mark West Creek in 1834. The sawmill was washed away by floods.

At 7600 River Road is the Mirabel Trailer Park, also an agency for Trowbridge canoe rentals. This family resort has trailer sites for full hookup and campsites for non-hookup vehicles; call 887-2383. Nearby Burke's Canoe Trips, at 8600 River Road, has canoe rentals, fifty campsites, and its own private beach. Cook's Hollydale Beach and Campground, six miles from Highway 101 on River Road, has free swimming at their beach. Parking is $2, camping $5.

Hilton Park and River Bend campgrounds, with the adjacent Russian River Pub, are popular riverside camping and dining sites. The Russian River Pub is an informal place for sandwiches, burgers, and Mexican food, plus Sunday brunch; 887-7932. Offices for both Hilton and River Bend campgrounds are at 11820 River Road in River Bend. You will find tent camping at Hilton; trailer, camper, and tent camping at River Bend; plus groceries and Trowbridge canoe rentals. Call 887-7662.

You can camp under the redwoods, hike, or swim at Schoolhouse Canyon Campground, 12600 River Road. The Schoolhouse Canyon Park Wildlife Sanctuary, part of the campground, is located across River Road on 200 acres near the Odd Fellows Park. It's a private reserve for the many birds and small animals that live near the River.

Antique-decorated rooms, continental breakfast from a country kitchen, and a hot tub await lucky vacationers at Ridenhour Ranch House Inn, 12850 River Road, 887-1033. This eleven-room house with five bedrooms (two with private bath) dates from 1906. Louis William Ridenhour came here from Missouri in 1856 as a homesteader, and his family owned the property until it was sold to Martha and Bob Satterthwaite in 1977. The Satterthwaites converted the home into a bed and breakfast inn.

Five hundred yards around the bend is F. Korbel and Bros., one of the region's premier wineries. Korbel is famous for champagne made in the classic *methode champenoise*—every stage of production takes place in the same bottle you buy. Champagne varieties include natural (bone dry), brut, extra dry, sec, rose, rouge, Blanc de Noir, and Blanc de Blanc. Korbel's brandy has been served for a century. Varietal wines—Cabernet Sauvignon, Gamay Rose, Johannisberg Riesling, Gewurztraminer, Chardonnay, Chenin Blanc, and Cabernet Rose—round out their wine roster.

The Bohemian-born Korbel brothers immigrated to California, where they made cigars, published a satirical magazine, raised dairy cattle, logged redwoods, and even raised tobacco before they started making wine in 1881. The Northwestern Pacific Railroad station beside the winery was the result of the brothers' efforts to get a rail line to their lumber mill.

Korbel's brick winery dates from 1886; the Norman tower is a replica of the prison tower where brother Francis spent some time in Europe. Birth year of Korbel champagne was 1898, with help from midwives Frank Hazek, a Prague champagne-maker, and Pilsen-trained Jan Hanuska.

In 1954, the Korbel family sold the winery to the Heck family, German Alsatians; new production facilities were added for better champagne production. F. Korbel and Bros. Cellars and Vineyards, 13250 River Road, Guerneville, 887-2294, hosts tours every hour from 9:45 to 3:45, tasting and retail sales 9-5 daily.

Rio Nido

A half mile from F. Korbel Cellars and fourteen miles from Highway 101 is Rio Nido (Spanish for "river's nest"), once the most exclusive of the River's resort towns. Today, the town is again known for its resorts and restaurants.

Rio Nido Lodge, tucked away amid the redwoods at 14580 River Road, 869-0821, features a menu with steak and Italian food, dancing and cocktails, and a variety of entertainers. Their lounge and dinner shows sport well-known performers from John Gary and Dennis Day to the Ink Spots and Barbara McNair. On summer nights, you can get chuckwagon-style dinners—barbecued beef, beans, baked potato, sourdough roll, and dessert—and live western entertainment, all out under the stars, part of the Circle T Chuckwagon.

Rio Nido Strip

The section of River Road between Rio Nido and Guerneville is called the Rio Nido Strip. Most of the beaches along here are private, but Reinhart's Campground (Roland's Sandy Beach) has free swimming; parking fee is $1.50. Burke's Canoe Trips has limited camping for users of their rental canoes, and Trowbridge Recreation plans to put a campground here. The Strip also contains a number of resorts, restaurants, and craft shops.

The resorts include the River Village, 14880 River Road, 869-9066, a predominately gay resort with cabins (full kitchens and living rooms), full bar, hot tub, swimming pool, and beach access to the River. Their indoor/outdoor dining area is a popular lunch and dinner spot. Nearer to Guerneville is the Willows, a gay guest house on five willowy acres. The Willows, 15905 River Road, has a private beach, canoes, hot tub, a dozen bedrooms, and a grand living room; 869-3279.

Ric and Jean Fullerton, local craftspeople, have a duo of shops that sell their own creations plus the crafts of other river artisans. Jean's Oak and Glass shop, 15105 River Road, features commissioned stained glass works; 869-3595. Ric's Russian River Woodcraft is a bazaar of handmade furniture for every room of your house. He's at 15149 River Road; 887-1775.

Guerneville

N ext stop is Guerneville (GURN-vil); with but a thousand souls, this is the biggest little town in the resort region. Guerneville has seen its share of change, from rowdy redwood logging camp to rustic resort mecca. Fire and flood have destroyed much of the town at one time or another, and its residents have been a parade of retirees, students, artists and craftspeople, bikers and fishermen, hippies, gays, and middle American families. Guerneville has survived it all.

238

The Pomo Indians avoided Guerneville's Big Bottom redwood region, calling it a "dark hole," but American settlers returning from Sierra gold mines found redwood gold here. George Emil Guerne, Swiss-born lumberman, and his brother-in-law, Tom Heald, started a sawmill in 1865. In the center of town was a maze of redwood stumps, and Stumptown became the name of the town. Parts of downtown Guerneville are built over these stumps. The name Guerneville dates from 1870.

Loggers worked in pairs to cut the huge redwoods. They lined up a tree to fall in a particular spot, then climbed a dozen or more feet up, past the swell of a burl, to fasten their "springboards"—pieces of flexible planking upon which they stood—and began chopping. Within an hour, their rhythmic cutting brought them to the tree's heartwood, and the pace slowed until the tree toppled. Many a logger was crushed by falling trees or runaway logs crashing down hillsides. Falling branches called "widow makers" took their toll.

After the trees were cut, teams of oxen "snaked out" the logs on "skid roads" made by placing logs together to form a path. Chinese laborers walked ahead of the ox teams, wetting the log roads to keep down dust and cut friction.

In 1877 the San Francisco and North Pacific Railroad (later the Northwestern Pacific Railroad) reached Guerneville, and a railroad locomotive called the "Coffee Grinder" hauled the logs away. In its prime, Guerneville rivaled Eureka as California's busiest logging camp; the rollicking frontier town boasted eight saloons in one block.

Within thirty-five years, the redwood forests had been logged. Railroad promoter A. W. Foster turned the logging camps into vacation sites, and thousands rode the rails to camp, swim, boat, and fish. Out of favor for several years, Guerneville is again a popular vacation destination. Many resorts have been revived, several with gay money, while local restaurants have been upgrading their cuisine. Guerneville's resorts and campgrounds are located on both sides of the Russian River, along River Road and Mill

Guerneville's Russian River Rodeo is one of several held annually in Sonoma County. (Russian River Chamber of Commerce)

Street in town, and off Armstrong Woods Road north of town.

Near Guerneville is Armstrong Woods State Reserve, the only virgin redwood grove in Sonoma County open to the public, and Guerneville beaches are among the best on the River. The town hosts several summer festivals, including the Russian River Country Music Festival, the Russian River Jazz Festival, the Korbel Concert series in Armstrong Redwoods' outdoor theater, as well as the Russian River Rodeo and Stumptown Days Celebration.

Downtown Guerneville

Downtown Guerneville fans out from the busy intersection of Highway 116 (from Forestville), River Road, and Armstrong Woods Road, which runs north out of town to

Armstrong Woods State Reserve. For a short distance through town, Highway 116 is Main Street; it continues west to Guernewood Park, Monte Rio, and Duncans Mills, and then joins Highway 1 near Jenner.

A good first stop is the Russian River Region office, 14034 Armstrong Woods Road, for resort, restaurant, camping, and fishing information, maps, and literature. Tickets for many local annual events are sold here. Out-of-area guests can find out which resorts cater to families, couples, or gays. The Russian River Region office is open 9-5, Monday through Saturday in the summer; 10:30-5, Monday through Saturday in the winter; 11-4 on Sundays. Call 869-9009.

Along Main Street are several restaurants, delicatessens, gift shops, and bars. The River Inn—a river institution for over three decades—is a classic, old-school coffee shop serving Swedish pancakes for breakfast, seafood and hamburgers at other meals. Pat's Restaurant and Bar is open daily for breakfast, lunch, and dinner; fishermen come here to check out the fishing spots pinpointed on the Russian River map decorating the restaurant wall. Otto's Guerneville Bakery, 16270 Main Street, features delicious Dutch crunch rolls and blueberry muffins.

A few steps off Main Street, at 13550 Church Street, is Rosemary's Garden, where one of California's leading herbalists, Rosemary Gladstar, dispenses more than four hundred herbs and scores of spices. Gladstar also holds herb walks, retreats, and seminars on an eighty-acre ranch south of Guerneville. For information, call 869-0972, or send $2 to California School of Herbal Studies, P.O. Box 350, Guerneville, CA 95445.

The Guerneville Safeway grocery store is a good orientation point for locating most of the in-town resorts and lodges. RVs can park in the rear of the Safeway parking lot, near First Street.

One block south of Main Street is First Street, fronting the Russian River and the location of two family resorts. The first is Johnson's Lodge, adjacent to Johnson's Beach, with river cottages (with and without kitchens) and camping; 869-2022. Next door, at First and Church streets, is Riverlane Resort, one of the River's oldest resorts, with fourteen housekeeping cabins for two to eight people, a heated pool, hot tub, and private river beach; 869-2323.

A block west of Safeway are three resorts—Brookside Lodge and Resort Motel, Fife's, and Ferngrove. Brookside, Highway 116 at Brookside Lane, borders Fife Creek. This family resort has beautifully landscaped grounds with a swimming pool, plus one- and two-bedroom motel units, a triplex, and several cottages. Call 869-2470.

Fife's, 16467 River Road, is Guerneville's most famous gay resort. Located on fourteen landscaped acres are cabins, cottages, camping facilities, pool, private beach, day-use facilities, full bar, disco, and restaurant. Call 869-0656. Across River Road is Ferngrove, an adult resort for straight and gay clientele, with eighteen cottages (some with fireplaces) and a pool. Call 869-9992.

Johnson's Beach

One block south of Main Street via Church Street is the entrance to Johnson's Beach. A temporary summer dam backs up the River at this point, forming a swimming lagoon. There's free parking here, and you can rent canoes. Johnson's Beach is a popular canoe launching spot and the site of several Guerneville festivals.

Guerneville's South Bank

The south bank is the center of family resorts and entertainment. From Main Street, follow Highway 116 over the Guerneville Bridge and you're there. Two neighboring family resorts are Southside Resort and Donovan's Resort. Southside, 13811 Highway 116, has roomy cabins, camping and RV spots, a private beach, rental canoes, and a tiny animal farm for kids. Call 869-2690. Around the corner on Drake Road is Donovan's Resort, with cabins, campsites for self-contained RVs, a private beach, and a boat dock. Be sure to make your reservations in advance: 869-2689.

Nearby stand two amusement parks, Abby's Playland and J's Amusements, with a super slide, Ferris wheel, go-karts, bumper cars, and such. They're generally open from 11 A.M. to 10 P.M. during the summer months. The adjacent Jack Wright Memorial Park, a good rest stop, has tennis courts; open daily during daylight hours.

The River Landing shopping complex is home to the Country Grounds Cafe, with indoor and outdoor tables for breakfast, lunch, and dinner. To work up an appetite, how about a bicycle ride? The Bike Shop, next to River Landing, sponsors tours on the second Saturday and last Sunday of each month. Tours leave at 9:30 A.M.; everyone is welcome.

Neeley Road, off Highway 116, leads to two other resorts and a restaurant with a fine river view. First is the Creekside Inn and Resort, 16180 Neeley Road. The inn's six guest rooms are reserved for adults only; a continental breakfast is served. The resort's nine housekeeping cottages welcome families, and special group rates are available. Creekside also has spots for trailers, campers, and tents, and there's a pool. Call 869-3623. Family-oriented Parker's Resort, 16220 Neeley Road, is on twenty-four acres with a lot of river frontage. Besides twelve housekeeping units, there are fifty campsites for trailers, tents, and RVs, plus a pool and playground. Nightly campfires are a popular attraction here. Call 869-2037.

Mexican cuisine and river vistas are yours at Casa de Joanna, 17500 Orchards Road off Neeley Road. Crab enchiladas are among the diners' favorites, as are wine margaritas. Reservations suggested, 869-3756.

Guerneville's Nightlife and Festivals

Downtown Guerneville is known for its busy nightlife, while resorts and campgrounds south of the River and along Armstrong Woods Road are quieter.

Garbo's, one-half mile west of Guerneville, at 17081 Highway 116 in Guernewood Park, is a popular disco with live bands. The bar opens at 6 P.M., the action starts at 10. Nearby is the Red Barn, 14120 Old Cazadero Road, off Highway 116, with live country music and dancing on weekend nights. Gay discos include Fife's, 16467 River Road, and The Woods (formerly the Hexagon House), 16881 Armstrong Woods Road.

Guerneville is also the River's entertainment center. Music lovers congregate at Johnson's Beach every June for the Russian River Country Music Festival and every September for the Russian River Jazz Festival. Country favorites such as Leon Russell, Lacy J. Dalton, and Doug Kershaw have had fans stompin' in the sands in years past, while jazz greats Stan Getz and Count Basie have played beats for boogieing. (There's no shade at the beach; bring hats and suntan lotion.) Outdoor summer concerts are held each Sunday in Armstrong Redwoods State Reserve's 1,200-seat amphitheater. Featured are Shakespearean plays and modern theater, string quartets and folk music, all part of the Korbel Armstrong Woods Concert Series.

Tickets for the country music, jazz, and summer concert series are available through the Russian River Creative Arts Foundation, 16320 First Street, beside Riverlane Resort in Guerneville, or by calling 887-7720. The mailing address is P.O. Box 763, Guerneville, CA 95446. BASS outlets also carry tickets for the country and jazz festivals, and the Russian River Region office has country music festival tickets.

The Russian River Rodeo and Stumptown Days Parade are held each June. The parade is in downtown Guerneville; the rodeo takes place at Birkhofer Field, south of town on Highway 116. Rodeo events include bull riding, bareback riding, saddle bronc riding, calf roping, and team roping. Admission is generally $6 adults, $3 children, for each day of the two-day events. Contact the Russian River Region office for information and tickets, 869-9009.

The Russian River Slug Off, honoring the dreaded forest beast, the banana slug, is held each Ides of March at

a different spot along the River. Events include the slug
derby and recipes featuring slug meat. Winning dishes
have included slug-a-roni (the Rio Nido treat), slugetti,
and stir-fried slugs. While the slug derby is well attended,
the "slug" tasting is marked by the judges' reluctance to
sample the delicacies. San Francisco *Examiner* columnist
Jeff Jarvis advises, "Never go to a Slug Fest when you have
a hangover." For more information, write *The Paper*,
Box 280-S, Monte Rio, CA 95462.

Armstrong Redwoods State Reserve

Armstrong Redwoods State Reserve and adjacent
Austin Creek State Recreation Area offer quiet
contrasts to bustling Guerneville streets. The
Armstrong redwoods are the last stand of coastal redwoods in Sonoma County in an area open to the public.
These trees were saved by Civil War Col. James Armstrong, who switched from logging to preservation. After
the Big Bottom redwoods had been logged, Armstrong
enlisted Luther Burbank's help in saving the threatened
giants. Armstrong's daughter, Lizzie Armstrong Jones,
fulfilled her father's dreams when the county bought the
site, later deeding it to the state in 1934.

To reach the park from Guerneville, take Armstrong
Woods Road off River Road/Main Street and drive north
2.3 miles. This is the old Big Bottom country, once damp
and dark from the shade of 300-foot redwood trees. Along
the way you'll pass near the Highlands Resort, 14000
Woodland Drive, a gay resort; and family-oriented trailer
parks like Deer Park Woods Lodge, the Little Big Horn
Trailer Heaven, and Ring Canyon Campground.

Before reaching the reserve, you'll spot The Woods,
formerly the Hexagon House, now a gay resort with hotel
rooms, large cabins, bunkhouse, two swimming pools,
hot tub, three bars, gourmet dining room, cabaret enter-

Hiker dwarfed by grove of virgin redwood trees. (Don Edwards)

tainment, and disco. It's at 16881 Armstrong Woods Road, 869-3991.

The hexagon-shaped main building at The Woods began as the Pond Farm, a rural retreat for artisan refugees from Hitler's Europe. Jane Brandenstein Herr, related to the Brandensteins of MJB coffee fame, bought the property in the 1940s; the hexagon art center was built in 1949.

Many aspiring actors, including Carol Burnett, have starred in the Stumptown Players' productions held here. After Jane Herr's death in 1952, the artists migrated to other Bay Area locales. Many northern California art movements trace their beginnings to the Pond Farm colony.

When you arrive at Armstrong Redwoods State Reserve, you can park free in the lot by the entrance and then walk into the park, or you can drive through for $2. Either way, stop between the ranger station and the entrance kiosk to examine an exhibit of the plants of the redwood forest. Three types of redwoods are planted here: the coastal redwood (*Sequoia sempervirens*), the Sierra redwood (*Sequoiadendron giganteum*), and the dawn redwood (*Metasequoia*). Feel the texture of their barks and note their different colored leaves. The coastal redwood is the tallest of the three, and the Sierra redwood the greatest in girth. The dawn redwood, the only deciduous redwood, is a survivor from prehistoric times. The dawn redwood is native only to China, coastal redwoods live in parts of California and Oregon, and the Sierra redwood is found in the California Sierra Nevada mountains.

Coastal redwoods love fog, thriving in the coastal ranges from sea level to elevations near 2,000 feet. Despite holding the title of the world's tallest tree, coastal redwoods have shallow root systems. They are unique among conifer (cone-bearing) trees because they reproduce from seeds and by sprouting from the roots or stump of a parent tree. On many older redwoods you'll notice gnarled lumps, called burls; these can be cut from the tree and placed in water to sprout new branches. Burls are also used to make unusual wooden gift items, and several shops in Guerneville sell burl creations.

Coastal redwoods can grow up to 2.5 feet per year for their first century, which is why many second-growth redwood forests in Sonoma County now sport 100-foot trees. The redwood's rapid growth shuts out light for the plants below. The plant exhibit notes the other flora that can live with redwoods. Prominent among these are

Douglas fir, prized for timber; tan oak, whose bark was sought by nineteenth-century loggers for tanneries; and redwood sorrel, resembling clover, which was eaten in many a pioneer salad. As you walk through the reserve, look also for the rare redwood orchid (calypso), which blooms underneath the redwoods each spring. And beware of poison oak, with its distinctive three-leaf arrangement and scarlet fall colors.

Follow the Pioneer Trail in the reserve to the Parson Jones Tree—310 feet high, 13.8 feet in diameter, and over 1,200 years old—named for W. L. Jones, Armstrong's preacher son-in-law. The Colonel Armstrong Tree, 14.5 feet around (the largest in the park), is 308 feet tall and 1,400 years old. Coastal redwoods can exceed 367 feet in height, live for 2,200 years, but seldom grow larger than 16 feet in diameter. Their cousins, the Sierra redwoods, grow to 325 feet in height, live up to 3,300 years, and can be 30 feet in diameter.

In the reserve are picnic tables and fire pits; some can be reserved for groups. Stop at the 1,200-seat amphitheater, site of the Korbel Sunday Concert Series, and a popular spot for weddings and other social events. The amphitheater can be reserved free of charge (including a shuttle to carry guests to and from the parking lot); call 869-2015 or write Austin Creek State Recreation Area, Armstrong Redwoods State Reserve, 17000 Armstrong Woods Road, Guerneville, CA 95446.

Austin Creek State Recreation Area

A rmstrong Woods Road ends at Redwood Lake Campground in the Austin Creek State Recreation Area, where you trade the shady redwood forest for open, sunny grasslands and oak forests ringing the tributaries of East Austin Creek. Spring unfolds here with the blooming of wild azaleas or California buckeye,

and the sight of fishermen angling for pan-sized trout or
steelhead. Wildlife in the park include black-tailed deer,
gray foxes, and even wild feral pigs, descendants of tame
swine the Russians kept at Fort Ross. Redwood Lake is
stocked with bluegill and black bass.

Hiking and riding trails branch out from Redwood
Lake. There are twenty-four campsites at the lake and four
primitive campsites elsewhere (one at Tom King Camp,
one at Gilliam Creek Camp, two at Manning Flat Camp).
Bring your own water to these smaller, hike- or ride-in
camps. Horse-trailer parking is located at the entrance to
Armstrong Redwoods.

Camping is available on a first-come, first-served basis.
Camping fees are $3 per vehicle, $2 extra vehicle, $1.50
seniors, $1 per dog per night (dogs must be on a leash and
have proof of rabies vaccination); firewood is $1.25. The
narrow road up to Redwood Lake can't be negotiated by
vehicles (or combinations of vehicles) over twenty feet
long.

Monte Rio

Four miles west of Guerneville on Highway 116 is the
resort town of Monte Rio (Spanish for "river
mountain"). Parts of the downtown area have been
destroyed by a series of unsolved arson fires, so much of
what passes for Monte Rio is on the outskirts of town.
Monte Rio has beaches and diverse but limited lodging
and dining stops.

Immediately west of Guerneville is the resort area of
Guernewood Park, with a popular sandy beach at Ginger's
Rancho, 17155 Highway 116. Free parking and swimming
are available here, plus canoe rentals, a restaurant and bar.

Monte Rio Beach, a free, public beach, is located one
block off Highway 116. Turn left at the stop sign beneath
the street-spanning sign saying "Welcome to Monte Rio—
Vacation Wonderland" and park beneath the Monte Rio
Bridge. The adjacent beach is open during the summer

months, with lifeguards on duty, a snack bar, and rental stands for canoes, inner tubes, and beach umbrellas. On the opposite side of the bridge is the Monte Rio Parks and Recreation District boat launch and an angling access for fishermen. It's open all year, 9-9 summer, 9-6 winter.

Riens Sandy Beach, 22900 Sylvan Way, is three miles west of Monte Rio. Besides swimming, boating, and fishing, Riens offers camping facilities for trailers, campers, and tent campers. All camping sites have water and picnic tables; some feature electricity and sewer connections. Call 865-2102.

The Northwood Lodge and the Northwood Golf Course, Restaurant and Lounge form the River's most glamorous complex, set amid the redwoods three miles west of Guerneville on Highway 116. The lodge and the golf course-restaurant operation are separately managed, but visitors see them as a self-contained resort for swimming, golfing, hot tub sitting, dining, and walking in the redwood groves. The L-shaped Northwood Lodge has twenty hotel rooms clustered around the pool, but visitors treasure the roomy cabins with Franklin stoves, kitchens, and plenty of privacy. Reservations can be made by calling 865-2126 or writing Northwood Lodge, P.O. Box 188, Monte Rio, CA 95462.

Northwood Golf Course, a nine-hole course, is rated par 69 for men, par 71 for women. It's open daily from 7 to 7, with hand and power carts, plus rental clubs. The Northwood Restaurant serves prime rib, crab, and roast lamb among its other dishes. It's now owned by Randy and Gretchen Neuman of Cazanoma Lodge fame in nearby Cazadero; their Sunday brunch draws many visitors to Northwood. Call 865-2454 for reservations.

The Village Inn, 20822 River Boulevard, Monte Rio, on the south side of the River, has all the ambience of the roomy, brown-shingled summer homes and resorts that once dotted the River. Their thirty rooms are furnished in antiques. The restaurant serves European cuisine, with seafood and vegetarian dishes, and has live entertainment daily and a full bar; 865-2738.

Farther down River Boulevard is Angelo's Resort and Restaurant. Enjoy a river view while dining on Italian dishes. There are one- and two-bedroom cabins if you'd like to stay the night. Call 865-2215. Yee's Restaurant, 20293 Highway 116, the *only* Chinese restaurant on the River, features Mandarin cuisine; 865-9956.

The Bohemian Grove

Ronald Reagan, Robert Kennedy, Prince Philip of England, and Germany's Helmut Schmidt have all visited tiny Monte Rio, as have captains of industry, Nobel Prize winners, top government officials, Hollywood entertainers, and well-known financiers. They've gathered at the Bohemian Grove, a private, 2,700-acre redwood-shrouded retreat where America's wealthy and influential men meet every July for an "encampment."

The Bohemian Grove, the wilderness branch of San Francisco's Bohemian Club, hosts what fellow member Herbert Hoover once called "the greatest men's party on earth." Members and guests in this all-male, heavily Republican group perform plays, host parties, and hold off-the-record meetings, including the Lakeside Talks (Henry Kissinger, Nelson Rockefeller, and Dwight Eisenhower have been among the speakers at the Talks). It's been said that among decisions reached in the Grove were the one to build the atomic bomb via the Manhattan Project, and a preconvention agreement between Ronald Reagan and Richard Nixon that Nixon be unchallenged for the 1968 Republican nomination.

The annual July encampment draws 2,000 men for two weeks to a miniature city within a virgin redwood grove. Besides the dining circle (which can seat 1,000), two outdoor theaters, a private beach, and an infirmary, the Grove contains 122 camps. Some of the "camps" are actually buildings designed by Bay Area architect Bernard Maybeck and include their own staffs and kitchens; other camps are just tents with flooring above the forest floor.

Women are not allowed to join the Bohemian Club, so

the encampment is a stag affair. Members have been known to seek female companionship, however, and in 1971 a scandal broke over members "jumping the river" to local red-light encampments. There will be women in the Grove next year, for a state commission has ruled that they must hire women employees.

During the encampment, some of the celebrities in attendance stage a benefit show in Monte Rio, but their names are kept secret until showtime. Among past performers were Bing Crosby, Dennis Day, and Edgar Bergen. The show is open to the public. Tickets can be purchased at the door or in advance through Torr Realty Company; call 865-2182.

Cazadero

Cazadero, tucked eight miles off Highway 116 in thick forests, has an alpine flavor though it is only 117 feet in elevation. Local resorts and restaurants accentuate this feeling by offering German dishes and cultivating a European ambience. Cazadero's resorts draw those who seek quiet rather than the bustle of Guerneville.

Cazadero, loosely translated from the Spanish as "hunter's camp," began as the terminus of the narrow-gauge Northwestern Pacific Railroad. Lumbering was the occupation here, and the Berry Mill, a family-owned sawmill, was established in the 1880s. Still in operation (though moved from its downtown site), Berry's Mill is one of five sawmills remaining in Sonoma County.

This is an area where families pride themselves on residing in these hills for generations, and recently there's been some conflict between natives and newcomers. Old-timers object to two cottage industries promoted by some recent settlers—marijuana growing and the construction of "illegal" nonconforming, owner-built homes.

To get to Cazadero from Highway 116, drive three miles west of Monte Rio to either of two roads that parallel Austin Creek on their way to Cazadero—Austin Creek

Road and Cazadero Highway. When you reach town, there are several interesting dining and resort choices.

Cazanoma Lodge is Cazadero's best-known dining and lodging spot. You can catch your own trout in their pond and have the chef prepare it, or try roulade, roast duck, and rabbit among the many menu choices. Owners Randy and Gretchen Neuman also serve Sunday brunch. Lodging is limited to the main building and two cabins. There's entertainment in the bar in summer months, and a swimming pool too. Cazanoma Lodge is at 1000 Kidd Creek Road, off Austin Creek Road. Call 632-5255.

Another dining-lodging combo is Double B's Mototel and Elim Grove Restaurant, at 5400 Cazadero Highway. Elim ("mile" spelled backward) was a mile from the end of the rail line. Double B's Mototel has studio and two-bedroom cabins. Elim Grove Restaurant dishes out an international cuisine, including churrasco argentino (steak with guasaca sauce); 632-5259.

Down the road, at 3650 Cazadero Highway, is the Austin Dell Resort, on Austin Creek. They have housekeeping cottages with fireplaces, a hot tub, swimming, playground. Children are welcome; 632-5273.

Cazadero is perhaps best known for its music festivals. The Cazadero Music and Arts Center, 5385 Cazadero Highway, has a large outdoor amphitheater where free summer concerts are performed. Music students come to the Center each vacation to perfect their skills in jazz, baroque, and other music forms. The Center is part of the city of Berkeley's Camp Department, and most students hail from that East Bay city. For program times, write to the Center (Box 140, Cazadero, CA 95421) or call 632-5211.

North of Cazadero is Fort Ross Road, which meets Highway 1 near Fort Ross State Historic Park. A second road, King Ridge Road, zigzags through the backcountry to Hauser Bridge Road, near the Kruse Rhododendron State Reserve. Both are rough roads, not much improved since the 1870s, when the Fort Ross stagecoach—plagued

by highwayman Black Bart—took this route to Guerneville. One day the stage arrived, minus $300 and bearing
this note from Black Bart:

> *I've labored long and hard for bread,*
> *For honor and for riches*
> *But on my corns too long you've tread,*
> *You fine-haired sons of bitches*
> —Black Bart

Black Bart continued his robberies across the state,
once telling a frightened female stagecoach passenger, "I
never rob passengers, Ma'am, only Wells Fargo." The
gentleman bandit, when corralled, was unmasked as
Charles Bolton, established San Francisco bon vivant who
had once been a Wells Fargo clerk.

Duncans Mills

The quickest way to the coast is back on Highway
116, following the winding River. Stop for a while
in Duncans Mills, a resurrected logging town and
stagestop.

Alexander and Samuel Duncan, two Irish Presbyterian
brothers, began one of the county's first lumber mills
along the coast at today's Bridgehaven, later moving the
mill upriver on a raft to meet the narrow-gauge railroad in
1877. Duncans Mills grew into an important sawmill
camp; her railroad business was second only to Santa
Rosa's. The trains stopped running in 1935, but the old
depot remains, restored and used as a museum and campground office.

Most of the town's surviving buildings have been
restored. The DeCarly Store, built in 1880, withstood the
1906 earthquake. Other equally old edifices house shops
such as Christopher Queen (wildlife prints), Pig Alley
(collectibles), and Anemone Culinary (kitchenware). The

Cheese Merchant dishes out deli delights and homemade specialties, while a good wine selection is found at the General Store.

Since nothing's far from anything else in Duncans Mills, you'll spot the Blue Heron Restaurant right off. The Blue Heron is well known for its vegetarian dishes, fish and chicken, and Sunday brunch, topped off with jazz or blue-grass, good listening from the bar.

Duncans Mills has two campgrounds, Duncans Mills Campground and the Casini Ranch Family Campground. The first, headquartered in the Duncans Mills Depot, is ideal for group camping. It has over a hundred campsites for campers, trailers, and tents, as well as canoe rentals. There's even a private redwood forest hiking trail; 865-2573.

Casini Ranch Family Campground, across the River off Moscow Road, offers 120 acres with a mile of river frontage complete with campsites for RVs, pickup campers, tents, and trailers. Also available here are a boat ramp, boat and canoe rentals, fishing and camping supplies, swimming, and fishing holes for steelhead, shad, black bass, stripers, silver salmon, trout, and catfish; 865-2255.

In corrals on the side of Highway 116, you'll notice a large string of horses. Clan Parmeter Livery Stable rents horses, has guided trail rides, and also arranges group rides with local summer camps. Write Clan Parmeter, P.O. Box 181, Cazadero, CA 95421, or call 865-9982 or 632-5602.

From Duncans Mills, it is about a five-mile drive to the coast. The road leaves the shady redwood forest and winds through open, grassy hills dotted with grazing sheep. As you near the coast, the air becomes crisp and cool, and fog is often pushed inland by the ocean-born winds. Just as the ocean comes into view, Highway 116 meets Route 1, the coastal highway. The tiny hamlet of Bridgehaven lies on the south side of the bridge that crosses the river here. This was the site of the original Duncan brothers' mill. Travelers wanting to go to Bodega Bay will cross the bridge, while motorists heading north will follow Route 1 to the nearby town of Jenner, a mile to the north.

At Jenner, the Russian River finally ends its journey, flowing into the Pacific Ocean. During the flood season, the river mouth frequently is closed by silt and has to be reopened by bulldozer. At the mouth of the Russian River is Penny Island, a good fishing spot for steelhead and salmon. Legend has it that Penny Island was once inhabited by a hermit, whose beautiful singing could be heard across the river on clear nights.

Redwood Empire Association

The Sonoma Coast

7

Wild and Rugged Shore

Stand on a bluff in the silence following a Pacific winter storm and gaze out to sea for a glimpse of a migrating whale. Dive into the frigid ocean to dislodge an abalone, or cast a line into the water and reel in a red snapper or lingcod. Run barefoot along a white sandy beach, or hike in a forest of redwood trees and blooming rhododendrons. Barbecue your ocean catch in a fire ring at the beach, or devour crab and salmon, with sips of Sonoma County wine, in a seaside restaurant. Spend the night in a cliff-hanging inn with the sound of the surf beneath you. The Sonoma Coast means many places, many moods.

The wild, uncluttered Sonoma Coast is a place where the land seems at war with the sea, where waves and wind have chiseled the earth into small coves, pocket beaches, steep cliffs, and tiny islands known as sea stacks. Earthquakes have also helped shape this coastline; the notorious San Andreas Fault cuts beneath Bodega Harbor, runs out to sea, and returns landward near the historic Russian enclave called Fort Ross.

The sixty-two miles of the Sonoma Coast remain as one of California's few undeveloped coastal regions, but its beaches, parks, and seaside villages can all be reached via Coast Highway 1. On the southern Sonoma Coast is the

New England-like fishing village of Bodega Bay; between
here and the little town of Jenner are a dozen secluded
beaches composing the Sonoma Coast State Beach. The
treeless, grassy hills extending inland provide excellent
pastureland for cattle and for tall, shaggy sheep of the
Romney strain.

From the mouth of the Russian River at Jenner to Fort
Ross, Highway 1 follows the coastline, clinging to steep
cliffs that seem to plunge straight into the sea, while
inland, the back roads in the Mendocino highlands offer
some of the coast's best vistas. The coast north of Fort
Ross to the Gualala River on the county border is marked
with tiny coves so popular with abalone divers that this
stretch is often called the abalone coast. This rugged,
windswept shoreline resembles the fierceness of Cornwall
or the Gaspe Coast of Maritime Canada, but it's called the
"banana belt" because it has fewer foggy days than the rest
of the north coast.

The Pacific waters along the Sonoma Coast rank
among the coldest outside of the Arctic. The earth's rota-
tion and strong northwest winds brush aside sun-warmed
surface waters to let water ten to fifteen degrees cooler
upwell to the surface, chilling the ocean's temperature to
as low as 50 degrees Fahrenheit. These subsurface waters
teem with minerals, nutrients to the sea creatures upon
which king and silver salmon, steelhead trout, rockfish,
Dungeness crabs, seals, and gray whales feast. The cold
upwelling waters also create coastal fogs, forming an offshore fog bank during summer months that moves inland
at night, only to be burned away by the midday sun.

Commercial and sport fishermen find the waters off the
Sonoma Coast prolific. Bodega Bay commercial fishermen
use trolling boats, called trollers, to catch salmon between
the Golden Gate and Crescent City, while boats labeled
draggers use nets to catch bottom fish, including over fifty
varieties of rockfish. All bottom fish caught in these waters
are edible.

Shellfish lovers are in luck along the Sonoma Coast:
there are abalone, gaper and Washington clams, mussels,

rock crab, and Dungeness crab, the famous crab of "walk-away" cocktails sold at San Francisco's Fisherman's Wharf. Dungeness crabs are ocean bottom dwellers and are caught commercially with crab pots lowered into the sea.

Bird-watchers find the coast alive with shorebirds, waterfowl, and land birds. The Madrone Audubon Society focuses its annual bird count, held on December 28, in western Sonoma County, including Bodega Bay and the Sonoma Coast up to Jenner. The 1980 census found 187 bird species living in the region.

Centuries ago, the peoples of the Western Coastal Miwok, the Southwestern Pomo and the Southern Pomo tribes fished these waters and hunted seabirds in the marshlands around Bodega Bay. Their first contact with Europeans occurred when England's Sir Francis Drake sailed along this coast in 1579, followed by Spanish explorer Sebastian Vizcaino in 1602. Juan Francisco de la Bodega y Cuadra arrived here in 1775 and anchored in the bay now named for him, Bodega.

In the early 1800s, Russian fur traders from Alaska, pursuing the sea otter herds, explored the Sonoma Coast for permanent settlements. They founded Fort Ross in 1812 and established ranches at Bodega and Bodega Bay. The Russians remained for three decades, until the near extinction of the sea otter and poor crop yields forced their retreat to Alaska.

Mexican attempts to control this area came only after the Russians had gone. In 1844, Capt. Stephen Smith, a native of Maryland, was granted the 35,000-acre Rancho Bodega, which stretched from the present-day Marin County line to the southern bank of the Russian River and included one-third of the Sonoma Coast. Smith's brother-in-law, Manuel Torres, obtained Rancho Muniz, which covered much of the Sonoma coastline north of the Russian River. Captain Smith transformed the area into a prosperous agricultural and shipping region when he imported California's first steam-operated sawmill to his Bodega home and constructed a gristmill nearby. New England and Irish settlers raised "Bodega red" potatoes

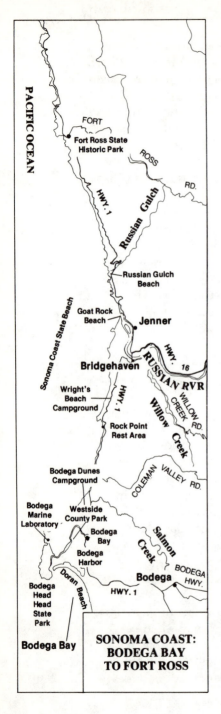

PACIFIC OCEAN

FORT
● Fort Ross State
Historic Park

ROSS

RD.

Russian Gulch

HWY. 1

Russian Gulch
Beach

Goat Rock
Beach

● **Jenner**

Sonoma Coast State Beach

Bridgehaven

HWY. 1

RUSSIAN RVR

HWY. 16

WILLOW

CREEK

RD.

Willow Creek

Wright's
Beach
Campground

Rock Point
Rest Area

Bodega Dunes
Campground

COLEMAN VALLEY RD.

Bodega
Marine
Laboratory

Westside
County Park

● Bodega
Bay

Bodega
Harbor

Salmon Creek

Bodega

BODEGA

HWY.

Bodega
Head
Head
State
Park

Doran Beach

HWY. 1

Bodega Bay

**SONOMA COAST:
BODEGA BAY
TO FORT ROSS**

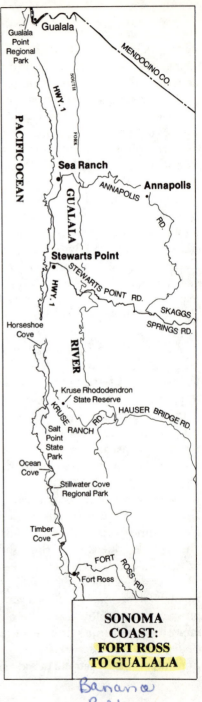

Gualala
Point
Regional
Park

Gualala

MENDOCINO CO.

HWY. 1

SOUTH FORK

PACIFIC OCEAN

Sea Ranch

GUALALA

ANNAPOLIS

Annapolis

RD.

Stewarts Point

HWY. 1

STEWARTS POINT RD.

SKAGGS

SPRINGS RD.

Horseshoe
Cove

RIVER

Kruse Rhododendron
State Reserve

KRUSE

HAUSER BRIDGE RD.

RANCH

RD.

Salt
Point
State
Park

Ocean
Cove

Stillwater Cove
Regional Park

Timber
Cove

FORT

ROSS

RD.

● Fort Ross

**SONOMA
COAST:
FORT ROSS
TO GUALALA**

Banana
Belt

here, and Swiss-Italian dairymen made cheese; these products were shipped from Bodega Bay to San Francisco.

Before the railroad reached the redwood groves, timber was shipped aboard lumber schooners that docked in the tiny coves of the Sonoma Coast called "doghole" ports. (It was said that "only a dog could turn around in them.") Villages like Stewarts Point and Gualala grew up around the lumber mills and doghole ports, then almost became ghost towns when lumber began to be shipped by rail. The Sonoma Coast slumbered, its trade limited by its sea access, until Highway 1 reached the area in the 1920s.

The opening of Highway 1 brought fishermen and vacationers to the coast, and later second-home developments were started at Bodega Bay, Carmet, and Sea Ranch. But in the 1980s, sections of the Sonoma Coast remain scarcely more populated than when Miwok villagers and Russian trappers lived here. The area's recent history has been riddled with controversies, all centered on protecting the area's unspoiled beauty: an epic battle to halt construction of a nuclear power plant on Bodega Head, a prolonged struggle between Sea Ranch homeowners and the state Coastal Commission over development and public access to the sea, and a yet unresolved conflict over offshore oil drilling.

Today's visitors to the Sonoma Coast can enjoy a multitude of activities—fishing, hiking, beachcombing, clamming, bird-watching, camping, picnicking, or whale-watching. Swimming is not advised, however; strong rip currents and cold water temperatures make even walking in shallow water dangerous. Much of the lower two-thirds of the Sonoma Coast is held by the state or the county as natural and historic parks, but the coast north of Salt Point State Park is mostly private land; owners sometimes allow use of their land, with payment of a trespasser fee. The major coast towns—Bodega Bay, Jenner, and Gualala —are your best spots for dining, lodging, shopping, and buying gas. Highway 1, which runs the entire length of the Sonoma Coast, is scenic, but be prepared for slow travel time, as the road is windy and there are few places to pass.

Bodega

The towns of Bodega and Bodega Bay are frequently confused, since both were settings for the 1962 filming of Alfred Hitchcock's thriller, *The Birds.* Bodega lies five miles inland from the bay and harbor of the same name. To reach the towns, take Highway 1 north out of Marin County, or Petaluma/Valley Ford Road west from Petaluma. The hamlet of Valley Ford lies a mile west of where Highway 1 joins Petaluma/Valley Ford Road. If you're planning a fishing or picnicking trip to the coast, you can stop at the Happy Hooker in Valley Ford for bait and tackle, marine and camping supplies, deli items, beer, and wine. They are open daily 6 to 6.

Three miles beyond Valley Ford is a right-hand cutoff onto Bodega Highway; a quarter-mile drive takes you to a pleasant valley and the village of Bodega. Bodega's entire business district can be taken in with a single glance: a general store, a garage, an antique store, a doll museum within a Victorian home, a church, and the old Potter School, now a restaurant and shops. Miwok Indians, Russians, and Mexicans all lived in the vicinity, but the village's structures date from California's pioneer American days. The town was originally known as Smith's Rancho, after its founding father, Capt. Stephen Smith, who arrived here in 1843 with his fourteen-year-old Peruvian bride and the state's first steam-powered sawmill. The name was soon changed to Bodega.

Smith began the coastal lumber trade by shipping redwood planks to San Francisco. Previously, Bay Area communities had imported lumber from Hawaii. His grandson, Capt. William Smith, started Sonoma's commercial fishing industry with a small sailboat based at Bodega Bay.

Bodega blossomed as a major trade center, funneling the goods shipped into Bodega Bay on to the inland towns of Sebastopol and Petaluma. The region's chief products were the "Bodega red" potato, well known for its bright maroon coat and fine flavor, and milk and cheese. In 1870, John Genazzi, a Swiss-Italian from Canton Ticino, started a successful dairy business in Bodega and soon attracted thousands of his countrymen to settle in southern Sonoma and northern Marin counties to create much of the North Bay's present-day dairy industry. Bodega's growth came to a halt after the narrow-gauge railroad bypassed the village in favor of Valley Ford, Freestone, and Occidental.

Today you can explore the tiny village and sample the full flavor of Bodega's history. Start at the white frame, much photographed church of St. Teresa of Avila. St. Teresa's was commissioned by Jasper O'Farrell, who hired New England ships' carpenters to build the church in 1859. Today it is Sonoma County's oldest continuously active Catholic church and has been designated a state historical landmark.

A stone's throw from the church lies the Potter School (1873); *sans* students today, it is a top spot for dining and shopping. On the ground floor is the Bodega Gallery Restaurant, where the menu is chalked on the blackboard; the rote includes lamb, veal, beef, and seafood. Reservations requested, 876-3257. On the same floor is the Greenery, a classroom stuffed with cacti, spider plants, plus many unusual plant species. Owners Chuck Stasek and Bob Hornback have extensive botanical backgrounds, and Hornback is considered one of the best authorities on Luther Burbank's plant studies. Phone 876-3497. Upstairs, Karel's Quilts has just what you need for cold coastal nights. The shop features locally sewn quilts, plus new and antique quilts from such spots as Pennsylvania's Amish country. The restaurant and shops are all open Thursday through Sunday.

Other historical spots-cum-businesses include Charlene's Yesterday Museum on Bodega Highway. This century-old Victorian home and its barn are filled with dolls, antiques, and memorabilia gathered worldwide. Charlene's is open Wednesday through Sunday, 11-5. Admission for adults is 75 cents; children, 25 cents. Phone 876-3282. Nearby is the Wooden Duck Antique Shop,

housing eighteenth- and nineteenth-century antiques;
open weekends. McCaughey's Store, next to the gas
station, dates from 1854 and is the oldest continuing
market in the county.

If you're in Bodega in mid-August, don't miss the Big
Event Old Time Country Fair. The shebang is a fund
raiser for the Bodega Volunteer Fire Department, a weekend full of fun that includes volleyball games, square
dances, an auction of homemade lunches, and a barbecue
(adults $4, children $2).

Picnickers will find an ideal spot two miles east of
Bodega on Bodega Highway, at the Watson School Wayside Park. The one-room schoolhouse went up in 1856; it's
now a county-run park open daily from sunrise until sunset. To get to Bodega Bay from here, retrace your steps
back to Highway 1 and proceed through the grassy coastal
hills until the bay comes into view.

Bodega Bay

The fishing and ranching village of Bodega Bay lies
perched on the bottom slopes of Mount Roscoe,
just where it meets Bodega Harbor. The harbor is
surrounded by a clawlike thrust of land jutting into the
Pacific, with Bodega Head facing the ocean and Doran
Beach fronting the bay.

Bodega Harbor's salt marshes, tidal flats, and shores
support an amazing diversity of wildlife—seventy-seven
kinds of birds, including great blue herons, snowy egrets,
and brown pelicans, at least seventy-five varieties of fish,
fourteen shrimp species, twenty-two crab varieties, and
three dozen types of clams. During October and November, flocks of orange and black Monarch butterflies
migrate to Bodega Bay.

The climate is changeable here—foggy, sunny, windy—
but temperatures vary less than at inland locales. Bodega
Bay is generally cool and foggy in summer, with daily afternoon breezes in spring and early summer. Bright, warm,

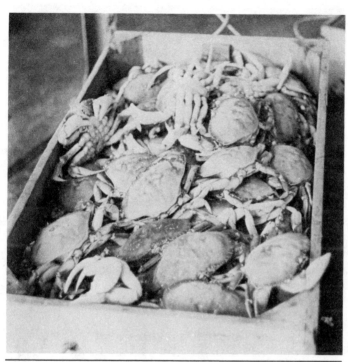

Dungeness crabs at Bodega Bay. (Don Edwards)

sunny days occur from September through November, while winter brings storms and rain, succeeded by clear, calm days. Bodega Bay is especially popular during summer months when visitors come to the coast to escape hot inland areas.

The village of Bodega Bay straddles Highway 1. At the water's edge are marinas filled with single-masted commercial fishing boats; perched on the hills above the harbor are stalwart frame homes. The village is a center for sportfishing, but if you're not a fisherman, you can dig clams at a nearby beach, feast on seafood, or play golf. Be sure to also take a look around the village.

Your first in-town stop should be the Bodega Bay Chamber of Commerce office, which is in the Gene Walker Realty building, 913 Highway 1, 875-3422. Here you'll find area maps and information.

Next, check out the Tides Resort, a Highway 1 landmark with its bright orange roof. The wharf at this restaurant/motel/fishing complex, a docking area for commercial fishermen, is also the spot where you can board a party boat for deep-sea fishing (see details in the Fishing section). Even if you never leave land, stroll around the Tides Wharf; in crabbing season it's lined with wire pots filled with live, freshly caught crabs. You can fish for free off the wharf pier or buy marine fuel and ice for your own boat. Stop in at the wharf store to buy fresh fish and shellfish in season, or to buy or rent tackle and bait.

The Tides Restaurant gives you harborside seats for drinking and dining. It's open for breakfast, lunch, and dinner. The Tides Treasure Chest sells gifts and souvenirs, but you can't buy the enormous whalebones outside the gift shop door. If you want to sack out, the Tides Motel has fourteen rooms, some with kitchenettes, and one cottage. The Tides Wharf number is 875-3595; restaurant and motel number is 875-3553.

South of the Tides Resort is Lucas Wharf, 595 Highway 1, which sells fresh fish, deli items and sandwiches to go, groceries, beer, and wine; open daily. Nearby, on Highway 1, is the Bodega Bay Lodge, 875-3525, with spacious rooms overlooking the harbor, complete with either fireplaces or kitchenettes.

The Bodega Bay Lodge frequently offers an overnight golf package, since the Bodega Harbour Golf Links borders the motel. This public nine-hole course, designed by Robert Trent Jones, is built on marshland and dunes, with views of the Pacific Ocean. Weekday green fees are $5 and $7.50 for nine and eighteen holes, respectively; weekend fees are $7.50 and $10. Bodega Harbour Golf Links, 21301 Heron Drive, 875-3538, is found in the exclusive Bodega Harbour residential community. A number of these refined redwood homes, some with hot tubs and saunas, can be rented for a week or weekend through local realtors listed in the Visitors Services section.

Bodega Bay's other restaurants and lodging are located north of the Tides Resort on Highway 1. Bernardo's Seafarer Inn is both a restaurant and a deli, while Russo's specializes in Italian food. The tiny Crab Pot sells fresh fish and crab in season, smoked fish, clams, lobster, prawns, and scallops. The Fisherman's Cafe, 1410 Bay Flat Road off Highway 1, serves hearty clam chowder, homemade pies, plus breakfast starting at six each morning.

Near Russo's and the Crab Pot, one-half block west of Highway 1 at 1588 Eastshore Drive, is the Bay Arts Gallery, a collection of paintings, antiques, pottery, jewelry, and home accessories, many from the hands of North Coast artisans. The gallery features paintings of the late Maurice Logan, who did many of the early covers for *Sunset* magazine. Open 11-5 every day except Tuesday; 875-3875.

A place to get away from it all, western style, is the Chanslor Ranch, a working cattle ranch two miles north of Bodega Bay on Highway 1. Bonnie and Bob Hardenbrook, East Bay expatriates who own this 705-acre spread, welcome singles, couples, and families in their varied accommodations for twenty-four guests. The Hardenbrooks dish up gargantuan breakfasts and family-style dinners which can be worked off by jaunts through the coastal hills on one of their Morgan horses. Lodging includes the ranchhouse and the more informal bunkhouse—great for families. Definitely call ahead, 875-3386. Nonguests can rent a horse, $7 first hour, $6 thereafter. You can board your own horse for $5 per day.

Doran Beach

The sand spit on the south edge of Bodega Harbor is Doran Beach, a good place for overnight camping or for just a day on the beach. You can fish off the rock jetty without a fishing license, or dig for gaper and Washington clams off the east bank of the spit. Divers can use the north end of the beach along the rock jetty. You can also visit the U.S. Coast Guard Station located here.

Take Doran Beach Road off Highway 1 near the Bodega Bay Lodge. Entrance fee to Doran County Park is

$2 for a single vehicle; 50 cents per person in a bus (over eight people); or get in free if you walk, ride a bike, or have a Golden Year Pass. The park has a boat-launching facility and 139 campsites—both drive-in and walk-in, plus some for groups—with rest rooms, showers, trailer sanitation facilities, and a fish cleaning station. Camping fees: overnight campsite, $5 Sonoma County resident, $6 out-of-county resident; extra vehicle $3; walk-in or bike $1 per night; dogs $1 per night; wood $2 per bundle. No reservations; first come, first served. Doran County Park is open all year. Call ahead for camping availability, tides, and weather; 875-3540.

The U.S. Coast Guard Station, located within Doran County Park, is open to visitors Saturday and Sunday, 1-4, for a fifteen-minute tour of the Coast Guard search-and-rescue station and its lifeboats, including the eighty-two-foot *Port Chico*. School groups should call two weeks in advance, 875-3596.

Bodega Head

Bodega Head, a windswept granite peninsula, is a geological cousin of Point Reyes and the Farallon Islands, for these chunks of land lie west of the San Andreas Fault and are unrelated to the rocks inland. Geologists believe Bodega Head was once located next to the Tehachapi Mountains, 300 miles south of Sonoma County. Like Point Reyes, Bodega Head has crept northward, sometimes violently, along the earthquake-prone faultline.

In 1958, Pacific Gas and Electric announced its plans to build a nuclear power plant almost directly over the San Andreas Fault line on Bodega Head. The indomitable Rose Gaffney, Polish-born property owner of the plant site, led a decade-long but successful struggle to stop construction, taking on a host of corporate and public officials. Today the only evidence of the unbuilt power plant is "The Hole in the Head," a 142-foot water-filled pit now home to wild ducks. Gaffney's collection of Indian stone tools, arrowheads, and relics (many from Bodega Head) is now part of the Indian Artifact Museum at Sebastiani Vineyards in Sonoma.

The roads out Bodega Head take you past private marinas, a county park, the University of California's Bodega Marine Laboratory, and Bodega Head State Park at the end of the peninsula. Take Bay Flat Road off Highway 1 to reach Bodega Head.

The first of two marinas is Masons Marina, 1820 Westshore Road, off Bay Flat Road, with 115 berths, a hoist, docks, fuel, and marine supplies. Phone 875-3811. Farther on is Porto Bodega, 1500 Bay Flat Road, with 95 berths, a boat dock and launch, bait and tackle, plus accommodations (with electric and water hookups) for thirty-one trailers. Phone 875-3550.

Westside County Park, on Bay Flat Road, features a no-fee boat-launching ramp, a day-use boating area, and forty-seven vehicle campsites with rest rooms, showers, and trailer sanitation facilities, plus picnic tables. This park is ideal for fishing and clamming. It's open year-round. Fees: $2 single vehicle; overnight campsite, $5 county residents, $6 non-county resident; walk-in or bike $1 per night. Call 875-3540.

Every April, the Bodega Bay Fisherman's Festival takes place with a weekend of activities centered at Westside County Park, including the blessing of the colorfully decorated fishing fleet by local clergymen, a bathtub race, art show, live entertainment, food, and drink. Call the Bodega Bay Chamber of Commerce for dates, 875-3422.

The Bodega Marine Laboratory, off Westside Road (follow signs off Highway 1), welcomes visitors between 2 and 4 P.M. on Fridays for tours of the lab. This isn't exactly the Steinhart Aquarium; what you'll see is a film, small research aquariums, and lobsters being raised for possible commercial use. In this private research facility, scientists study aquaculture (food production from the sea) as well as ocean pollution and the decline of crab catches. Here, Dr. Robert Risebrough discovered and exposed the chemical DDT as the culprit in the diminishing brown pelican population. Call 875-2211 for information on the no-fee tours.

Westside Road leads to the end of the peninsula and Bodega Head State Park, an exposed, rocky, windy place. Hiking trails fan out from the centralized parking lot. Bodega Head gives tantalizing views of the Sonoma and Marin coastlines and is a popular whale-watching spot during the annual winter migrations. Scuba divers hike down to sheltered beaches for excellent diving when the weather is calm. Sure-footed anglers cast for perch and kelp greenling along the rocky shore. Bodega Head State Park is a day-use park only.

Fishing on the Coast

The village of Bodega Bay is the busiest harbor between San Francisco and Fort Bragg, the Pacific Coast's second largest salmon fishery and a prime crabbing area. Commercial and sport fishermen also catch prodigious numbers of the many varieties of rockfish, and the shores yield enough species of shellfish to make delicious stews.

King and silver salmon flourish in the abundant feeding grounds around the drowned mountains which peak as the Farallon Islands. Their rich diet of high iodine shrimp gives a striking pink color to the salmon's meat. Salmon migrate from the sea up fresh water creeks to spawn, then die, leaving the hatchlings to find their own way back to the ocean. The average netted salmon weighs about ten pounds, and they are delicious grilled, baked, or smoked. Salmon season is normally from April 15 to September 15.

Rockfish, also called Pacific snapper, come in all colors and can weigh up to thirty pounds. Among the best for eating are the orange, the yellowtail, the Bocaccio, and the red; the fish have a firm, white flesh that can be broiled, baked, fried, poached, barbecued, or used in soups and stews.

Sportfishing party boats leave the Tides Wharf all year long for bottom fishing; some boats offer salmon trolling in season or half-day whale-watching voyages in winter. Individual rates on all boats are the same: $25 for bottom fishing, $30 for salmon fishing, $3 rod and reel rental aboard the boat. Anglers must furnish their own hooks, sinkers, and bait (squid, sardines, or shrimp). These can be purchased at the Tides Wharf Bait and Tackle Shop. You'll need a short rod, star drag reel, and plenty of terminal tackle (hooks, sinkers, bait) to rig to your thirty- or forty-pound test line. A California sportfishing license is required; you can buy it at the Bait and Tackle Shop before boarding.

Party boats leave the Tides Wharf at 7 A.M. and return at 2:30 P.M. The Pacific can be rough, so remember your seasickness pills and dress warmly. Bottom fishing is normally done in waters forty to fifty feet deep. Your catch can be cleaned and filleted for a fee at the Tides Wharf after docking. Most boats have room for forty people; reservations are required with deposit. Call 875-3595 for reservations, or write to the Tides Wharf, P.O. Box 547, Bodega Bay, CA 94923.

If you'd rather stay on land, you can either surf fish or fish from the rocks and jetties just about anywhere up and down the Sonoma Coast. (Beware of "sleeper" waves that can pull fishermen out to sea.) All kinds of bottom fish are reeled in. In the summer, when the foot-long smelt come to spawn in the inland streams, fishermen simply scoop them up with an A-frame net that resembles the "squaw net" used by the Miwok Indians centuries ago. Smelt can be dipped in batter and pan-fried like trout.

Another type of fishing is done in the intertidal areas with a rig called a "poke pole." A poke pole is fashioned from a stout pole (such as bamboo), rigged with a heavy, looped wire, a fishing line, and a #4 or #6 snelled hook. Bait the hook with squid, shrimp, or shellfish guts and lower it into tidepools and rock crevices where lingcod, cabezon, striped perch, rockfish, greenlings, and eellike blennies lurk. You may take ten fish of any one species or twenty in combination of species.

The nooks and crannies of Bodega Bay and the Sonoma Coast are excellent places to gather sea creatures for your cioppino or bouillabaisse pot. In the intertidal zone, between low and high tide, live mussels, cockles, and rock crabs. You can round out your stew with Washington clams from Bodega Harbor, and horseneck and geoduck clams from Bodega Bay and nearby Tomales Bay. Mussels can't be taken from state beaches.

Sturdy boots are needed when poke pole fishing, gathering mussels from rocks, or clam digging. Abalone divers in Bodega Bay should be aware that they are diving in one of the favorite habitats of the great white shark.

Another hazard to be aware of is the "red tide." Mussels and Washington clams are especially vulnerable to this form of plankton called *gonyaulax catanella,* which causes paralytic shellfish poisoning in humans. The poisoning can be fatal, so don't harvest mussels or Washington clams between May 1 and October 31. Other sea creatures are unaffected by the "red tide," and commercially harvested shellfish are safe to eat.

The rich fishing grounds around Bodega Bay are threatened by efforts of oil companies to obtain offshore oil drilling rights. If allowed to proceed, both the inevitable leakage and a potential oil spill disaster could endanger the abundant sea life found here. In the fall of 1980, former President Jimmy Carter's Interior Secretary Cecil Andrus scrapped plans to lease offshore sites to the oil companies, but these plans were revived by President Ronald Reagan's Interior Secretary James Watt. The House of Representatives voted in August of 1981 to prohibit Watt from using Interior Department funds to proceed with the sale of offshore tracts to oil companies, but Watt vowed to offer the Bodega Bay tract for sale again in 1983. Local conservationist groups have joined commercial and recreational fishermen and concerned citizens in the fight against oil drilling.

Whale-Watching

The California gray whale, the most commonly seen whale along the California coast, makes a lengthy migration between its summer feeding grounds in the Bering Sea and its winter breeding grounds along Baja California, passing south along the Sonoma Coast from November to February, then north in the spring. The 13,000-mile round trip, longest migration of any mammal, brings the whales within about one-half mile of shore. The whales swim in small groups, traveling about four knots per hour. Scientists believe the shore-hugging whales navigate by using such points of land as Bodega Head.

Big as a Greyhound bus, the gray whale is toothless, using its baleen or whalebone to scoop up crustaceans, crabs, and other small organisms from the sea floor. The baleen filters seawater and mud, allowing only tiny sea life down the whale's grapefruit-sized throat.

In Baja California, at such spots as Scammon's Lagoon, the whales bear their young. Infant whales look like wrinkled pickles at birth but are twenty feet long by the time they accompany their mothers past the Sonoma Coast on the trip north.

During the nineteenth century, New England whaler Charles Melville Scammon discovered both the lagoon that bears his name and a method of killing the gray whales with a bomb gun. Scammon retired to a farm near Sebastopol, wrote a classic literary book about the grays, and became an early-day "save the whales" advocate. In 1938, an international treaty gave the gray whales complete protection. Blue whales (largest of all whales), humpback whales, minke whales, and a variety of dolphins and porpoises also visit the Sonoma shoreline.

Bodega Head State Park, Salt Point State Park, and the bluffs of the Sonoma Coast State Beach are the best land sites for viewing the grays. California State Park rangers are at Bodega Head on winter weekends between 1 and

3 P.M. to talk about whales, and with a two-day notice the state Park and Recreation Department will provide a whale expert for group tours. Call 865-2391 or 875-3483. Salt Point rangers are available to talk about whales on winter weekends starting at 10:30 A.M. The Sierra Club also offers whale-watching trips from Bodega Head; write to Redwood Chapter, Sierra Club, P.O. Box 466, Santa Rosa, CA 95402. For either land or sea whale-watching, wear warm clothing, sturdy boots, and bring your camera and binoculars.

To see the whales at sea, you can plunk down $20 per person and climb aboard the sixty-five-foot *Mary Jane*, courtesy of the Marine Mammal Fund of San Francisco. The boat leaves the Tides Wharf for half-day trips, mornings and afternoons on weekends. Call (415) 664-6665 for information and reservations, or write the Marine Mammal Fund, P.O. Box 16041, San Francisco, CA 94116.

Sonoma Coast State Beach

The ten-mile stretch of Highway 1 between the village of Bodega Bay and the hamlet of Bridgehaven on the Russian River's south side takes you past thirteen state-owned beaches collectively called Sonoma Coast State Beach. This park begins at Mussel Point on Bodega Head, encompasses the mouth of the Russian River, and ends north of Jenner at Russian Gulch Creek.

The secluded, sandy beaches lie hidden from the road by steep bluffs, but once you've reached the sheltered beach coves, you'll enjoy windswept headlands, water-carved arches and sea stacks, plus a riotous variety of marine life and seabirds. These beaches are ideal for fishing, beachcombing, picnicking, beach parties, diving, hiking, and wading, but the chilly waters are unsafe for swimming due to a strong undertow, rip currents, and sleeper waves. There are no lifeguards on the beaches.

Each beach has parking and a path leading to it; many

Sonoma Coast State Beach. (Redwood Empire Association)

have rest rooms. Duncan's Landing, Portuguese Beach, Schoolhouse Beach, Carmet Beach, and Coleman Beach all have especially steep trails. Often foggy and windy in summer, these beaches can be warm and sunny in winter. Dress warmly and remember you can get sunburned even on overcast days.

Beach bluffs, dunes, and slopes support a profuse variety of salt and fresh water vegetation such as pickle-weed and salt marsh daisies. In spring, lupine, Indian paintbrush, sea figs, western iris, and wild strawberries bloom. Shorebirds, waterfowl, and land birds commingle along the shores, while the ocean waters and coastal streams teem with rockfish, perch, salmon, steelhead, and smelt for eager surf and poke pole fishermen. Clams and abalone can be taken in state park waters and beaches, but not mussels or sea urchins. Be sure to have your current sportfishing license.

Beach headquarters are at Salmon Creek, one and a half miles north of Bodega Bay on Highway 1. You can get maps and information at the Salmon Creek Ranger Station, and park rangers offer nature and whale-watching walks, plus campfire talks. Interested groups should call ahead, 875-3483.

The Sonoma Coast State Beach contains two campgrounds: Bodega Dunes, south of the ranger station; and Wright's Beach Campground, halfway between Bodega Bay and Jenner on Highway 1. Bodega Dunes (formerly Cypress Dunes) is a secluded campground, one-half mile north of Bodega Bay, popular with hikers and equestrians. The campground has ninety-eight campsites, a campfire center, picnic tables, showers, and a trailer sanitation station.

Wright's Beach Campground features an expansive sandy beach that's popular with surf fishermen, seashell collectors, and divers. One of the few campgrounds right on the beach, it's fine in good weather but can be uncomfortable in windy weather. There are picnic tables and thirty campsites.

Fees for both campgrounds: $2 day-use fee; $5 per campsite per night (limit eight people per campsite), $2 second vehicle, $1.25 fuel, $1 dogs. Ticketron handles camping reservations; write Ticketron, P.O. Box 26430, San Francisco, CA 94126, or call (415) 495-4089. For local fishing regulations, call the state Fish and Game Department, 944-2443.

Both southern and northern accessways lead to Salmon Creek Beach, a large, well-used sandy beach and lagoon that draws salmon and steelhead fishermen in winter and smelt fishermen in summer. North of the beach headquarters lies Miwok Beach, followed by Coleman Beach (Coleman Valley Road leads inland to Occidental). Next lies Arched Rock Beach, then Carmet Beach and the summer home community of Carmet. Schoolhouse Beach is adjacent to Portuguese Beach, a sandy beach bordering rocky headlands, a good rockfish and surf fishing spot. Salmon Creek, Schoolhouse, and Portuguese beaches all have rest rooms; Schoolhouse and Portuguese also have rings for beach fires.

Gleason Beach, four miles north of Bodega Bay, has a state-maintained trail to the beach. All other trails lie on private land; don't trespass. Nearby Rock Point on a headland above the shoreline sports several picnic tables.

Duncan's Landing is the approximate midpoint between Bodega Bay and Jenner, interrupting the string of beaches along the coast. From 1862 until 1877, rocky Duncan's Landing and Cove was a doghole port for lumber schooners loading timber from the sawmills of Alexander and Samuel Duncan. The hand-forged iron rings once used to secure the doghole schooners can still be seen on the north side of the cove. When the railroad reached the Russian River, the Duncan brothers moved their mill by raft upstream from today's Bridgehaven to present Duncan Mills. Potatoes, butter, and produce were then shipped from the cove; later it served rumrunners during Prohibition. Today it is known as an excellent diving area.

278

In the last thirty years, over fifty shoreline-related drownings have occurred between Duncan's Landing and Goat Rock Beach, many happening at Death Rock. Unexpectedly large and powerful "sleeper" waves come quietly in and drag surf waders and beachcombers into the ocean. Heed the signs warning hikers and fishermen not to venture too near Death Rock's waters. In case of an emergency, call Goat Rock residence, 865-2457.

Diving and fishing improve near the mouth of the Russian River. Wright's Beach Campground lies past Duncan's Landing, followed by Shell Beach, a popular spot for rock fishermen and one of northern California's best sites for marine life study. Shell Beach's tidepools teem with jellyfish, snails, sea urchins, starfish, clams, scallops, squid, octopuses, abalone, mussels, sea anemones, and rock crabs. Many marine organisms will die if handled or moved; take pictures instead. Tidepool invertebrates are protected by state law, and only those species designated in the annual California sportfishing regulations may be taken.

Blind Beach and Goat Rock Beach form the southern lip of the mouth of the Russian River and can be reached by taking State Park Road off Highway 1. Blind Beach is a good smelt fishing spot. The first parking lot at Goat Rock Beach brings you to a mile-long sandy beach that draws steelhead fishermen in early winter. A second parking lot lies at the foot of Goat Rock, another good spot for shore fishing.

Harbor seals, as their name implies, love bays, harbors, and river mouths. Goat Rock Beach is a favorite "hauling out" spot for these mammals, who give birth here between March and June. Seal pups frequently appear abandoned, but their parents are usually fishing nearby. Beware: both pups and adult harbor seals can bite.

Rock Point near Gleason Beach is a roadside rest stop and picnic spot; Gleason, Wright's, Shell, and Goat Rock beaches all have rest rooms. Rings for beach fires are located at Wright's and Goat Rock beaches.

Jenner

ighway 116 joins Highway 1 on the north bank
of the Russian River, and a mile drive north
brings you to the coastal community of Jenner.
The town is named for Charles Jenner, who arrived in
1868; by tradition, Jenner was a literary man looking for
material for a book. The homes in this village cling to the
bluffs overlooking Penny Island, a popular steelhead
fishing spot.

Jenner is known for its restaurants, and the town also
has lodging, gift shops, and gas stations. Murphy's Jenner-
by-the-Sea Restaurant, 10400 Highway 1, specializes in
fresh local seafood, continental cuisine, cioppino, and
even Boston clam chowder, a reflection of Boston-born
Richard Murphy's Irish-Italian heritage. Murphy's is open
for lunch, dinner, and Sunday brunch, with live music
and dancing on weekends. Call 865-2377. Adjacent to the
restaurant is Murphy's Jenner Inn, with a variety of lodg-
ings from the quaint Crew's Quarters to the spacious
Taylor House. Same phone as restaurant.

River's End, Highway 1 in Jenner, is a dining, lodging,
and recreational complex owned by chef Wolfgang Gra-
matzki, a German who has prepared and catered meals for
the Emperor and Empress of Japan, Nelson Rockefeller,
and Henry Kissinger. You can dine on kedgerry (Oriental
seafood curry), coconut fried shrimp, or hasenpfeffer
(braised hare in spiced red wine sauce), or you can learn
how to make some of these dinner delights through Gra-
matzki's River's End School of Cooking. The course,
limited to twelve participants, is set up in a series of six
three-hour sessions or three six-hour sessions for $360.
Call 865-2484 or 869-3252, or write River's End School of
Cooking, Highway 1, Box 32, Jenner, CA 95450. River's
End Restaurant and Tavern hours vary summer and
winter; call 865-2484 for reservations. Open for dinner
and weekend brunches. River's End cabins overlook the

ocean, and other facilities include a day-use beach with lifeguard, a concrete boat launch ramp, fishing, and camping.

From Jenner to Russian Gulch is a 2.5-mile stretch of state-owned beaches that can be reached by steep trails down the eroding bluffs. The mouth of the Russian River is a favorite spot for jet skiers and hard-core wet-suited surfers. Russian Gulch is a good hiking, picnicking, and diving area, with a sandy beach reached by a path leading down from Highway 1. Near here, a high-living Cornishman, John Rule, built a sawmill and ranch but died before his home was completed. The house and outbuildings still stand, visible from Highway 1. Some say they're haunted by Rule's ghost.

The rugged Mendocino highlands that run north of the Russian River rise straight from the sea between Russian Gulch and Fort Ross State Historic Park. Highway 1 zigzags over the hills in a series of switchbacks that offer spectacular ocean views but call for attentive driving. A slower 7.5-mile alternate route is Meyers Grade Road to Fort Ross Road, which leads down to the park, or you can continue on via Seaview Road for seven miles to the old stage stop town of Plantation and down to Highway 1 via Kruse Ranch Road. Seaview Road follows Campmeeting Ridge, with vistas of the Mendocino highlands to the east and the Pacific to the west.

Eight miles north of Jenner on Highway 1 are three primitive campgrounds popular with abalone divers. The Pedotti Campgrounds, 18000 Highway 1, consist of two exposed shoreline areas for self-contained RVs. Pedotti Campground South offers access to a rocky beach, as does the main Pedotti Campground, which has pit toilets and picnic tables. Day-use is $3; camping is $5. No dogs allowed. Phone 847-3263. The Eckert Acquisition, partly within Fort Ross State Historic Park, has a campground with fire pits. From here, trails lead to a beach at Fort Ross and to Timber Gulch beach. Day-use fee is $3; camping is $5.

Fort Ross
State Historic Park

The weathered, wooden walls that visitors first see
when approaching Fort Ross State Historic Park
stand as starkly alone and isolated as in the days
when Russian trappers and explorers lived on this bluff
above the ever-windy sea. For three decades, the Russian
presence centered at this rectangular fort was so powerful
that the Mexican government sent soldiers, priests, and
settlers across the northern San Francisco Bay to check
them. An alarmed President James Monroe issued his
famous Doctrine partly as a warning to the czar to quit the
continent. But in the end the Russians left as quietly as
they first landed.

The Russian explorer Vitrus Bering, who laid claim to
Alaska, discovered the soft-furred sea otters in the sea that
now bears his name. Russian fur trappers stalked the otters
down the Pacific coastline to California, then returned to
tell of the fertile, frost-free land that could grow food for
their Alaskan colonies. In 1806, Count Nikolai Rezanov
sailed for Spanish Yerba Buena (San Francisco) to trade
furs for beef.

The youthful, dashing, sandy-haired Rezanov captured
the heart of fifteen-year-old Maria "Concha" Arguello,
daughter of the Presidio's commandant, and promised to
return for her. Rezanov died in Siberia on the return trip,
and Concha waited in vain for many years, learning of his
death decades later. Their love story fueled the pens of
novelist Gertrude Atherton and poet Bret Harte.

Russian adventurer Ivan Kuskov returned, used
Bodega Bay as a base to scout the Sonoma Coast for a
permanent settlement, and, on a 110-foot-high bluff overlooking two coves, founded Fort Ross (from the archaic
word for Russia, *Rosiya*) in 1812.

The Russian and Aleut settlers, acting not under the

czar's orders but as employees of the Russian-American
Fur Company, constructed a rectangular redwood fort
with fourteen-foot-high walls, two blockhouses, a chapel, a
commandant's house (Rotchev House), a fur barn, a
citadel (Kuskov House), employees' barracks, and a
kitchen. Today's visitors can see the fort walls, blockhouses, commandant's house, chapel, plus a museum.
Some structures are original; others are restorations, with
more to be constructed.

The Aleuts hunted sea otters in kayaklike *baidarkas*,
while Russian settlers grew grain, planted apples (possibly
Gravensteins among them), and traded—first with the
Spanish, then with their successors, the Mexicans. During
one of the Russian-Mexican meetings, Mariano Vallejo's
protege, Chief Solano of the Suisun Indians, attempted to
kidnap the beautiful Princess Elena Garagina, wife of the
fort's commander.

Russian scientists used Fort Ross as a base for exploring
northern California. One of these men, Johan F. Esch-
scholtz, collected specimens of the California poppy and
named it for himself, *Eschscholtzia Californica.*

By 1841, the otters had been hunted to near extinction,
and the Russians—faced with mounting crop failures—
departed, selling the property to a feisty Swiss-German
buyer from the Sacramento Valley named John Sutter. He
removed most of the fort's assets. One of the few remaining
Russian hunters, Finnish sea captain Gustave Nybom
(Niebaum), went inland to the Napa Valley to start the
Inglenook Winery.

In 1873, Ohio-born George Washington Call and his
Chilean wife and family bought Fort Ross. The Call
Ranch that grew up around the Russian fort is now pre-
served, leaving a vivid picture of nineteenth-century
Sonoma Coast ranch life.

Like other North Coast ranchers and lumbermen, Call
shipped his produce and timber from a doghole port—Fort
Ross's North Cove—via a wooden chute-and-wire cable
system to waiting schooners below. Loading the schooners
was a dangerous job. A "clapperman" at the lower end of

Fort Ross State Historic Park (Redwood Empire Association)

the chute operated a braking device to stop oncoming produce, timber, even farm animals from overshooting the deck. Animals that fell from the chute got a bone-crushing welcome from sharks waiting in the cove below.

Two-masted lightweight schooners sailed the waters between San Francisco and the doghole ports as far north as Oregon, hauling timber, butter, animals, abalone, and quarried stone. Vicious rip currents, sandbars, shallow reefs, and fierce storms challenged the "Scandinavian

284

Navy" sea captains who guided the schooners just as they'd done on their native North Sea. In 1908, the steamship *Pomona* struck a rock near Fort Ross and sank; the Call family housed the survivors.

Since 1903, the Call family has sold various portions of its ranch to the state, including Fort Ross and the Call Ranch buildings. The chapel, twice destroyed by fire and now rebuilt, is the site of Russian Orthodox church services on the Russian Easter, Memorial Day, and the Fourth of July. The commandant's house, oldest extant wooden building west of the Mississippi River, houses a museum, plus a gift and book shop. Picnickers can lunch in the garden next to the Call ranchhouse; many of the plants were started by Mercedes Leiva Call, a friend of Luther Burbank.

Fort Ross State Historic Park is open 10-4:30 daily except major holidays. Fees: $2 per car, $1 for seniors; tickets usable at other state parks. Phone 847-3286.

North of Fort Ross lie many coves, originally home to abalone-loving sea otters, then doghole ports, and now the haunts of abalone divers. One mile north of Fort Ross on Highway 1 is Kolmer Gulch, owned by Louisiana-Pacific, a timber company that hopes to have a demonstration forest and campground here. At present, for a nominal fee, divers can park and hike to a gravel beach. One-half mile farther lies Fort Ross Store, a pit stop for dining, deli items, groceries, beer, wine, gas, and some rental and replacement diving equipment. Open daily.

The Abalone Coast

A balone is the real lure of the northern Sonoma Coast; when "abalone fever" strikes, divers descend on the coves between Jenner and Gualala. The abalone is a giant marine snail cursed with a powerful, and powerfully delicious, foot, which can lock a strong grip on rock surfaces but can't carry it an inch away from danger. One of these mollusks can yield up to one and a half pounds of pure white meat; the moundlike shell is coarse on the outside but lined with beautiful mother-of-pearl within.

Red abalone is the most frequently taken species, but seven other species live on the North Coast. The abs thrive from the intertidal zone to depths of about thirty-five feet. In northern California, ab divers cannot use scuba equipment; instead, they must "free dive," often in dense kelp beds, wearing wet suits to protect them from the frigid waters, and then pry the abs loose with a legal-size abalone iron. (It's illegal to use knives, screwdrivers, or pointed, sharp instruments for taking abalones.) About 90 percent of the abs pried loose will be reds, which must have a shell seven inches in diameter to be kept. Under-sized abs must be replaced on the same rocks immediately or they may not survive. That's the law, although it's no easy trick in the cold, choppy waters.

It takes a dozen years for a red abalone to reach legal size, and though its mother laid a million or more eggs, most of its siblings will have become dinner for other sea creatures before humans get a crack at them. Once plenti-ful abalone beds are being depleted and state regulations are strictly enforced. Abalone season runs from April through November, with a break in July. The limit is four abalones in any combination. Legal diameters: red, seven inches; green, pink, and white, six inches; black, five inches; all others, four inches.

The abalone's edible part is its foot, which is trimmed, sliced into thin steaks, and pounded until tender. Each softened steak is dipped into egg and bread crumbs, then quickly fried in a hot skillet. Many an abalone has met its end on the Sonoma Coast, in good company with salad, French bread, wine, and fruit.

All along the Sonoma Coast are coves where divers can find abalone, and, for a fee, divers can also have access to many of the privately owned coves on the coast. After a long drive to the coast, it is tempting for divers to cast aside common sense and enter choppy, stormy waters in search of abs. Last year seven divers drowned.

286

Timber Cove

Two miles north of Fort Ross is Timber Cove. A thriving doghole port a century ago, it is now noted for the Timber Cove Inn, a campground popular with divers, and a subdivision of expensive homes tucked away in the pine forests off Highway 1.

The landmark Timber Cove Inn, a forty-seven-room retreat with a massive timbered lobby and bar, is decorated with Ansel Adams photographs and Benny Bufano sculptures, including "Peace," an eighty-five-foot-high statue beside the inn. San Francisco sculptor Bufano, an ardent pacifist, protested America's entry into World War I by cutting off his trigger finger and mailing it to President Woodrow Wilson.

About half of Timber Cove Inn's rooms focus on fireplaces and sunken tubs; none offer TV or phones. The Inn's restaurant spotlights sauerbraten, scampi, and steaks; it's open for breakfast, lunch, and dinner. The Inn is frequently used as a conference spot. The Timber Cove Inn is at 21790 Highway 1, Jenner; 874-3231.

Just before the Inn is Timber Cove Boat Landing and Campground, 21350 Highway 1, a privately owned day-use and overnight stop popular with divers. Owner Dave Verno offers boat rentals and sales, guided boat tours, and a boat launch. Divers can rent or buy equipment; there's a scuba air station, too. Bait and tackle are for sale, along with fishing licenses. The cove is used by many skin diving classes. Fees: $3 per person for day use, $7-$8 per vehicle overnight.

Verno also rents private homes, cabins, and chalets; all have fireplaces, some have hot tubs. Write Sea Coast Hide-a-Ways, 21350 North Coast Highway 1, Jenner, CA 95450, or call 847-3278. You can also call this number to check on weather and water conditions.

Stillwater Cove

One and a half miles north of Timber Cove is Stillwater Cove, now a county-operated park with privately owned lodging at nearby Stillwater Cove Ranch. Stillwater Cove Regional Park is a small, pine-forested preserve with a long stairway to the beach. Divers, rock fishermen, and tide-poolers all use the park, and a number of diving classes are held here. There are twenty-two campsites with rest rooms and showers, and a large day-use area with picnic tables. Day use is $1.50 per car; camping is $5. A paved wheel-chair ramp provides access to the cove.

Near the Old Fort Ross School is Stillwater Cove Ranch, 22555 Coast Highway 1, 847-3227, once a boys' school, now a coastal retreat where guests can unwind in cozy rooms in the cook's cottage, the teacher's cottage, the dairy barn, and other converted school buildings.

Ocean Cove

Ocean Cove Reserve, one mile north of Stillwater Cove, is a privately owned bluff and beach with excellent diving, picnicking, fishing, and camping. Pay your nominal day-use or camping fee between dawn and dusk at the Ocean Cove Store, which sells diving gear, bait and tackle, groceries, beer, wine, and gasoline; then take a dirt road one-half mile to the beach. Calm waters and easy access make Ocean Cove Reserve a fine place for novice divers. The campground features a hundred primitive campsites with fire pits.

Near the Ocean Cove Store is the Salt Point Lodge, sheltered by redwoods, offering sixteen units with fireplaces, hot tubs, sauna, informal bar, and restaurant. The Lodge is located at 23255 Coast Highway 1, Jenner, CA 95450; 847-3234.

Salt Point State Park

Less than a mile north of Ocean Cove, you cross the southern boundary of Salt Point State Park. Here you'll find 4,300 acres of shoreline, forests, and grasslands for diving, fishing, camping, picnicking, hiking, and horse-back riding. Gerstle Cove, one of the state's first underwater preserves, and Stump Beach Cove are outstanding diving places. You're not allowed to take anything from Gerstle Cove, just look.

Along the park's coast are rock-lace honeycomb formations called tafoni, formed by the rise and fall of tides on sandstone shelves. Local rock was quarried here and shipped by schooner to San Francisco in the last century.

Elevations in the park reach up to 1,000 feet, and you can hike through the bishop pine and Douglas fir forests to a pygmy forest, created when poor soil conditions stunted tree growth. Mature redwoods and other species grow no taller than a man here.

The park contains thirty primitive campsites, with another overflow campground for sixty self-contained RVs or tenters. Horseback riders can leave their horses at a barn within the park for $2 per horse. Camping is on a first come, first served basis. Fees: $3 per night, $2 extra vehicle, $3 overflow, $1 dogs, $1.25 firewood; $2 day-use fee, 50 cents day-use fee for dogs. The park office number is 847-3221. Call 847-3222 for diving and weather conditions. Park ticket is good at other state parks.

Kruse Rhododendron State Reserve

Adjacent to Salt Point State Park is the Kruse Rhododendron State Reserve, where twenty-foot-high rhododendrons bloom from mid-April to mid-June. This 317-acre reserve of second-growth redwood and Douglas fir contains five miles of equestrian and hiking trails, but no picnic facilities. The reserve, part of the German Rancho, the state's northernmost Mexican land grant to be recognized by the U.S. Land Commission, was donated by Edward P. O. Kruse in memory of his father, a founder of San Francisco's German Bank. It's open one-half hour before sunrise to one-half hour after sunset; admission is free.

From Salt Point State Park and Kruse Rhododendron State Reserve, it's a six-mile drive to the village of Stewarts Point. Along this length of coastline are several privately

owned access areas to diving spots. First up is Kruse
Ranch, just beyond the park, with nominal fee access.
Obtain permission to trespass at the ranch house. Next is
North Horseshoe Cove, one and a half miles south of
Rocky Point on Highway 1. Pay fee at the ranch house
approximately one mile north on the east side of Highway 1. Last is Richardson's Ranch or the Red Box Accessways. Place $2 in an envelope with your car license number
written on it in one of the red boxes and follow red signs.
The north cove here, called Backwards Cove, is a favorite
of many divers.

Stewarts Point

tewarts Point, once known as Fisherman's Bay, is
only a shell of its former glory as a busy doghole port
in lumbering days. Stewarts Point Store (1868) and
gas station has been run by the Richardson family for
generations. Open daily 8-6, it now sells fishing and diving
equipment.

From Stewarts Point it's a thirty-mile drive to Highway 101 via Skaggs Springs Road, but you can take a
twenty-mile drive back to Highway 1 by making a loop on
Stewarts Point and Annapolis roads. These routes cross
the south fork of the Gualala River, where you'll find good
trout fishing waters, the same ones Jack London fished
eighty years ago.

Five miles inland along Stewarts Point Road is the
Stewarts Point Indian Rancheria, home of the Kashaya
Pomo, descendants of the people who met the Russians at
Fort Ross. The Kashaya occasionally perform dances at
the Old Adobe Days Celebration in Petaluma, held each
August. Please respect their privacy.

Two miles more bring you to Annapolis Road, a
thirteen-mile trek back to Highway 1. Annapolis is noted
for its diminutive, wisteria-covered post office, the pioneer
Horicon School, and the Hollow Tree Store and picnic
grounds.

Sea Ranch

Located on the final ten miles of the Sonoma Coast is Sea Ranch, a privately developed second home and condominium community distinguished by its magnificent buildings, which have received many architectural honors. The Sea Ranch Lodge, Restaurant, general store, and land office are located on Highway 1 about four miles north of Stewarts Point.

The Sea Ranch Lodge features seasonal (May 1 to October 1) and off-season rates for its modern accommodations overlooking the Pacific from Black Point. Lodge guests can enjoy the Sea Ranch beaches and recreational facilities (swimming pool, tennis courts, golf course, fishing, and hiking trails) by requesting a visitor's pass upon arrival. Call 785-2371 or write Sea Ranch Lodge, P.O. Box 44, The Sea Ranch, CA 95497.

For breakfast, lunch, or dinner, stop at the Sea Ranch Restaurant. Your evening repast of fish, steak, or lamb will be complemented by an overpowering Pacific sunset. Reservations accepted for groups of seven or more; call 785-2371.

You can rent a Sea Ranch home with use of the community's facilities through one of several agencies listed in the Visitors Services section. If you simply want to study the architecture and landscape, then follow the roads off Highway 1. Sea Ranch dwellings aren't marked with numbers. One of the most impressive buildings is the Condominium I at the end of Seawalk Drive, near the Lodge and Restaurant.

The developers of Sea Ranch, Oceanic California (Castle and Cooke), hired city planner Lawrence Halprin to create a master plan that included all-underground utilities, clustered dwellings to maintain open space, and design restrictions on structures. Many of the Sea Ranch property owners contracted noted architectural firms—such as Moore and Turnbull, and Joseph Esherick—to design functional, yet abstract homes.

Sea Ranch plans for 5,200 dwellings along the coast helped fuel the passions that culminated in the 1972 passage of Proposition 20, the Coastal Initiative, which gave birth to the California Coastal Commission and the requirement that public access to the sea be a condition of coastal development. In a classic struggle between public coastal access and private property rights, the Coastal Commission ruled that the right to access meant no building. Sea Ranch's home population was frozen at 308 dwellings.

After an eight-year fight, the resulting compromise now allows building to begin again at Sea Ranch, while five public trails from Highway 1 to the sea will pass through the community. At present, the Salal Trail is the only route through Sea Ranch; this is a three-quarter-mile trail from the Gualala Point Regional Park to a small cove.

Gualala

D irectly north of Sea Ranch on Highway 1 is Gualala Point Regional Park, located on a sand-spit of land between the Pacific Ocean and the Gualala River. The park borders the river, which runs parallel to the Pacific shoreline for two miles west of Highway 1. On the north bank of the river, in Mendocino County, is the town of Gualala.

The origin of the name Gualala is uncertain. Some feel it derives from the Pomo word *awala-li* ("water coming down place"), while others trace its roots to Valhalla, home of slain heroes in Germanic mythology, a transplanted term given by early-day German settlers. The town started as a lumber port, but now it's frequented by fishermen and vacationers who like to stay in Gualala's turn-of-the-century refurbished hotels.

Land for the Gualala Point Regional Park was donated to the county by Sea Ranch officials during the prolonged public access controversy. The park has redwood forests, beaches, and excellent whale-watching spots. It's open year-round for steelhead and rock fishing, beachcombing, hiking, picnicking, and camping. The visitor center boasts a wind-powered generator that furnishes electricity to the structure. A paved trail leads to the beach. East of Highway 1 there are eighteen car campsites and seven walk-in campsites. Day-use fee is $1.50; camping costs $5, with $2 for each additional vehicle staying the night. For information, call 785-2377.

In winter the Gualala River is a favorite of steelhead fishermen; in early spring canoeists come to try their skills on the south fork of the river. Unlike the Russian River, the Gualala is little used, and a canoe trip will take you through a lovely redwood forest. You can put in your canoe either at the bridge on Stewarts Point/Skaggs Springs Road, for a five-mile river trip, or at the bridge on Annapolis Road, for a nine-mile run to a take-out point south of Gualala near Highway 1.

The town of Gualala, just beyond the Sonoma County line, appears to travelers like a metropolis after the many miles of thinly settled coastline. It's a place to find locally created arts and crafts, to dine on seafood, or to dream away in a seaside inn after a day of swimming, fishing, or canoeing on the river.

Visitors Services

The following selective listings are intended as a guide for visitors and a convenient reference for residents. All telephone numbers have a 707 prefix unless otherwise noted.

Maps and Information

Sonoma County Wineries Map. County-wide list of wineries open to the public. Free from chambers of commerce.

Russian River Wine Road. Winery map of the Russian River Valley. Send 25 cents to Russian River Wine Road, P.O. Box 127, Geyserville, CA 95441.

Sonoma County Farm Trails Map. Where to buy fresh products directly from the farmer. Free from local chambers of commerce or Farm Trail outlets, or send stamped, self-addressed, legal-sized envelope to P.O. Box 6674, Santa Rosa, CA 95406.

Sonoma County Crafts Map. County-wide map of local artisans and craftspeople. Send a self-addressed, stamped envelope to Lincoln Arts Center, 709 Davis Street, Santa Rosa, CA 95401.

California Sport Fishing Regulations. Legal limits of fish and invertebrate species, types of bait and gear, seasons and hours. Available at sporting goods stores, bait and tackle shops, or by writing Publications Section, Office of Procurement, General Services, P.O. Box 1015, North Highlands, CA 95660, or call (916) 445-1020.

Old Petaluma Walking Tour. Self-guided tour of downtown Petaluma. Free from Petaluma Chamber of Commerce, 314 Western Avenue, Petaluma, CA 94952.

Sonoma Walking Tour. Self-guided tour of downtown Sonoma. Send $1 to Sonoma League for Historic Preservation, 129 E. Spain Street, Sonoma, CA 95476.

Sonoma County Stay-A-Day Booklet. County-wide tour guide and map. Free from local chambers of commerce.

Guide to Petaluma Antique Shops. Free from Petaluma Chamber of Commerce.

Navigational Information for the Petaluma River. Free from the Petaluma Chamber of Commerce.

Tours and Excursions

Partyboat Sport Fishing, The Tides, P.O. Box 547, Bodega Bay, CA 94923 (875-3595). Group charters for bottom fishing, salmon trolling, whale watching.

Vintage Touring Company, 563 Michael Drive, Sonoma, CA 95476 (938-2100). Customized half-day or longer tours of wineries and cheese factories in the Sonoma Valley.

California Rivers, 21001 Geyserville Ave., P.O. Box 468, Geyserville, CA 95441 (857-3872). Guided trips and canoe classes on Russian River.

Hot Air Balloon Flights

Airborn of Sonoma County, 727 Mendocino Ave., Santa Rosa (528-8133); Skyline Balloons, P.O. Box 2152, Santa Rosa (539-3209); Thunder Pacific, 114 Sandalwood Ct., Santa Rosa (546-7124); Sonoma Thunder, 4039 White Oak Ct., Sonoma, 95476 (996-1112 or 938-5131); Flights of Fantasy, London Lodge, Glen Ellen (996-6306 or 415-921-5280).

Airplane Flights

Redwood Aviation (546-5546) or Sonoma Valley Flyers (546-1084), Sonoma County Airport, offer round-trip flights from Santa Rosa to other points in Sonoma County. Aerosport, Schellville Airport, 23982 Arnold Drive, features biplane tours over the Sonoma Valley (938-2444).

Rentals

Airplanes

Corporate Air Service, Inc., 175 Airport Blvd., Santa Rosa (544-9405); Let's Fly, Inc., 2238 Airport Blvd., Santa Rosa (546-9362); Nation Air, Sonoma County Airport (546-5659); Pyramid Aviation Ltd., 8299 Old Redwood Highway, Cotati (664-0292); Wings West, 21870 8th Street East, Sonoma (996-0006).

Bicycles

The Bicycle Factory, 143 Kentucky Street, Petaluma (763-7515); Spoke Folk Cyclery, 249 Center Street, Healdsburg (433-7171).

Boats

Lakeville Marina, 5688 Lakeville Highway, Lakeville (762-4900), rowboat rentals on Petaluma River; Recreation Rentals, 1077A Lakeville Highway, Petaluma (763-2525), one-day minicruise on Petaluma River; Port Sonoma Sail Boat Rentals (778-7245); Howarth Memorial Park, Santa Rosa (528-5115), sailboat, canoe, rowboat, paddleboat rentals; Spring Lake Concessions, Spring Lake Park, Santa Rosa (539-8092), canoe, sailboat, rowboat, paddleboat rentals; California Rivers, 21001 Geyserville Ave., P.O. Box 468, Geyserville, 95441 (857-3872), canoes, kayaks, rafts for rent by day or longer on Russian River; W. C. Bob Trowbridge Canoe Trips, 20 Healdsburg Ave., Healdsburg, 95448 (433-7247), canoe rentals for one- to five-day Russian River trips; Burke's Canoe Trips, 8600 River Road, Box 602, Forestville, 95436 (887-1222), canoe rentals for one- and two-day Russian River trips.

Cars

Avis Rent-A-Car, 501 College Ave., Santa Rosa (546-1965); Budget Rent-A-Car, 2642 Santa Rosa Ave., Santa Rosa (545-8013); Hertz Rent-A-Car, 1075 Santa Rosa Ave., Santa Rosa (542-5500) or Sonoma County Airport (528-0834); National Car Rental System, 2244 Airport Blvd., Santa Rosa (523-4240); also Bob Benson Buick-Pontiac-GMC Trucks in Petaluma, W. C. Sanderson Ford-Mercury in Healdsburg, Sonoma Subaru in Sonoma, and C and W Ford in Sebastopol.

Horses

El Adobe Rancho, 3268 Old Adobe Road, Petaluma (763-1011); Cloverleaf Ranch, 3890 Old Redwood Highway, Santa Rosa (545-5906); Palace Hill Ranch Wagon Tours, 4701 Dry Creek Road, Healdsburg, 95448 (433-3211), farm wagon and buggy tours of local vineyards and wineries; Clan Parmeter Livery Stable, Box 181, Cazadero, 95421 (865-9982 or 632-5602), trail rides, pony rides, hay rides, and horsemanship classes; Chanslor Ranch, P.O. Box 327, Bodega Bay, 94923 (875-3386).

Lodging

This selective list, arranged alphabetically by area, gives a choice of hotels, motels, resorts, country inns, and home rentals. Many are booked well in advance on summer holidays; a few Russian River resorts close in winter. Price ranges for a typical double room are as follows:

296

Hotels, motels, resorts: Inexpensive, under $25
                         Moderate, $26-$40
                         Expensive, $41 and up
Country inns: Inexpensive, under $40
                         Moderate, $41-$65
                         Expensive, $66 and up

County-wide

Wine Country Bed and Breakfast, P.O. Box 3211, Santa Rosa, 95403 (539-1183). Guests are matched with a variety of individualized accommodations, from Victorian homes to ranches. Moderate to expensive.

Bodega Bay (zip 94922)

Hotels, Motels, Resorts: Bodega Bay Lodge (Best Western), Highway 1, Box 357 (875-3525), expensive; The Tides Motel, Highway 1, Box 547 (875-3553), moderate to expensive.

Country Inns: Chanslor Ranch, two miles north of Bodega Bay on Highway 1 (875-3386), ranchhouse and bunkhouse accommodations on working cattle ranch, moderate.

Boyes Hot Springs (95416)

Resorts: Sonoma Mission Inn, 18140 Sonoma Highway (800-862-4945 or 996-1041), lavish country retreat, expensive.

Country Inn: J&D Bottling Works, 239 Boyes Blvd. (996-3777), fourteen antique furnished rooms, inexpensive.

Cazadero (95421)

Hotels, Motels, Resorts: Double B's Mototel and Elim Grove Restaurant, Box 320, 5400 Cazadero Highway (632-5259), moderate; Austin Dell Resort, 3650 Cazadero Highway (632-5273), moderate.

Country Inn: Cazanoma Lodge, 1000 Kidd Creek Road, Box 37 (632-5255), moderate.

Cloverdale (95425)

Motel: The Oaks Motel, 123 S. Cloverdale Blvd. (874-2404), moderate.

Country Inn: Vintage Towers, 302 North Main St. (894-4535), moderate.

Forestville (95436)

Country Inn: Russian River Lodge, 7871 River Road (887-1524), predominately gay resort, moderate to expensive.

Freestone (95472)

Country Inn: Green Apple Inn, 520 Bohemian Highway (874-2526), bed and breakfast in a Lincoln-era farmhouse.

Geyserville (95441)

Country Inns: Isis Oasis, 20889 Geyserville Ave. (857-3524), inexpensive; Hope-Bosworth House, 21238 Geyserville Ave. (857-3356), inexpensive; Hope-Merrill House, 21253 Geyserville Ave. (857-3945), moderate; The Campbell Ranch, 1475 Canyon Road (857-3476), moderate.

Glen Ellen (95442)

Motel: London Lodge, 13740 Arnold Dr. (938-8510), moderate, location of Jack London museum.

Country Inn: Beltane Ranch, 11775 Sonoma Highway (996-6501), newly opened country inn in Mammy Pleasant's old ranch home.

Gualala (95445)

Country Inns: Gualala Hotel, downtown Gualala, Box 78 (884-3441), European style accommodations, inexpensive; Old Milano Hotel, 38300 Highway 1 (884-3256), expensive; St. Orres, Coast Highway 1, Box 523 (884-3303), moderate to expensive.

Guerneville (95446)

Hotels, Motels, Resorts: River Village, 14880 River Road, Box 368 (869-9066), predominately gay resort, moderate to expensive; The Willows, 15905 River Road, Box 465 (869-3279), moderate; Johnson's Resort, near Guerneville Bridge, Box 386 (869-2022), family resort, inexpensive; Riverlane Resort, 16320 Church St., Box 313 (869-2323), family resort, moderate; Southside Resort, 13811 Highway 116 (869-2690), family resort, RV hookups, camping, moderate to expensive; Donovan's Resort, 16124 Drake Road, Box 738 (869-2689), family resort, moderate to expensive; Parker's Resort, 16220 Neeley Road (869-2037), family resort, camping and 50 campsites for self-contained vehicles, moderate; Brookside Lodge and Resort Motel, Highway 116 and Brookside Lane, Box 382 (869-2470), family resort, expensive; Ferngrove, 16650 River Road (869-9992), adult resort for gays and non-gays, moderate to expensive; Fife's, 16467 River Road, Box 45 (869-0656), gay resort, expensive; Schoolhouse Lodge, 14060 Mill Street, Box 607 (869-2082), moderate; Sleepy Hollow, 14220 Mill St., Box 169 (869-0888), moderate; Hetzel's Resort, Fourth and Mill Sts., Box 785 (869-2678), moderate; Camelot Resort, Fourth and Mill Sts., Box 467 (869-2538), adult resort, moderate to expensive; Highlands Resort, 14000 Woodland Dr., Box 346 (869-0333), gay resort, moderate to expensive; The Woods, 16881 Armstrong Woods Road (869-0111), gay and nongay resort, expensive.

Country Inns: Ridenhour Ranch House Inn, 12850 River Road (887-1033), moderate; Creekside Inn and Resort, 16180 Neely Road (869-3623 or 869-9978), inexpensive to expensive.

Healdsburg (95448)

Motels: Fairview Motel, 74 Healdsburg Ave. (433-5548), moderate; L & M Motel, 70 Healdsburg Ave. (433-9934), moderate.

Country Inns: Wine Bibbers Inn, 603 Monte Vista (433-3019), moderate to expensive; Belle du Jour, 16276 Healdsburg Ave. (433-2724 or 433-7892), moderate; Grape Leaf Inn, 539 Johnson St. (433-8140), moderate; Madrona Knolls Inn, 1011 Westside Road (433-4231), bed and breakfast in century-old mansion, expensive; Raford House, 10630 Wohler Road (887-9573), moderate.

Jenner (95450)

Hotels, Motels: Murphy's Jenner Inn, 10400 Coast Highway 1, Box 69 (865-2377), cabins and homes, moderate to expensive; River's End Restaurant and Tavern, Highway 1, Box 32 (865-2484), cabins and campground, expensive.

Country Inns: Timber Cove Inn, 21780 Coast Highway 1 (847-3231), expensive; Stillwater Cove Ranch, 22555 Coast Highway 1 (847-3227), moderate; Salt Point Lodge at Ocean Cove, 23255 Coast Highway 1 (847-3234), inexpensive to moderate.

Monte Rio (95462)

Resort: Northwood Lodge, 19400 Highway 116, Box 188 (865-2126), expensive.

Country Inn: Village Inn, 20822 River Blvd., Box 1 (865-2738), moderate.

Occidental (95465)

Motels: Negri's Occidental Lodge, 3700 Bohemian Highway (874-3623), moderate; Union Hotel, 3703 Main St. (874-3635), moderate.

Petaluma (94952)

Motels: Petaluma Inn Motel (Best Western), 200 McDowell Blvd. (763-0994), moderate; Motel Six, 5135 Old Redwood Highway (795-8000), inexpensive.

Country Inn: Garden Valley Ranch, 498 Pepper Road (778-7001), moderate to expensive.

Rio Nido (95471)

Resort: Balaika Cottages, 14691 Canyon Seven Road, Box 122 (869-2148), family resort, moderate.

Rohnert Park (94928)

Motel: Best Western Inn, 6500 Redwood Drive (584-7435), moderate.

Santa Rosa

Hotels, Motels, Resorts: Los Robles Lodge, 925 Edwards Ave. (545-6330), moderate; El Rancho Tropicana, 2200 Santa Rosa Ave. (542-3655), moderate to expensive; Flamingo Hotel, Fourth and Farmers Lane (545-8530), moderate to expensive; Hillside Inn (Best Western), 2901 Fourth St. (546-9353), moderate; Sandman Hotel, 3421 Cleveland Ave. (544-8570), moderate; Chantilly Motel, 1880 Mendocino Ave. (542-5993), moderate; Best Western Garden Inn, 1500 Santa Rosa Ave. (546-4031), moderate; Santa Rosa Travelodge, 1815 Santa Rosa Ave. (542-3472), moderate.

Country Inns: Pygmalion House, 331 Orange Street (526-3407), moderate; Western Hotel, 10 Fourth Street in Old Railroad Square (546-7900), expensive.

Sea Ranch (94597)

Country Inn: The Sea Ranch Lodge, Highway 1, Box 44, The Sea Ranch (785-2371), moderate to expensive.

Sonoma (95476)

Motels: El Pueblo Motel, 896 W. Napa St. (996-3651), moderate; Vineyard View Village, 23000 Arnold Dr., Schellville (938-2350), moderate.

Country Inns: Sonoma Hotel, 110 West Spain St. (996-2996), inexpensive to moderate; The Chalet, 18935 Fifth Street West (996-0190 and 938-3129), bed and breakfast, moderate.

Home Rentals

Bodega Bay area: George Haig Realty, P.O. Box 38, Bodega Bay, 94923 (875-2221); Bodega North Property Management, P.O. Box 68, Bodega Bay (875-3302).

Russian River area: Dede Scovell, Wiener and Associates, 1213 W. Steele Lane, Santa Rosa (523-4500—office, 887-1633—home).

Timber Cove: Sea Coast Hide-a-Ways, 21350 Coast Highway 1, Jenner, 95450 (847-3278).

Sea Ranch: Ralph Kerr's Sea Ranch Rentals, The Sea Ranch, 94597 (785-2579); Rams Head Realty, Box 123, The Sea Ranch (785-2417); Holley Realty, 1000 Annapolis Road, The Sea Ranch (785-2327).

Recreational Vehicle and Camping Facilities

Be sure to reserve a campground well in advance for your summer visits. Typical fees are $5 to $9 per night per campsite; county campgrounds charge a slightly higher fee for non-county residents. Fees for dogs are $1 to $1.50. In state parks, dogs must be on a leash and have proof of rabies vaccination. Note that most campgrounds do allow dogs, while few resorts do. Camping is also allowed at many resorts; check with owners.

Bodega Bay (94923)

Bodega Bay RV Park, Highway 1 (875-3701), full service; Porto Bodega, 1500 Bay Flat Road, Box 456 (875-3550), trailer camping space, elec./water hookups; Doran Regional Park, Bodega Bay (875-3540), camping, boat launch; Westside Park, Bay Flat Road (875-3540), boat launch, campsites; Bodega Dunes Campground, Sonoma Coast State Beach 1 mile north of Bodega Bay, campsites, showers, dump station (875-3382); Wright's Beach Campground, Sonoma Coast State Beach 6 miles north of Bodega Bay (875-3483), campsites.

Cloverdale (95425)

Boucher's Liberty Lake R.V. Resort, 225 Theresa Dr. (894-5512), tent and RV camping with lake, golf course, laundry, pools, tennis; KOA Campground, 26460 River Rd., Box 600 (894-3337), campsites, recreational facilities and pool.

Duncans Mills (95430)

Duncans Mills Campground, Duncans Mills Depot, Box 57 (865-2573), campsites for campers, travel trailers, and tents; some full hookups, showers, some group campsites; Casini Ranch Family Campground, 22855 Moscow Road, Duncans Mills, Box 522, Monte Rio 95462 (865-2255), RV/tent campsites, some full hookups, elec./water, dump station.

Forestville (95436)

Mirabel Park, 7600 River Road, Box 681 (887-2383), full hookups and non-hookup sites, showers, barbecue pits, canoe rentals; Burke's Canoe Trips, 8600 River Road, Box 602 (887-1222), family camping sites for self-contained units and tents; Cook's Campground, Hollydale Beach, River Road near Forestville, camping and canoe rentals; Hilton Park and River Bend Trailer Park, 11820 River Road (887-7662), campsites for self-contained vehicles and RV hookups.

Gualala (95445)

Gualala Point Regional Park, Highway 1 (785-2377), campsites for vehicles and walk-in campers; Gualala River Redwood Park, Road 501, Box 101-DM (884-3533), open May 1 to Sept. 7, campsites, elec./water hookups available, showers, laundry.

Guerneville (95446)

Schoolhouse Canyon Campground, 12600 River Road (869-2311), campsites, bathhouse; Austin Creek State Recreation Area, 17000 Armstrong Woods Road (869-2015), vehicle campsites and backpack campsites.

Healdsburg (95448)

Alexander Valley Campground, 2411 Alexander Valley Rd. (433-1320), camping, non-hookup RVs, picnic facilities, Saturdays reserved for canoe trips; Thunderbird Ranch, 9455 Highway 128 (433-3729), camping, non-hookup RVs, showers, pool, closed July and August for private summer camp.

Jenner (95450)

Bridgehaven, south bank of Russian River on Highway 1, Box 30 (865-2020), cabins, camping and boating; River's End, Highway 1 (865-2484), day use, camping, boat launch; Pedotti Campgrounds, 18000 Highway 1 (847-3263), campsites, open camping; Timber Cove Boat Landing and Campground, 21350 Highway 1 (847-3278), campsites, with and without elec. hookups, day use also; Stillwater Cove Regional Park, 3 miles north of Fort Ross (847-3245, 785-2377), day use or overnight camping; Ocean Cove Reserve Campground, 23125 Coast Highway 1 (847-3422), campsites, pay at Ocean Cove Store; Salt Point State Park, 25050 Highway 1 (847-3221), campsites, no hookups.

Kenwood (95452)

Sugarloaf Ridge State Park, 2605 Adobe Canyon Rd. (833-5712), primitive campsites; Hood Mountain Regional Park, 6 miles east of Santa Rosa on Los Alamos Road, walk-in camping.

Petaluma (94952)

San Francisco North/Petaluma KOA Campground, 20 Rainsville Rd. (763-1492), RV campsites, store, dump station, pool, hot spa, picnic tables.

Santa Rosa

Spring Lake Regional Park, camping access from Newanga Ave. or to Violetti Rd. (539-8092), family-type campsites, walk-in campsites, one large group campsite; Mobile Home Estates, 5761 Old Redwood Highway (546-1065), 8 overnight spaces; Plaza Mobile Home Park, 3350 Santa Rosa Ave. (546-6543), 40 overnight spaces.

Sonoma (95476)

Acacia Grove, 18629 Sonoma Highway (996-6313), 6 overnight mobile home spaces.

Windsor (95492)

Camperlodge R.V. Park, 8225 Conde Lane (838-4195), sites for RVs, full hookups, dump station, laundry, showers, pool; Windsor Land, 9290 Old Redwood Highway (838-4882), full hookups, tent spaces, laundry, pool.

Transportation

Airlines

WestAir, 2310 Airport Blvd., Santa Rosa (542-2941), offers regularly scheduled flights from Santa Rosa to San Francisco Airport, Sacramento, Chico, Redding, Eureka/Arcata, and Crescent City.

Airport Transportation

Airport Express (526-1360), service to San Francisco and Oakland airports from Santa Rosa; Santa Rosa Airporter, Inc. (545-8015), service to San Francisco Airport from Santa Rosa; Sonoma Airporter, Inc. (938-4246), Sonoma to San Francisco Airport.

Buses

Petaluma Municipal Transit (762-2783), service around Petaluma and to Cotati, Rohnert Park, Sonoma State University; Santa Rosa Municipal Transit (528-5306 or 528-5238), routes begin/end at Old Courthouse Square; Healdsburg Transit (433-9425), inter-city service, service to Windsor; Sebastopol Transit Service (823-7863), weekday service; Russian River Express (415-435-5286), weekend resort express between San Francisco and the Russian River resorts; Sonoma County Transit (527-7665), Route 20—Russian River/Sebastopol/Santa Rosa, Route 30—Sonoma/Santa Rosa; Golden Gate Transit (544-1323), service to Marin County and San Francisco from Petaluma, Cotati, Rohnert Park, Santa Rosa, Sebastopol; Greyhound Bus Lines (542-6400), serves Petaluma, Sonoma, Santa Rosa, Sebastopol, Healdsburg, Russian River; Mendocino Transit Authority (847-3421), Gualala, Sea Ranch, Stewarts Point, Timber Cove, Seaview Road, Jenner, Santa Rosa; Yellow Cab: Santa Rosa, 544-4444, Petaluma, 763-1533, Sonoma, 996-6733; London Transport of Sonoma (996-1212), British cabs.

Index

Stevenson, Robert Louis, 79, 116
Stewarts Point, 261, 289
Stillwater Cove, 286-87
Stillwater Cove Regional Park, 287
Sugarloaf Ridge State Park, 180, 183-84
Summer Repertory Theatre, 60
Sunsweet Growers, 96

Temelec Hall, 138-39
Timber Cove, 286
Tours and excursions, 296
Train Town, 139
Transportation, 304
Trione, Henry, 70, 78
Tubbs Island Bird Sanctuary, 138

Ugly Dog Contest, 5, 19
U.S. Coast Guard Station, 267, 268
U.S.Coast Guard Training Center, 29-30
Utopian colonies, 78-79, 106-7, 108, 109, 218-19

Vallejo, Mariano Guadalupe, 2, 21-24, 34, 41, 89, 132, 140, 141, 145,
    157-58, 164, 168, 176, 188, 189
Valley Ford, 213-14, 262
Valley of the Moon. *See* Sonoma Valley
Villa Chanticleer, 94
Vintage Festival, 159
Visitors Services: calendar of annual events, 305-6; lodging (hotels,
    resorts, country inns), 297-302; maps and visitor information,
    295-96; recreational vehicle and camping facilities, 302-4; rentals
    (airplanes, bicycles, boats, cars, horses), 296-97; tours and
    excursions, 296; transportation, 304.

Warm Springs Dam, 123-25
Watson School Wayside Park, 264
West Petaluma Regional Park, 26-27
Westside County Park, 269
Westside Road, 126-29; winery tour, 126-29
Whale watching, 273-74
Windsor, 86-89; winery tour, 87-89
Windsor Waterworks and Slides, 86-87
Winery Tours: Alexander Valley, 113-15; Asti, 106-7; Cloverdale,
    111-12; Dry Creek Valley, 120-23; Forestville, 210-12; Geyserville,
    102-6; Glen Ellen, 177, 178-79; Guerneville, 235-36; Healdsburg,
    96-99; Kenwood, 181-82; Petaluma, 20; Santa Rosa, 66; Sebastopol,
    208, 209; Sonoma Valley, 159-64, 167-68; Westside Road, 126-29;
    Windsor, 87-89
Wristwrestling contests, 5, 11

Acknowledgments:

This book is the result of the assistance of hundreds of people who answered questions, made intelligent suggestions, and read portions of the manuscript. Special thanks goes to Joan Griffin, senior editor at Presidio Press, who gave utmost support to this book from its birth. Also of tremendous assistance were Geets Vincent, journalism instructor at Santa Rosa Junior College, Dennis Hall, Dennis Machado, and Jay Gordon of Pan Am, all of whom worked as consultants and helped me meet deadlines. Directors, officers, and employees of historical societies, chambers of commerce, state and county parks, and county offices were of immeasurable assistance.

I would particularly like to thank: John Ash, John Ash and Company; Don Bennett, publisher, *North Country Journal*; Gracelyn Blackmer, Simi Winery; Dee Blackman and Sherman Boivin, Luther Burbank Property Advisory Committee; David Bolling, publisher, Santa Rosa *News-Herald*; Roger Bowlin, Italian Swiss Colony; Glen Burch, State of California Department of Parks and Recreation; Mary Carey, public information officer, Santa Rosa Junior College; Hannah Clayborn, Edwin Langhart Museum; Gene Cuneo, grape grower; Louis M. Foppiano, Foppiano Vineyards; Edward Fratini, historian; Nicky Frye, Robert L. Ripley Museum; Herman Goertz, Green Hill Berry Farm; Harvey Hansen, history instructor, Santa Rosa Junior College; Jack Healy, Santa Rosa city councilman; William Heintz, wine historian; Mildred Howie, public relations; Darrel Hurst, Twin Hill Ranch; Eric Jorgeson, Santa Rosa Parks and Recreation; Russ Kingman, author and authority on Jack London; Harry Lapham, historian; Gaye LeBaron, columnist, Santa Rosa *Press Democrat*; Steve Lee, Applied Photographic Laboratory; Ed Mannion, historian; John McKenzie, former ranger, Fort Ross State Historic Park; Bob McLaughlin, Petaluma River authority; John Melvin, ranger, Sonoma Coast State Beach; Ross Miller, Miller Ranches; Bob Mosher, Souverain Winery; Stuart Nixon, Redwood Empire Association; Gloria Oster, director of special events, Sonoma State University; Steven Phelps, park manager, Lake Sonoma and Warm Springs Dam; Dee Richardson, Luther Burbank Property Advisory Committee; John Schubert, historian; the Sonoma County Planning Department; the Sonoma County Regional Parks Department; Harry Sullivan, grower representative, California North Coast Grape Growers; Jack Trotter, geothermal specialist, Pacific Gas and Electric Company; William Trowbridge, Trowbridge Recreation, Inc.; Jean Valentine, Wine Institute; Joe Vercelli, wine consultant; Bruce Wakelee, manager, First Interstate Bank; Jim Webb, Heritage Homes of Petaluma, Inc.; Paul Wright, manager, Santa Rosa Chamber of Commerce.